The Construction of Logical Space

The Construction
of Logical Space

Agustín Rayo

OXFORD
UNIVERSITY PRESS

Great Clarendon Street, Oxford, OX2 6DP,
United Kingdom

Oxford University Press is a department of the University of Oxford.
It furthers the University's objective of excellence in research, scholarship,
and education by publishing worldwide. Oxford is a registered trade mark of
Oxford University Press in the UK and in certain other countries

First Edition published in 2013
Impression: 1

British Library Cataloguing in Publication Data
Data available

ISBN 978-0-19-966262-3

Printed and bound in Great Britain by
CPI Group (UK) Ltd, Croydon, CR0 4YY

For Carmen

Preface

What is logical space? And in what sense is it constructed?

Let me start with the notion of truth. To set forth a statement is to make a *distinction* amongst ways for the world to be, and to single out one side of this distinction; for the statement to be *true* is for the region singled out to include the way the world actually is. To set forth the statement that snow is white, for example, is to distinguish between white-snow and non-white-snow ways for the world to be, and to suggest that the world falls on the white-snow side of this distinction; for the statement to be true is for the world to actually fall on the white-snow side of the distinction—for it to actually be the case that snow is white.

Our search for truth is therefore inextricably linked to our search for distinctions amongst ways for the world to be. *Logical space*, as I shall understand it here, is the set of all such distinctions. (To specify a *region* in logical space is to take sides with respect to some of these distinctions; to specify a *point* in logical space is to take sides with respect to every such distinction.)

In order to develop a useful conception of logical space, it is not enough to come up with a set of distinctions. One must also get clear about which pairs of distinctions coincide, and which ones do not. Consider the distinction between water-containing and water-free ways for the world to be, on the one hand, and the distinction between H_2O-containing and H_2O-free ways for the world to be, on the other. Do these distinctions come to the same thing? We think that to be composed of water *just is* to be composed of H_2O, so we think that they do. But if we had different views about the chemical composition of water, we would think they do not.

One of the main themes of this book is the idea that our conception of logical space is shaped by our acceptance or rejection of 'just is'-statements—that it is by accepting or rejecting a 'just is'-statement that one settles the question of when distinctions coincide, and when they do not.

To accept a 'just is'-statement is to close a theoretical gap. By accepting 'to be composed of water *just is* to be composed of H_2O', for example, one closes the theoretical gap between being composed of water and being composed of H_2O. A bit more colorfully: one comes to think that when God created the world and made it the case that the Earth was filled with water, she *thereby* made it the case that the Earth was filled with H_2O; and that when God made it the case that the Earth was filled with H_2O, she *thereby* made it the case that the Earth was filled with water. There was nothing *extra* that God needed to do, or refrain from doing. For there is *no difference* between creating water and creating H_2O.

The acceptance of a 'just is'-statement comes with costs and benefits. The benefit is that there are less possibilities to rule out in one's search for the truth, and therefore less explanatory demands on one's theorizing; the cost is that one has less distinctions to work with, and therefore fewer theoretical resources. In deciding whether to accept a 'just is'-statement one strives to find a balance between these competing considerations. Different 'just is'-statements can be more or less hospitable to one's scientific or philosophical theorizing. So the decision to accept them should be grounded on their ability to combine with the rest of one's theorizing to deliver a fruitful tool for scientific or philosophical inquiry. And because of the crucial role of 'just is'-statements in shaping one's conception of logical space, this yields the result that one's conception of logical space cannot be constructed independently of the rest of one's theorizing.

Philosophy of Mathematics

One reason to be interested in this way of thinking about logical space is that it can help us address a family of stubborn problems in the philosophy of mathematics. It opens the door to new ways of defending Mathematical Platonism (the view that mathematical objects exist), and to new ways of thinking about the epistemology of mathematics.

Much of the material in this book can be thought of as an extended argument for *Trivialist Platonism*, a form of Mathematical Platonism according to which the following 'just is'-statement is true:

DINOSAURS

    For the number of the dinosaurs to be Zero *just is* for there to be no dinosaurs.

and, more generally,

NUMBERS
> For the number of the Fs to be *n just is* for there to be exactly *n* Fs.

My argument for Trivialist Platonism has three main components. The first is a thesis in the philosophy of language, and is developed in Chapter 1. I defend a conception of reference according to which there is no *linguistic* obstacle for the truth of a 'just is'-statement such as DINOSAURS. I then argue that the resulting conception of language won't lead to an unattractive metaphysics.

The second component of my argument is an account of 'just is'-statements, and is developed in Chapter 2. I argue that 'just is'-statements play a central role in shaping our conception of logical space, as suggested above, and defend an account of the sorts of considerations that might ground the acceptance or rejection of a 'just is'-statement.

The resulting picture is one according to which there are significant theoretical pressures for accepting NUMBERS. For although the acceptance of NUMBERS comes with costs, they are far outweighed by the benefits. Significantly, NUMBERS allows one to dismiss the following as an illegitimate demand for explanation:

> I can see that there are no dinosaurs. What I want to understand is whether it is *also* the case that the number of the dinosaurs is Zero.

For in accepting NUMBERS one rejects the idea that there is a theoretical gap between there being no dinosaurs and their number being Zero. One thinks there is *no difference* between the number of the dinosaurs being Zero and there being no dinosaurs.

The third component of my argument is a defense of the claim that Trivialist Platonism can be developed into a viable philosophy of mathematics. In Chapter 3 I argue that one can construct a semantics for mathematical discourse whereby 'just is'-statements such as NUMBERS turn out to be true. In Chapter 4 I show that the resulting proposal has the resources to explain how mathematical knowledge is possible.

Metaphysics without Foundationalism

Like many of my peers, I see the work of David Lewis as a great source of inspiration. At the same time, I have become increasingly skeptical of some of the foundationalist assumptions that guided his philosophy.

Lewis's foundationalism is based on three main theses:

PROPERTY FUNDAMENTALISM
> Some properties are, metaphysically speaking, 'fundamental': they 'carve the world at the joints'. Fundamental properties are intrinsic, and render their instances 'perfectly similar'. (Lewis 1983a, 2009)

HUMEAN SUPERVENIENCE
> No two possible worlds just alike in their spatio-temporal distributions of point-sized instantiations of fundamental properties could differ in any other way. (Lewis 1986b, 2009)

MODAL REDUCTIONISM
> Modally rich claims can be analyzed as claims about the intrinsic features of possible worlds, given a suitable counterpart relation. (Lewis 1986a)

These three claims come together to ensure that a modally rich claim like 'Humphrey didn't win the election but might have' is ultimately grounded on spatio-temporal distributions of fundamental properties. By MODAL REDUCTIONISM, our modally rich claim can be broken down into claims that are 'modally flat': they each depend only on how matters stand in one particular world. Relative to a suitable counterpart-relation, the original claim might be analyzed as the requirement that: (a) the actual world verify the modally flat claim that there is an election-losing Humphrey, and (b) that there be a possible world verifying the modally flat claim that there is a Humphrey-counterpart that wins a counterpart election. By HUMEAN SUPERVENIECE, each modally flat component of the analysis can be cashed out as a claim about the distribution of fundamental properties across the space-time manifold of the relevant world. PROPERTY FUNDAMENTALISM completes the picture by delivering the requisite notion of fundamentality.

Lewis's foundationalist assumptions deliver a tidy metaphysics. But they are also potentially problematic. A first problem is emphasized by Lewis himself: the identities of the fundamental properties turn out to be unknowable (Lewis 2009). For Lewis is committed to a combinatorial principle of possibility: if you cut out any region of any world, keeping its intrinsic properties fixed, and put it together with any other such regions, intrinsic properties also fixed, you get a genuine possibility. This yields the result that connections between fundamental properties and their effects are always contingent. So we have no way of distinguishing the fundamental properties that are actually responsible for the phenomena we observe from rival fundamental properties that could have had the same effects. Like Kant's noumena, Lewis's fundamental properties turn out to be irremediably beyond our reach. The price of Lewisian foundationalism is that one must remain ignorant of the identities of the relevant foundations.

To see what an alternative picture might look like, consider the property of having negative charge. Particles with negative charge have certain dispositional properties: they are, for example, disposed to repel other particles with negative charge. Lewis's foundationalism commits him to the claim that such dispositions can ultimately be cashed out as distributions of purely intrinsic properties across the space-time manifolds of various worlds. And because of his combinatorialism, he also thinks that these intrinsic properties can be rearranged in arbitrary ways. So the intrinsic properties of negatively charged particles float free of their dispositional properties. On an alternative picture, the property of negative charge cannot be separated from its theoretical role: part of *what it is* to be a negatively charged particle is to be disposed to repel other negatively charged particles. This threatens the foundationalism, since it is no longer clear that the property of being negatively charged can be factored into modally flat components, and it is no longer clear that such components would be decomposable into spatio-temporal distributions of intrinsic properties. But there is no longer any reason to think that the property is beyond our reach.

A second problem with Lewis's foundationalist picture is that HUMEAN SUPERVENIENCE may well be inconsistent with our best physical theorizing. Consider the relation of quantum entanglement. In order for HUMEAN SUPERVENIENCE to be true, such a relation must supervene on the distributions of point-sized instantiations of intrinsic properties. But, as Maudlin (1998) points out, it is far from obvious that this is so. Lewis's foundationalist picture gets us metaphysical tidiness, but it does so by incurring empirical liabilities. (Lewis is aware of this as a potential problem, and partly for that reason thinks of HUMEAN SUPERVENIENCE as a contingent truth; see Lewis (1986b: x.)

A third problem concerns PROPERTY FUNDAMENTALISM. Notions of metaphysical fundamentality such as Lewis's have played an increasingly important role in contemporary metaphysics (Fine 2001; Schaffer 2009; Sider 2012). But, as we will see in Sections 1.2 and 2.1.4, reliance on such notions comes at a cost. When one buys into a notion of metaphysical fundamentality one gains access to additional distinctions, and therefore to additional theoretical resources. But the additional distinctions also give rise to potentially awkward questions. One is forced, for example, to elucidate the connection between objective fundamentality and fundamentality by the lights of a particular theoretical framework. To my mind, at least, it is not obvious that this is a price worth paying.

A fourth problem concerns MODAL REDUCTIONISM. By presupposing that no property resists factorization into modally flat components, Lewis is making a non-trivial assumption—an assumption that one might have good reason to resist for reasons that go beyond any concerns one might have about PROPERTY FUNDAMENTALISM or HUMEAN SUPERVENIENCE. This is a point that will be developed in detail in Section 5.2.

Because of these worries, I will make a concerted effort to steer clear of Lewis's foundationalist assumptions in this book. In so doing, I will be developing a brand of metaphysics that is distinctly unlewisian. But the book is certainly not an attempt to produce *anti*-Lewisian metaphysics. What I hope to show is that one can do interesting philosophy without committing oneself to Lewis's foundationalist assumptions, not that the assumptions are mistaken.

Rather than assuming from the outset that there is sense to be made of metaphysical fundamentality—as PROPERTY FUNDAMENTALISM requires—I will remain *neutral* with respect to matters of metaphysical fundamentality. Rather than assuming from the outset that every truth about the world supervenes on a particular kind of foundation—as HUMEAN SUPERVENIENCE requires—I will let supervenience relations be determined by whatever 'just is'-statements are suggested by our best overall theorizing. And rather than assuming from the outset that there must be a way of factoring modally rich claims into modally flat components—as MODAL REDUCTIONISM requires—I will develop a conception of modality that does not depend on a reduction of the modal to the non-modal.

How to Read this Book

I have divided the book into three parts:

Part I: Main Texts (Chapters 1–4)
Part II: Detours (Chapters 5–8)
Part III: Appendices (A–C)

All the of main themes of the book are developed in Part I. If you'd like to see the overall picture while limiting your time-commitment, what I recommend is that you focus on Chapters 1–4. (If you have time for only one chapter, I recommend Chapter 1.)

Part II is for enthusiasts. It discusses issues arising from Part I that are important for a detailed understanding the project, but may be skipped by less committed readers. These detours should not be thought of as extended footnotes, though. Each of them develops a self-standing idea of independent interest. In Chapter 5, I explore the connection between 'just is'-statements and metaphysical possibility, and argue that a limited class of 'just is'-statements can be used to fix the truth-value of every sentence in a first-order modal language. In Chapter 6, I characterize the *dot-function*: a device for simulating quantification over merely possible objects. In Chapter 7, I describe the expressive resources that would be needed to supply nominalistic paraphrases for the language of arithmetic. In Chapter 8, I offer an account of linguistic stipulation in mathematics.

If you are tempted by the material in Part II, what I recommend is that you read it in conjunction with other parts of the book. You'll find plenty of pointers in the text, but here are some suggestions:

Table 0.1 How to Read This Book

Read …	in conjunction with …
Chapter 5	Section 2.2.1
Chapter 6	Section 3.3.1 or Section 5.2.2
Chapter 7	Section 1.4 or Section 3.3.1
Chapter 8	Section 1.3 or Chapter 3

Part III consists of technical appendices, and is intended only for the true aficionado.

Acknowledgements

I wish to thank an editor and two publishers for granting permission to reprint some of the material in this book:

- An earlier version of Chapter 1 is forthcoming as 'Absolute Generality Reconsidered', Karen Bennett and Dean W. Zimmerman (eds.), *Oxford Studies in Metaphysics*, vol. 7 (Oxford University Press), and is reprinted here by permission of Oxford University Press.
- An earlier version of some of the material in Chapter 3 is forthcoming as 'Neo-Fregeanism Reconsidered', Philip A. Ebert and Marcus Rossberg (eds.), *Abstractionism* (Oxford University Press), and is reprinted here by permission of Oxford University Press.
- An earlier version of Chapter 6 and Appendix B, is forthcoming as 'An Actualist's Guide to Quantifying-In', *Crítica: Revista Hispanoamericana de Filosofía* (forthcoming), and is reprinted here by permission of the editor.
- An earlier version of Appendix A appeared as an appendix to 'On Specifying Truth-Conditions', *The Philosophical Review* 117 (2008), and is reprinted here by permission of Duke University Press. The text is also forthcoming as an appendix to 'An Actualist's Guide to Quantifying-In', *Crítica: Revista Hispanoamericana de Filosofía*.

For their many helpful comments, I am grateful to Elizabeth Barnes, George Bealer, J. C. Beall, Karen Bennet, Phillip Bricker, Stephen Biggs, Susanne Bobzien, Denis Bonnay, Alex Byrne, Ross Cameron, Matti Eklund, Adam Elga, Michael Friedman, Javier García Salcedo, Andrew Graham, David Gray, Caspar Hare, Benj Hellie, Øystein Linnebo, Jack Marley-Payne, Vann McGee, Charles Parsons, Alejandro Pérez Carballo, Graham Priest, Steve Read, Michael Rescorla, Damien Rochford, Marcus Rossberg, Alice Phillips Walden, Josh Schechter, Brad Skow, Paulina Sliwa, Jönne Speck, Bob Stalnaker, Zoltán Gendler Szabó, Gabriel Uzquiano, Robbie Williams, Tim Williamson, Jessica Wilson, Steve Yablo, and Dean Zimmerman.

I am also grateful to participants in the New England Logic and Language Colloquium, the Cambridge 'Mexican Food' Reading Group, and seminars at MIT, the Institut Jean-Nicod, the National University of Mexico and the University of Buenos Aires. Thanks are due to audiences at the Oxford and Harvard-MIT Graduate Conferences, the annual meetings of the American Association of Mexican Philosophers, the American Mathematical Society, the Central and Eastern APA and the Mexican Philosophical Association, and to audiences at Cornell University, McGill University, Stanford University, UC Santa Barbara, the University of Leeds, the University of Southern California, the University of St Andrews and the University of Toronto. Portions of this book were written during the tenure of an ACLS Burkhardt Fellowship at Harvard University's Radcliffe Institute for Advanced Study, for which I am very grateful.

Special thanks are due to Sally Haslanger, who first suggested that I write this book, to Jack Marley-Payne, who was in charge of indexing and helped prepare the final version of the manuscript, to six anonymous referees for *Oxford University Press*, who produced extremely useful comments, and to Peter Momtchiloff, for his patience and encouragement.

My greatest intellectual debt is to Bob Stalnaker. Alex Byrne once quipped that this book is a *reductio* of Stalnaker: "it starts with Bob's views, and develops them to the point of absurdity." There can be little doubt that at least half of Alex's statement is correct.

Contents

Part II Detours

Part III Appendices

PART I

Main Texts

1

Language and Metaphysics

Consider the following 'just is'-statements:

1. SIBLING
   For Susan to be a sibling *just is* for her to share a parent with someone else.
2. WATER
   For the glass to be filled with water *just is* for it to be filled with H_2O.
3. PHYSICALISM
   For such-and-such a mental state to be instantiated *just is* for thus-and-such brain states and environment conditions to obtain.
4. PROPERTIES
   For Susan to instantiate the property of running *just is* for Susan to run.
5. DEATH
   For Socrates's death to take place *just is* for Socrates to die.
6. TABLES
   For there to be a table *just is* for there to be some things arranged tablewise.
7. DINOSAURS
   For the number of the dinosaurs to be Zero *just is* for there to be no dinosaurs.

Statement 1 is utterly uncontroversial. Statement 2 should be pretty uncontroversial too, at least if we ignore certain complications (such as the possibility of impurities). Statement 3 is somewhat controversial (Chalmers 1996), but it seems to be the dominant view amongst contemporary analytic philosophers.

Statements 4–7, on the other hand, are all highly controversial metaphysical theses. My own view is that they are all true, but I won't try to convince you of that in this chapter. The aim of the chapter is to argue that they shouldn't be rejected *on general linguistic or metaphysical grounds*. I will proceed by defending a conception of language I call 'compositionalism', and showing that it makes room for Statements 4–7. I will then argue that a compositionalist who accepts Statements 4–7 won't thereby be left with an unattractive metaphysics.

The plan for the chapter is as follows. I will start by explaining how I think the 'just is'-operator should be understood (Section 1.1). I will then introduce my foil: a view I refer to as *metaphysicalism*. Metaphysicalists believe that in order for an atomic sentence to be true, there needs to be a certain kind of correspondence between the logical form of the sentence and the 'metaphysical structure' of reality. I will explain why I think metaphysicalism is bad philosophy of language (Section 1.2), and develop compositionalism as an alternative (Section 1.3). Attention will then turn to metaphysics. I will argue that compositionalism does not lead to untoward metaphyical consequences, even if one accepts 'just is'-statements such as 4–7 (Sections 1.4 and 1.5).

1.1 The 'Just is'-Operator

Before mounting my defense of compositionalism, it will be useful to say something about how I will be understanding the 'just is'-operator, as it occurs in Statements 1–7.

Consider SIBLING as an example. What it takes for SIBLING to be true is for there to be *no difference* between Susan's having a sibling and Susan's sharing a parent with someone else. If Susan is a sibling it is *thereby* the case that she shares a parent with someone else, and if she shares a parent with someone else it is *thereby* the case that she is a sibling. More colorfully: when God created the world, and made it the case that Susan shared a parent with someone else, there was nothing *extra* she had to do, or refrain from doing, in order to ensure that Susan was a sibling. She was already done. And when God created the world, and made it the case that Susan was a sibling, there was nothing *extra* she had to do, or refrain from doing, in order to ensure that Susan shared a parent with someone else. She was already done.

In the special case in which Susan is, in fact, a sibling, there is an additional way of clarifying the meaning of SIBLING. For SIBLING to be true is for 'Susan is a sibling' and 'Susan shares a parent with someone else' to be full and accurate descriptions of the *same feature of reality*.

Other 'just is'-statements should be understood in the same sort of way. For DEATH to be true is for there to be *no difference* between Socrates's dying and his death's taking place. When Socrates dies it is *thereby* the case that his death takes place, and when his death takes place it is *thereby* the case that he dies. The feature of reality that is fully and accurately described by saying 'Socrates's death has taken place' is also fully and accurately described by saying 'Socrates died'.

It is useful to compare SIBLING and DEATH with an identity-statement such as 'Hesperus is Phosphorus'. If you accept 'Hesperus is Phosphorus', then you believe that there is no difference between traveling to Hesperus and traveling to Phosphorus. Someone who travels to Hesperus has *thereby* traveled to Phosphorus, and someone who travels to Phosphorus has *thereby* traveled to Hesperus. The feature of reality that is fully and accurately described by saying 'A Soviet spaceship traveled to Hesperus' is also fully and accurately described by saying 'A Soviet spaceship traveled to Phosphorus'.

Since I will be treating 'just is'-statements as equivalent to the corresponding 'no difference' statements, I will be treating the 'just is'-operator as *symmetric*. There is a different reading of 'just is' on which it fails to be symmetric. One could suggest, for example, that a 'just is'-statement should only be counted as true if the right-hand-side 'explains' the right-hand-side, or if it is in some sense 'more fundamental'. This is *not* the reading that will be relevant for present purposes. If you find the asymmetric reading more natural than the symmetric reading, please substitute a suitable 'no difference'-statement for each 'just is'-statement in the text.

There is a lot more to be said about 'just is'-statements, but further discussion will be postponed to Chapter 2.

1.2 Metaphysicalism

I this section I will introduce my foil: *metaphysicalism*. It makes no difference for present purposes whether there are any actual metaphysicalists.

The point of introducing metaphysicalism is that it will make it easier to explain what compositionalism amounts to, and why it is an attractive thesis. (We will return to the question of whether metaphysicalism has any actual adherents in Section 1.5.)

Metaphysicalism is the conjunction of two theses. The first concerns metaphysics; the second concerns reference.[1]

Metaphysics A metaphysicalist believes that there is a 'metaphysically privileged' way of carving up reality into its constituent parts. Suppose, for example, that Susan runs. As long as one is suitably deflationary about fact-talk, one might think of the relevant feature of reality as a *fact*: the fact that Susan runs. Let us agree that this fact can be divided into distinct *constituents*; as it might be: Susan and the property of running. Someone might argue that there are other ways of carving up this very fact into distinct components. Perhaps it can also be carved up into the property of running and the (second-order) property of being instantiated by Susan. The first metaphysicalist thesis is the claim that only one such carving would successfully 'carve the world at the joints'. Even if it is in some sense true that a given fact can be carved up into constituents in more than one way—something that the metaphysicalist need not concede—only one of these carvings will correspond to what the world is like 'fundamentally speaking'. Only one of them would correspond to the world's 'metaphysical structure'.

Reference A metaphysicalist believes that in order for an atomic sentence to be true, there needs to be a certain kind of correspondence between the logical form of a sentence (i.e. its semantically operative lower-level syntactic structure) and the metaphysical structure of reality (i.e. the metaphysically privileged carving of reality into constituent parts). Consider, for example, the sentence 'Susan runs'. Let us agree that in order for this sentence to be true, it must supply a full and accurate description of some feature of reality—in this case, the fact that Susan runs. According to the metaphysicalist, 'Susan runs' can only supply an accurate description of the fact that Susan runs if the logical form of 'Susan runs' is in sync with the particular way in which the world's metaphysical

---

[1] For further discussion of metaphysicalist conceptions of language, see Heil 2003; for criticism, see Eklund 2009.

structure carves up the fact that Susan runs. In particular: metaphysical structure must have carved up the fact into an object and a property such that 'Susan' refers to the object and 'runs' expresses the property.

More generally, the second metaphysicalist thesis is the claim that in order for an atomic sentence $\ulcorner F(t_1, \ldots, t_n) \urcorner$ to constitute a full and accurate description of a given feature of reality, the following three conditions must hold:

1. The world's metaphysical structure carves up the relevant feature of reality into the objects $a_1, \ldots, a_n$ and the property P.
2. For each i, the singular term $\ulcorner t_i \urcorner$ refers to a_i.
3. The predicate F expresses P.

Metaphysicalism is a substantial view. Notice, in particular, that metaphysicalists are immediately barred from accepting certain 'just is'-statements. Consider 'for Socrates's death to take place *just is* for Socrates to die'. The embedded sentences are both atomic, but they have different logical forms. Suppose for *reductio* that they both describe the same feature of reality, as the 'just is'-statement would have it. How does the relevant feature of reality get carved up by the world's metaphysical structure? At most one of the following can be true:

- It gets carved up into Socrates and the property of dying.
- It gets carved up into Socrates's death and the property of an event's taking place.

If the former is true, then the relevant feature of reality can be accurately described by 'Socrates is dying', but not by 'Socrates's death is taking place'. If the latter is true, then the relevant feature of reality can be accurately described by 'Socrates's death is taking place', but not by 'Socrates is dying'. Either way, the 'just is'-statement turns out to be false.

Here I am taking for granted that the logical form of a sentence can be read off more or less straightforwardly from the sentence's surface grammatical structure. This is a non-trivial assumption. Say you believe that proper logical analysis of 'Socrates is dying' reveals it to have the same logical form as 'Socrates's death is taking place'. Then you should think that the metaphysicalist could accept 'for Socrates's death to take place *just is* for Socrates to die' after all. Contemporary linguistics does suggest that there are certain cases in which there is a real mismatch between surface structure and semantically operative lower-level syntactic structure.

(See, for instance, the treatment of semantics in Heim and Kratzer 1998.) But, as far as I can tell, it is not the sort of mismatch that would allow the metaphysicalist to claim that sentences like 'Socrates is dying' and 'Socrates's death is taking place' have the same logical form. So the assumption that logical form can be read off more or less straightforwardly from grammatical structure is a harmless simplification in the present context.

There are certain 'just is'-statements that the metaphysicalist *is* in a position to accept. She is free to accept 'for the glass to be filled with water *just is* for it to be filled with H_2O', for example. For, as long as she is happy to identify the property of being filled with water with the property of being filled with H_2O, she will be in a position to claim that the logical forms of *both* 'the glass is filled with water' and 'the glass is filled with H_2O' are in sync with the metaphysical structure of the fact that the glass is filled with water. For similar reasons, the metaphysicalist is free to accept SIBLING and PHYSICALISM, from Section 1.

The metaphysicalist is, however, barred from accepting PROPERTIES. And, on reasonable assumptions about the treatment of non-atomic sentences, she is also barred from accepting DINOSAURS and TABLES. As I noted above, these are all controversial metaphysical theses. What is striking about metaphysicalism is that it rules them out *merely on the basis of syntactic considerations*.

1.2.1 Metaphysical Structure

Metaphysicalism is a hybrid of linguistic and metaphysical theses. It deploys a metaphysical assumption—the existence of metaphysical structure—to impose a constraint on reference. It is not obvious to me, however, that the notion of metaphysical structure is in good order. I would like to make a few remarks about that before turning to my official argument against metaphysicalism.

Let me start by talking about objectivism. Most of us are objectivists about astronomy. We believe that it makes sense to speak of what is objectively the case concerning celestial bodies, as something over and above what is true *according* to one person or another. Many philosophers, but not all, are objectivists about morality. They believe that it makes sense to speak of what is objectively good, as something over and above what would be good *with respect to* some value system or other. Few philosophers, if any, are objectivists about fashion. You may think that ascots are fashionable. But it would be preposterous to suggest that they are *objectively* fashionable: fashionable over and above the tastes of some community or other.

Objectivism comes at a cost. An objectivist about fashion, for example, would be faced with the awkward task of elucidating a non-trivial connection between what is objectively fashionable and what various communities take to be fashionable. She would also have to choose between coming up with an explanation of what it takes for something to be objectively fashionable and burdening her picture of the world with the view that there are brute facts about objective fashion. And the rewards for her efforts would be decidedly meager. For it is not clear what theoretical advantages fashion objectivism could bring. As far as I can tell, interesting theoretical questions concerning fashion can all be addressed by using a community-relative notion of fashionability.

When the price of objectivism is not worth paying, one should do more than simply deny that the relevant objectivist notion has any instances. One should deny that the notion *makes sense*. For someone who claims to understand the notion of objective fashionability faces the burden of elucidating the connection between objective and community-relative fashionability, whether or not she thinks the world happens to contain any instances of objectively fashionable outfits. What gives rise to the explanatory burden is the assumption that objective fashionability makes sense, not the assumption that there are any instances. (In some cases, of course, the price of objectivism *is* worth paying. Objectivism about astronomy is fruitful enough that few would feel unduly burdened by the need to explain the connection between objective astronomical truth and astronomical truth according to an agent.)

Metaphysics is filled with objectivist views. There are metaphysicians who believe that it makes sense to speak of objective similarity, as something over and above what might strike an agent as similar (Lewis 1983a, 1984). There are metaphysicians who believe it makes sense to speak of objectively fundamental vocabulary, as something over and above the role a piece of vocabulary plays in some scientific theory or other (Fine 2001; Schaffer 2009; Sider 2012). And—most relevantly for present purposes—a metaphysician might think that it makes sense to speak of the objectively correct way of carving up reality into objects, as something over and above the syntactic properties of the various representations one might use to describe the world.

Before embracing a form of metaphysical objectivism, it is important to be mindful of the costs. When it comes to metaphysical structure, it is not obvious to me that the price is worth paying. For I suspect that many of the most interesting metaphysical questions can be addressed without having to appeal to the notion of metaphysical structure. If so, the need to elucidate the connection between an objectively correct way of carving up reality and the ways in which reality gets carved up by our representations may be too high a price to pay for the resulting theoretical benefits. (I do not claim, however, that it would be irrational to think otherwise; see, for instance, Schaffer 2009 and Sider 2012; for a critique of certain forms of metaphysical objectivism, see Hofweber 2009.)

1.2.2 Bad Philosophy of Language

Even though I worry that the notion of metaphysical structure may turn out to be senseless, I will not be relying on such a claim anywhere in the book. My official argument against metaphysicalism will be based on the claim that it is bad philosophy of language.

Metaphysicalism is a close cousin of the 'picture theory' that Wittgenstein advocated in the *Tractatus*.[2] And it ought to be rejected for just the reason Wittgenstein rejected the picture theory in his later writings. Namely: if one looks at the way language is actually used, one finds that usage is not beholden to the constraint that an atomic sentence can only be true if its logical form is in suitable correspondence with the metaphysical structure of the world.

It is simply not the case that ordinary speakers are interested in conveying information about metaphysical structure. The sentences 'a death has occurred' and 'someone died', for example, are used more or less interchangeably in non-philosophical contexts. An ordinary speaker might choose to assert one rather than the other on the basis stylistic considerations, or in order to achieve the right emphasis, or in order to create the right context for a future assertion. But it would be tendentious to suggest that her choice turns on her views about metaphysical structure. It is not as if an ordinary speaker would only be prepared to assert 'a death has taken place' instead of 'someone died' if she has a certain metaphysical

---

[2] Here I have in mind a traditionalist interpretation of the *Tractatus* (Hacker 1986; Pears 1987). See, however, Goldfarb 1997.

view about *events* (namely, that they are amongst the entities carved out by the world's metaphysical structure). Think about how inappropriate it would be to respond to an assertion of 'a death has occurred' in a non-philosophical context by saying 'I am certainly prepared to grant that someone died, but I just don't think that the world contains events amongst its ultimate furniture'. Your interlocutor would think that you have missed the point of her assertion, and gone off to a different topic.

If ordinary *assertions* of 'a death has taken place' are not intended to limn the metaphysical structure of the world, what could be the motivation for thinking that the truth-conditions of the *sentence asserted* play this role? As far as I can tell, it is nothing over and above the idea that logical form ought to correspond to metaphysical structure. Remove this idea and there is no motivation left. To buy into metaphysicalism is to start out with a preconception of the way language ought to work, and impose it on our linguistic theorizing from the outside—from beyond what is motivated by the project of making sense of our linguistic practice.

1.2.3 Moderate Metaphysicalism

There is a *moderate* form of metaphysicalism according to which the constraint that there be a correspondence between logical form and metaphysical structure applies only to assertions made by philosophers in the 'ontology room'. When I use the term 'metaphysicalism' here, the view I have in mind is always *non-moderate* metaphysicalism. My arguments for the claim that metaphysicalism is bad philosophy of language do not apply to moderate metaphysicalism. For all I know, there is a special convention governing discourse in the ontology room, which demands correspondence between semantic and metaphysical structure.

Although I am not myself a moderate metaphysicalist, moderate metaphysicalism is compatible with all the main theses of this book. In particular, a moderate metaphysicalist is free to accept a 'just is'-statement such as 'for Socrates's death to take place *just is* for Socrates to die'. All she needs to do is insist that at most one side of the 'just is'-statement is taken in an ontology-room spirit. To avoid confusion, moderate metaphysicalists might consider introducing a syntactic marker for ontology-room discourse (Fine 2001). Accordingly, they could use something along the lines of

DEATH (Fundamentalist Version)
   What it is, *fundamentally speaking*, for Socrates's death to take place
   is for Socrates to die

or

   what it *really is* for Socrates's death to take place is for Socrates to
   die

to indicate that the feature of reality described by 'Socrates's death has
taken place' gets carved by the world's metaphysical structure in a way
that corresponds to the logical form of 'Socrates died'.

Just to be clear: this is *not* what I intend when I use 'just is'-statements
in this book. The fundamentalist version of DEATH consists of two claims:
(1) that there is no difference between Socrates's death taking place and
Socrates's dying, and (2) that the logical form of 'Socrates dies' is in sync
with the metaphysical structure of the fact that Socrates dies. When I use
a 'just is'-statement like DEATH in this book, I intend to express the first
of these claims while remaining *neutral* on the second.

Why such neutrality? Why not follow neo-Aristotelian approaches
to metaphysics, and distinguish between more and less fundamental
descriptions of reality? (Schaffer 2009) Why not claim that the truth of
'Socrates's death took place' is, in some sense, 'grounded' in the fact that
Socrates died?

I wish to remain neutral for two reasons. The first is that none of the
answers to philosophical puzzles that I offer in this book will depend on
taking a stand on issues of fundamentality. So why burden the view with
unnecessary commitments? The second reason is that it is not obvious to
me that the relevant notion of fundamentality makes sense—and not just
because I do not feel like I have a good handle on it myself. As I noted
above, objectivism comes at a cost, and objectivism about fundamentality
is no exception. In conceding that it makes sense to say that some
descriptions of reality are more fundamental than others, one burdens one's
picture of reality with an additional primitive (objective fundamentality)
and incurs additional explanatory commitments (there is, for example,
the need to explain what it means to say that a piece of vocabulary is
'fundamental', as something over and above the role it plays in some
scientific theory or other). Such costs may well be worth paying, since

the introduction of a new primitive could certainly prove fruitful, and there may well be satisfying answers to the added explanatory commitments. But it is not obvious to me whether the costs are indeed worth paying.

1.3 Compositionalism

I would now like to consider an alternative to metaphysicalism: the view I shall refer to as *compositionalism*.

Suppose you introduce the verb 'to tableize' into your language, and accept 'for it to tableize *just is* for there to be a table' (where the 'it' in 'it tableizes' is assumed to play a dummy role). Then you will think that what would be required of the world in order for the truth-conditions of 'it tableizes' to be satisfied is precisely what would be required of the world in order for the truth-conditions of 'there is a table' to be satisfied. In both cases, what would be required is that there be a table (equivalently: that it tableize). So you will think that for the purposes of stating that there is a table, object-talk—our system of singular terms, and corresponding variables and quantifiers—is *optional*. One can state that there is a table by employing a quantifier that binds singular-term positions—as in 'there is a table'—but also by employing an essentially different logical form—as in 'it tableizes'.

If object-talk is optional, what is the point of giving it a place in our language? The right answer, it seems to me, is 'compositionality'. A language involving object-talk—that is, a language including singular terms and quantifiers binding singular-term-positions—is attractive because it enables one to give a recursive specification of truth-conditions for a class of sentences rich in expressive power. But there is not much more to be said on its behalf. In setting forth a language, we want the ability to express a suitably rich range of *truth-conditions*. If we happen to carry out this aim by bringing in singular terms, it is because they supply a convenient way of specifying the right range of truth-conditions, not because they have some further virtue.[3]

---

[3] For relevant discussion, see Burgess 2005; for a statement of a view similar to the one developed here, see Dummett 1981: 497.

Compositionalism—as I shall understand it here—is the conjunction of two claims, one concerning singulartermhood, the other concerning reference:[4]

Singulartermhood The following three conditions are jointly sufficient for an expression *t* to count as a genuine singular term:

1. SYNTAX

   t behaves *syntactically* like a singular term: it generates grammatical strings when placed in the right sorts of syntactic contexts.

2. TRUTH-CONDITIONS

   Truth-conditions have been assigned to every sentence involving *t* that one wishes to make available for use.

3. LOGICAL FORM

   This assignment of truth-conditions is such as to respect any inferential connections that are guaranteed by the *logical forms* of the relevant sentences. In particular:

   > If ϕ and ψ have been assigned truth-conditions, and if ψ is a logical consequence of ϕ (that is, if logical form guarantees that ψ is true if ϕ is), then satisfaction of the truth-conditions assigned to ϕ is at least as strong a requirement on the world as satisfaction of the truth-conditions assigned to ψ.[5]

---

[4] It is worth noting that our definition of compositionalism presupposes notions that are better understood in formal languages than in natural languages—notions like 'behaves syntactically like a singular term', 'is a logical consequence of' and 'is an inferential analogue of "$\exists x(x = t)$"'. The result is that our definition of compositionalism does not, on its own, deliver a compositionalist characterization of singulartermhood and reference for natural languages. It is important to keep in mind, however, that such a characterization is more than our definition is meant to achieve. While it would certainly be desirable for a compositionalist to be in a position to formulate a general theory of singulartermhood and reference, such a theory is not required for the purposes of this book. What we need is enough of an understanding of compositionalism to argue that compositionalism is a genuine alternative to metaphysicalism, and to argue that a compositionalist would see no linguistic obstacle to accepting 'just is'-statements such as those listed in Section 1.1. The task of articulating a compositionalist characterization of singulartermhood and reference for natural language would require a detailed discussion of the vagaries of natural language, and therefore a shift from philosophy to linguistics. That would be an interesting project, but it is not the project of this book.

[5] Actually, the principle we need is slightly more general:

> If the sentences in Φ and Ψ have all been assigned truth-conditions, and if it is a logical consequence of the sentences in Φ that at least one of the sentences in Ψ must be true, then joint satisfaction of the truth-conditions assigned to any sentences

Reference   Assume *t* satisfies Conditions 1–3 above. Then the following additional condition is sufficient for *t* to have a *referent*:

4. TRUE EXISTENTIAL

The world is such as to satisfy the truth-conditions that have been associated with the sentence '$\exists x(x = t)$' (or an inferential analogue thereof).

Compositionalism is a substantial view. The best way to see this is to imagine the introduction of a new family of singular terms ⌜the direction* of *a*⌝, where *a* names a line. The only atomic sentences involving direction*-terms one treats as well-formed are those of the form 'the direction* of *a* = the direction* of *b*', but well-formed formulas are closed under negation, conjunction and existential quantification. A sentence ϕ is said to have the same truth-conditions as its nominalization $[\phi]^N$, where nominalizations are defined as follows:[6]

> in Φ is at least as strong a requirement on the world as the requirement that the truth-conditions of at least one sentence in Ψ be satisfied.

From the more general principle it follows that:

> (a) a logical truth—that is, a logical consequence of the empty set—is assigned trivial truth-conditions (if assigned truth-conditions at all); and
>
> (b) a logical falsehood—that is, a sentence that logically entails the empty set—is assigned impossible truth-conditions (if assigned truth-conditions at all).

If one is working with a classical first-order object-language (and a classical metalanguage), one also gets the result that the logical connectives are assigned their standard interpretations, if assigned truth-conditions. In particular:

> (c) what it takes for the truth-conditions of a conjunction to be satisfied is for the truth-conditions of each conjunct to be satisfied; and
>
> (d) what it takes for the truth-conditions of a negation to be satisfied is for the truth-conditions of the negatum to fail to be satisfied.
>
> [*Proof*: any logical truth entails $\{\phi, \neg\phi\}$, so if the truth-conditions of one of ϕ and $\neg\phi$ fail to be satisfied, the truth-conditions of the other must be satisfied. But it cannot be that the truth-conditions of both are satisfied because $\{\phi, \neg\phi\}$ entails a logical falsehood.]

For reasons famously articulated by Putnam 1980 the general principle does *not* suffice to guarantee that the quantifiers receive their standard interpretations.

It is also worth emphasizing that, in a standard first-order system, '$\exists x(x = t)$' is counted as a logical truth. So our general principle would deliver the result that the truth-conditions of '$\exists x(x = t)$' must be trivial. This should be regarded as undesirable by anyone who rejects the claim that everything exists necessarily. It is also undesirable for present purposes because it trivializes Condition 4 of our characterization of compositionalism. I shall therefore assume that the compositionalist works with a (negative) free logic.

[6] It is worth noting that the nominalizations of open formulas are open formulas, and therefore lack truth-conditions. Fortunately, all that is required for present purposes is an assignment of truth-conditions to *sentences*.

- $[\ulcorner\text{the direction}^\star\text{ of }a = \text{the direction}^\star\text{ of }b\urcorner]^N = \ulcorner a\text{ is parallel to }b\urcorner$.
- $[\ulcorner x_i = \text{the direction}^\star\text{ of }a\urcorner]^N = \ulcorner z_i\text{ is parallel to }a\urcorner$.
- $[\ulcorner x_i = x_j\urcorner]^N = \ulcorner z_i\text{ is parallel to }z_j\urcorner$.
- $[\ulcorner\exists x_i(\phi)\urcorner]^N = \ulcorner\exists z_i([\phi]^N)\urcorner$.
- $[\ulcorner\phi \wedge \psi\urcorner]^N = \text{the conjunction of }[\phi]^N\text{ and }[\psi]^N$.
- $[\ulcorner\neg\phi\urcorner]^N = \text{the negation of }[\phi]^N$.

It is easy to verify that every condition on the compositionalist's list is satisfied. Notice, in particular, that since $['\exists x(x = \text{the direction}^\star\text{ of }a)']^N$ is '$\exists z(z\text{ is parallel to }a)$', and since every line is parallel to itself, all that is required for the truth-conditions of '$\exists x(x = \text{the direction}^\star\text{ of }a)$' to be satisfied is that a exist.

Accordingly, the compositionalist will claim that the existence of a is enough to guarantee that the singular term 'the direction* of a' has a referent. Moreover, by employing the newly introduced vocabulary in the metalanguage, the compositionalist will claim that the referent of 'the direction* of a' is the direction* of a, and therefore that the existence of a is enough to guarantee the existence of the direction* of a.[7]

How is this possible? How could a linguistic stipulation, together with the existence of lines, guarantee the existence of *directions**? There is nothing deep or mysterious going on. As a result of the linguistic stipulation, the fact that is fully and accurately described by saying 'a is parallel to b' can now also be fully and accurately described by saying 'the direction* of a = the direction* of b'. Similarly, the fact that is fully and accurately described by saying 'a is parallel to a' can now also be fully and accurately described by saying 'the direction* of a = the direction* of b'. So *of course* the existence of lines is enough to guarantee the existence of directions*: for the direction* of a to be self-identical (equivalently: for the direction* of a to exist) *just is* for a to be self-parallel (equivalently: for a to exist).

---

[7] For closely related views, see Frege 1884; Dummett 1981; Wright 1983; and Rosen 1993. Discussion of compositionalism amongst contemporary metaphysicians in the United States has tended to focus on the work of Eli Hirsch, who draws on earlier work by Hilary Putnam. (See Putnam 1987 and Hirsch 2002; for criticism, see Eklund 2008 and Bennett 2009.) It is worth keeping in mind, however, that some of Hirsch's linguistic theses go significantly beyond anything defended here, and that his general attitude towards metaphysics is profoundly different from my own. (See, in particular, the discussion in Section 1.3.1 of the present text.)

Needless to say, the metaphysicalist would insist that such a linguistic stipulation is inadmissible. She would insist, in particular, that 'a is parallel to b' and 'the direction* of a = the direction* of b' cannot be full and accurate descriptions of the *same* fact. For they are atomic sentences with distinct logical forms. So they cannot both be in sync with the way in which the fact that a is parallel to b gets carved up by the world's metaphysical structure. According to the metaphysicalist, there can't be directions* unless some fact gets carved up into directions* by the world's metaphysical structure. And even if the existence of lines is taken for granted, no stipulation can tell us that directions* are amongst the objects carved out by the world's metaphysical structure.

The compositionalist, on the other hand, believes that an atomic sentence can be true even if there is no correspondence between logical form and metaphysical structure. So there is no immediate obstacle to atomic sentences with different logical forms delivering full and accurate descriptions of the same fact. We needn't check whether directions* are amongst the objects carved out by the world's metaphysical structure in order to determine whether there are any directions*. It is enough to observe that 'a is parallel to a' and 'the direction* of a = the direction* of a' are full and accurate descriptions of the same fact, and that a is indeed parallel to itself. (Notice, incidentally, that it is no part of compositionalism that there is no such thing as metaphysical structure. The point is simply that the notion of metaphysical structure does not figure in a proper account of the reference of singular terms.[8])

It is important to be clear that compositionalism does not entail any interesting 'just is'-statements unless it is supplemented with further claims. Notice, in particular, that compositionalism does *not* entail that all it takes for the direction of a (as opposed to the direction* of a) to exist is for a to exist. In order to get that conclusion we would need a substantial hypothesis about the truth-conditions of sentences involving the ordinary word 'direction'. In particular, we would need to help ourselves to the claim that the ordinary sentence 'the direction of a exists' has the same

---

[8] It is also worth noting that compositionalism is not in tension with the view—first suggested by Lewis (1983a, 1984)—that problems of referential indeterminacy can sometimes be resolved by attending to metaphysical naturalness. Compositionalism is a view about what it takes for a singular term to be in good order, not about the sorts of considerations that might be relevant to fixing the reference of singular terms. In fact, there is room for thinking that Lewis himself was a compositionalist (Lewis 1980).

truth-conditions as 'a exists'. And this is a non-trivial assumption. We would, in effect, be assuming that for the direction of a to be identical to the direction of b *just is* for a to be parallel to b, which is a controversial metaphysical claim. It is true that we made the analogous assumption in the case of directions*. But back then we were introducing a new term, and were therefore free to introduce truth-conditions by stipulation. (For a detailed discussion of linguistic stipulation from a compositionalist's point of view, see Chapter 8.)

Although compositionalism does not commit one to the acceptance of any interesting 'just is'-statements, it does *eliminate an obstacle* for the acceptance of 'just is'-statements. One is no longer barred from accepting a 'just is'-statement merely on the basis of syntactic considerations. But there is substantial work to be done before one can make a case for accepting any particular statement.

1.3.1 'Just is'-Statements in Metaphysics

Some of the 'just is'-statements a compositionalist is in a position to accept constitute interesting metaphysical theses: for the number of the dinosaurs to be Zero *just is* for there to be no dinosaurs; for Susan to instantiate the property of running *just is* for Susan to run. Let me say something about the sorts of considerations that might be relevant to deciding whether to accept 'just is'-statements such as these. (My discussion is very much indebted to Block and Stalnaker 1999 and Block 2002.)

When one accepts a 'just is'-statement one closes a theoretical gap. Suppose you think that for a gas to be hot *just is* for it to be have high mean kinetic energy.[9] Then you should think there is no need to answer the following question. 'I can see that the gas is hot. But why does it also have high mean kinetic energy?' You should think, in particular, that the question rests on a false presupposition. It presupposes that there is a *gap* between the gas's being hot and its having high kinetic energy—a gap that should be plugged with a bit of theory. But to accept the 'just is'-statement is to think that the gap is illusory. There is no need to explain how the gas's being hot might be correlated with its having high mean kinetic energy because there is no difference between the two: for a gas to be hot *just is* for it to be have high mean kinetic energy.

---

[9] This is a badly inaccurate statement of the thermodynamic theory of heat. Fortunately, the inaccuracies are harmless in the present context.

The decision whether to treat the gap as closed is partly a terminological issue. (How should we use the word 'heat'?) But in interesting cases the terminological issue is tied up with substantial theoretical issues. (Is the thermodynamic theory of heat superior to the caloric theory of heat?) And it isn't always easy to separate the two.

Rejecting a 'just is'-statement comes at a cost, since it increases the range of questions that are regarded as rightfully demanding answers (why does this gas have high kinetic energy, in addition to being hot?), and therefore the scenarios one treats as open possibilities (there is a hot gas with low mean kinetic energy). But having extra scenarios to work with can also prove advantageous, since it makes room for additional theoretical positions, some of which could deliver fruitful theorizing. (A proponent of the caloric theory of heat, for example, would want to make room for a scenario in which a substance is hot because it contains high quantities of caloric fluid, even though it is not made up of particles with high kinetic energy.) Disagreement about whether to accept a 'just is'-statement is best thought of as disagreement about whether the additional theoretical space would be fruitful enough to justify paying the price of having to answer a new range of potentially problematic questions. (I will return to this in Chapter 2.)

We have been focusing on an example from the natural sciences, but our conclusions carry over to 'just is'-statements in metaphysics. One has to balance the cost of rejecting the relevant statement—an increase the range of questions that are regarded as rightfully demanding answers—with the cost of accepting the statement—a decrease in the range of theoretical resources one has at one's disposal.

There is no quick-and-easy criterion for determining whether the extra theoretical space is fruitful enough to justify paying the price of having to answer a new range of potentially problematic questions. The only reasonable way to proceed is by rolling up one's sleeves and doing metaphysics (Graham 2011).

Suppose we are considering whether to accept 'for a time to be present *just is* for it to have a certain relational property'. (To keep things simple, I will ignore Einsteinian relativity.) By accepting the 'just is'-statement one would eliminate the need to answer an awkward question: what does it take for a time to be present *simpliciter*, as opposed to present relative to some time or other? But there may be a price to be paid, because it is not immediately obvious that one will have the theoretical resources to explain the feeling that there is something special about the present. By rejecting the 'just is'-statement, on the other hand, one would be left with a gap to fill—one needs to explain what it is for a time to be present *simpliciter* as something over and above being present relative to some time or other. One could try to fill the gap by saying something like 'to be present *simpliciter* is to be at the edge of objective becoming', and thereby introduce a new theoretical resource. It is not immediately obvious, however, that such a move would lead to fruitful theorizing, or be especially effective in explaining the feeling that there is something special about the present (Skow 2011). The decision whether to accept the 'just is'-statement is a decision about how to best negotiate these competing theoretical pressures. (As evidenced by Hare (2009), this debate can also be played out with respect to the case of the self, rather than time.)

Here is a second example. Suppose we are considering whether to accept 'to experience the sensation of seeing red *just is* to be in a certain brain state'. What sorts of considerations might be used to advance the issue in an interesting way? Jackson's Knowledge Argument immediately suggests itself:[10]

Mary is confined to a black-and-white room, is educated through black-and-white books and through lectures relayed on black-and-white television. In this way she learns everything there is to know about the physical nature of the world... If physicalism is true, she knows all there is to know. For to suppose otherwise is to suppose that there is more to know than every physical fact, and that is just what physicalism denies... It seems, however, that Mary does not know all there is to know. For when she is let out of the black-and-white room or given a color television, she will learn what it is like to see something red, say. (Jackson 1986: 29)

What Jackson's argument brings out is that physicalists face a challenge. They must somehow accommodate the fact that it seems like Mary acquires information about the world—information she did not already possess—when she first experiences the sensation of seeing red, even though physicalism appears to entail that she does not. My own view is that the challenge can be met (see Section 4.5). But someone who thinks that the challenge cannot be met might see the argument as motivating the introduction of possibilities that a physicalist would regard

---

[10] See Jackson 1982 and Jackson 1986; for a review of more recent literature, see Byrne 2006.

as unintelligible. According to the variety of physicalism I have in mind here, to experience the sensation of seeing red *just is* to be in a certain brain state. So it makes no sense to consider a scenario in which someone is in the brain state but lacks the sensation. If, however, one were to give up the physicalistic 'just is'-statement and countenance the intelligibility of such a scenario, one might be able to relieve some of the pressure generated by Jackson's argument. For one could claim that even though Mary knew all along that she would be in the relevant brain state when she was first shown a ripe tomato, she did not yet know if she would *also* experience the relevant sensation. It is only after she is actually shown the tomato, and experiences the relevant sensation, that she is in a position to rule out a scenario in which she is in the brain state without having the sensation. And this ruling out of scenarios substantiates the claim that Mary does indeed acquire information about the world when she is first shown the tomato.

I think there are good reasons for resisting this way of addressing the puzzle (Lewis 1988). But suppose one takes it to work. Suppose one thinks that by creating a gap between being in the relevant brain state and experiencing the relevant sensation—and thereby making room for the possibility of being in the brain state without having the sensation—one can adequately account for a case like Mary's. Then one will be motivated to give up the 'just is'-statement that keeps the gap closed ('to experience the sensation of seeing red *just is* to be in a certain brain state'). But doing so comes at a cost because it opens up space for awkward questions. For instance:

> I can see that Mary is in the relevant brain state. What I want to know is whether she is also experiencing the relevant sensation. I would like to understand, moreover, how one could ever be justified in taking a stand on this issue, given that we would find Mary completely indistinguishable from her zombie counterpart, or from someone with 'inverted' sensations.

1.3.2 *Avoiding the Metaphysicalist Legacy*

The metaphysicalist can be expected to reject statements 4–7 from Section 1. But it seems to me that these are all cases in which the advantages of accepting the 'just is'-statement far outweigh the disadvantages. Consider TABLES. By accepting the claim that for there to be a table *just is* for there to be some things arranged tablewise, one eliminates the need to address an awkward question: what would it take for a region that is occupied by some things arranged tablewise to also be occupied by a table? It is true that one also loses access to a certain amount of theoretical space, since one is no longer in a position to work with scenarios in which there are things arranged tablewise but no tables. It seems to me, however, that this is not much of a price to pay, since the availability of such scenarios is not very likely to lead to fruitful theorizing. But not everyone would agree (van Inwagen 1990).

For similar reasons, it seems to me that PROPERTIES, DEATH, and DINOSAURS are all eminently sensible 'just is'-statements. Again, not everyone will agree. But I hope to have convinced you that these statements shouldn't be rejected merely on the basis of *syntactic* considerations. They should be rejected only if one thinks that the resulting theoretical space leads to theorizing that is fruitful enough to pay the price of answering awkward questions.

And the relevant questions can be very awkward indeed. By rejecting DINOSAURS, for example, one is is forced to concede—with Benacerraf (1973)—that the following is a legitimate line of inquiry:

> I can see that there are no dinosaurs. What I want to know is whether it is *also* true that the number of the dinosaurs is Zero. And I would like to understand how one could ever be justified in taking a stand on the issue, given that we have no causal access to the purported realm of abstract objects.

If, on the other hand, you accept DINOSAURS you will think that such queries rest on a false presupposition. They presuppose that there is a *gap* between the non-existence of dinosaurs and dinosaurs' having Zero as a number—a gap that needs to be plugged with a philosophical account of mathematical objects. DINOSAURS entails that the gap is illusory. There is no need to explain how the non-existence of dinosaurs might be correlated with dinosaurs' having Zero as a number because there is no difference between the two: for the number of the dinosaurs to be Zero *just is* for there to be no dinosaurs.

Of course, you won't see the closing of this theoretical gap as a real benefit unless you think that the resulting theory is consistent with a sensible metaphysical picture of the world, and unless you think that it gives rise to a sensible philosophy of mathematics. The remainder of this chapter will be devoted to addressing the first of these two challenges: I will argue that a compositionalist incurs no untoward metaphysical commitments by accepting a 'just is'-statement like DINOSAURS. The second challenge will be addressed in Chapters 3 and 4, where I develop a semantics for mathematical discourse and an account of mathematical knowledge.

1.4 Life as an Anti-Metaphysicalist

Let an *anti-metaphysicalist* be a compositionalist who accepts metaphysically contentious 'just is'-statements. (Like metaphysicalism, but unlike compositionalism, anti-metaphysicalism is a hybrid of linguistic and metaphysical theses.)

Anti-metaphysicalism has a distinguished provenance. When Frege claims that the sentence 'there is at least one square root of 4' expresses the same thought as 'the concept *square root of 4* is realized', and adds that 'a thought can be split up in many ways, so that now one thing, now another, appears as subject or predicate' (Frege 1892: 199), it is natural to interpret him as embracing the 'just is'-statement:

> For the concept *square root of 4* to be realized *just is* for there to be at least one square root of 4.

And when he claims, in *Grundlagen* §64, that in treating the judgement 'line *a* is parallel to line *b*' as an identity, so as to obtain 'the direction of line *a* is identical to the direction of line *b*', we 'carve up the content in a way different from the original way', it is natural to interpret him as embracing the 'just is'-statement:

> For the direction of line *a* to equal the direction of line *b just is* for *a* and *b* to be parallel.

Other authors with broadly anti-metaphysicalist sympathies include Parsons (1974); Dummett (1981); Wright (1983); Rosen (1993); Stalnaker (1996); and Burgess (2005).[11] My impression is that many contemporary metaphysicians are nonetheless suspicious of anti-metaphysicalism. The

---

[11] Hirsch (2002) is a compositionalist, but it is not clear to me that he is also an anti-metaphysicalist.

purpose of this section is to get clear about what the view entails, and what it does not.

Realism A metaphysicalist might be tempted to complain that if anti-metaphysicalism were correct, there would fail to be a definite fact of the matter about how the world is. I have sometimes heard arguments such as the following:

> Say you believe that for the number of the dinosaurs to be Zero *just is* for there to be no dinosaurs. You believe, in other words, that a single fact can be described fully and accurately by asserting 'the number of the dinosaurs is Zero' and by asserting 'there are no dinosaurs'. This presupposes that a single fact can get carved up into objects and properties in different ways. When the fact is described by asserting 'the number of the dinosaurs is Zero', it gets carved up into an individual (the number Zero), a first-order property (the property of being a dinosaur), and a second-order function (the function taking first-order properties to their numbers); when it is described as 'there are no dinosaurs', it gets carved out into a first-order property (the property of being a dinosaur) and a second-order property (non-existence).
>
> But if this is so, there can't be an objective language-independent fact of the matter about whether there are numbers. It all depends on how we choose to describe the world.

I am happy to grant everything in the first paragraph of this argument (as long as the metaphor of fact-carving is spelled out properly; see Section 1.5). The argument's second paragraph, on the other hand, strikes me as deeply misguided.

The anti-metaphysicalist is certainly committed to the view that a single feature of reality can be fully and accurately described in different ways. But this does not entail that there is no fact of the matter about how the world is. On the contrary: it is strictly and literally true that the number of the dinosaurs is Zero, and therefore that there are numbers. And this is so independently of which sentences are used to describe the world—or, indeed, of whether there is anyone around to describe it. The point is simply that the relevant feature of the world could also be fully and accurately described in another way: by asserting 'there are no dinosaurs'.

Moral: If realism is the view that there is a definite, subject-independent fact of the matter about how the world is, then anti-metaphysicalism is no less of a realist position than metaphysicalism.

The world as a structureless blob   'Wait a minute!'—you might be tempted to reply—'Isn't the anti-metaphysicalist still committed to the view that the world is a structureless blob?'

Absolutely not. The anti-metaphysicalist believes that it is strictly and literally true that there are tables, that a death took place, that the number of the dinosaurs is Zero, and so forth. So if the strict and literal existence of tables, deaths and numbers is enough for the world not to be a structureless blob, then it is no part of anti-metaphysicalism that the world is a structureless blob.

Perhaps what you mean when you say that the world might be a structureless blob is that the world might fail to be endowed with metaphysical structure. In that case, you should think that anti-metaphysicalism is *neutral* with respect to the question of whether the world is a structureless blob. It is compatible with anti-metaphysicalism that reality be carved up by the world's metaphysical structure. The point is simply that such a carving is not presupposed by ordinary language.

A brief aside: I don't really understand what Putnam has in mind when he talks about Internal Realism. But perhaps one could interpret some of what he says as an endorsement of an anti-metaphysicalist form of realism. (See, for example, Putnam 1987: 18–19).

Comprehensivism   Comprehensivism is that view that it is in principle possible to give a comprehensive description of the world—a description such that: (1) there is precisely one way for the world to be that would satisfy the description, and (2) the world, as it actually is, satisfies the description.

A critic might be tempted to think that anti-metaphysicalism is incompatible with comprehensivism. 'According to anti-metaphysicalism'—the critic might argue—'the same fact can be described in many different ways. One can say that there is a table, or that some things are arranged tablewise, or that the world tabelizes, or that tablehood is instantiated, or that two half-tables are put together in the right sort of way, and so forth, with no natural end. But one hasn't given an exhaustive description of the world until one has described it in all these ways. So the anti-metaphysicalist could never give a comprehensive description of the world.'

To see where the critic goes wrong, it is useful to consider an example. Suppose I hand you a box and ask you to give me a comprehensive description of its contents. You examine it and say: 'There is a hydrogen-1 atom in such-and-such a state, and nothing else.' It would be inappropriate for me to respond by complaining that your answer is incomplete on the grounds that it failed to mention at least two objects: a proton and an electron. Such a response would be guilty of double-counting. Part of what it is for there to be a (non-ionized) hydrogen-1 atom is for there to be a proton and an electron. So when you mentioned that there was a hydrogen-1 atom, the presence of protons and electrons was *already included* in the information you gave me. It is true that you never mentioned protons and electrons explicitly. But that was not required for your description to be comprehensive. All that comprehensiveness requires is that there be precisely one way for the contents of the box to be such that it would satisfy your description.

Moral: Anti-metaphysicalism does not entail that comprehensivism is false. What it entails is that there is more than one way of giving a fully comprehensive description of the world.

Paraphrase   It is tempting to think that in accepting a 'just is'-statement one commits oneself to the availability of a *paraphrase-method* for translating vocabulary that appears on one side of the statement into vocabulary that appears on the other. Consider, for example, an anti-metaphysicalist who accepts every instance of the following schema:

NUMBERS
>   For the number of the Fs to be *n just is* for there to be exactly *n* Fs.

It is tempting to think that she should also be committed to the claim that arbitrary arithmetical statements can be paraphrased as statements containing no mathematical vocabulary.

It seems to me that this would be a mistake. The availability of a suitable paraphrase-function depends on the expressive richness of one's non-mathematical vocabulary. And the decision to accept NUMBERS should be based on a cost-benefit analysis of the sort suggested above, not on whether one has access to a powerful enough stock of non-mathematical linguistic resources.

It is easy to overestimate the importance of paraphrase when one sees things from the perspective of a *nominalist*: someone who thinks that numbers don't exist. For a nominalist might think that non-mathematical paraphrases are needed to give an adequate statement of our best scientific theories, and of the real content of our mathematical accomplishments. But a friend of NUMBERS is no nominalist, and would see little value in stating our scientific theories or mathematical accomplishments in a non-mathematical language. Suppose, for example, that 'there is an even number of stars' can be paraphrased as a non-mathematical statement, ϕ. In all likelihood, ϕ will be significantly more cumbersome than its mathematical counterpart. And a friend of NUMBERS will think that its truth-conditions impose no less of a demand on the world, since she will think that for ϕ to be the case *just is* for there to be an even number of stars (Alston 1957). She will therefore see little point in reformulating her scientific or mathematical theorizing in terms of ϕ.

The question of whether it is possible to paraphrase arbitrary mathematical statements as statements containing no mathematical vocabulary is an interesting one, and will be taken up in Chapter 7. The present point is simply that one should not confuse NUMBERS with the view that a suitable paraphrase-function exists. Accepting a 'just is'-statement is one thing; committing oneself to the availability of paraphrase-functions relating vocabulary on either side of the statement is another.

1.5 Absolute Generality

In this section I will consider the question of whether anti-metaphysicalists should think that there is a complete and final answer to the question of what there is.

There are several different ways of understanding the question:

FIRST READING
> Is there is a definite fact of the matter about *how* the world is, and is it in principle possible to give a fully comprehensive description of its contents? (For short: can one be a realist and a comprehensivist?)

SECOND READING
> Is there a definite fact of the matter about which entities are carved

out by the world's metaphysical structure, and is it in principle possible to give a complete list? (For short: is there such a thing as a *fundamental* domain?)

THIRD READING

Is there a definite fact of the matter about which entities the world might get carved into, and is it in principle possible to give a complete list? (For short: is there such a thing as a *maxi*-domain?)

We have seen that anti-metaphysicalism is compatible with both Realism and Comprehensivism. So, on the first of the three readings, there is no tension between anti-metaphysicalism and the view that there is a complete and final answer to the question of what there is.

What about the second reading? Anti-metaphysicalism is *neutral* with respect to the existence of a 'fundamental domain'. To address the issue of a fundamental domain would require deploying the notion of metaphysical structure, and anti-metaphysicalism does no such thing.

Let us therefore turn our attention to the third reading. The anti-metaphysicalist believes that there are tables. So a 'maxi-domain' would have to include tables. But according to the anti-metaphysicalist, the fact that there are tables could also be described by saying that there are half-tables put together in the right sort of way, or that the property of tablehood is instantiated, or that some mereological simples are arranged tablewise, or that the set of tables is non-empty, or that the number of tables is greater than Zero. So the maxi-domain would also have to include half-tables, and instantiated properties of tablehood, and mereological simples arranged tablewise, and non-empty sets, and numbers greater than Zero, and Zero itself, and so forth.

Could such a list ever be completed? It seems to me that anti-metaphysicalists should be skeptical of the claim that it could. It is not that an anti-metaphysicalist should think that the world is somehow *incomplete*. The problem is that there is no reason to think that our concept of 'carving the world into objects' is determinate enough to allow for a final answer to the question of how it might be possible to carve up reality into objects. Let me explain.

Unpacking the 'carving' metaphor   As I think it should be understood, a 'carving' of the world is nothing more than a compositional system of representation for describing the world. In the most familiar case, a carving is a compositional system of *linguistic* representation: a language in which the truth-conditions of sentences are generated recursively from the semantic values of a restricted set of basic lexical items. To say that a subject carves the world into *objects* is simply to say that she represents the world using a language that contains *singular terms*, or variables that take singular-term-positions. Similarly, to say that a subject carves the world into *properties* is simply to say that she represents the world using a language that contains *predicates*, or variables that take predicate positions.

Carving up the world is not like carving up a turkey. For the purposes of spelling out the carving-metaphor, one is *not* to think of the world as a big object—the mereological fusion of everything there is—and of a carving as a way of subdividing the world into smaller parts. The world, for these purposes, is to be thought of as 'the totality of facts, not of things', and a carving is to be thought of as a compositional system for describing these facts. (Compare Eklund 2008.)

When the carving-metaphor is spelled out in this way, the existence of a maxi-domain would require a final answer to the question of what counts as a possible system of compositional representation. And I see no *prima facie* reason to think that our notion of representation (and our notion of linguistic representation, in particular) are constrained enough for this question to have a definite answer. From the perspective of metaphysicalism, the range of admissible compositional languages is restricted by metaphysical structure, since only languages whose logical form is in correspondence with the metaphysical structure of the world are potential vehicles for truth. From the perspective of anti-metaphysicalism, on the other hand, the only constraint on logical form is that it deliver an assignment of truth-conditions to sentences from the semantic values of basic lexical items. So it is hard to say in advance what would count as a possible compositional language. Whenever we dream up a new mechanism for representing reality, the potential for a new compositional language—and hence for a new way of carving up the world—will be in place.

An analogy   An analogy might be helpful. Suppose you are told that the ordinals* are built up in stages. One starts with a 'base' ordinal*, and at each stage one gets a new ordinal* by pooling together all the ordinals* that have been constructed so far. The process is to be carried out indefinitely.

In the absence of further constraints, your understanding of 'ordinal*' (which may or may not be the same as your understanding of 'ordinal') will be hopelessly incomplete. It will be consistent with taking the ordinals* to be isomorphic with the natural numbers. But it will also be consistent with taking the ordinals* to be isomorphic with the natural numbers followed by an additional copy of the natural numbers—or two additional copies, or three, or as many copies of the natural numbers as there are natural numbers. In fact, one's understanding of 'ordinal*' will be consistent with taking the ordinals* to be isomorphic with any limit von Neumann ordinal.

Notice, moreover, that assuming that there is a definite plurality of von Neumann ordinals wouldn't bring a natural end to the process. For although your understanding of 'ordinal*' is consistent with taking the ordinals* to be isomorphic with the von Neumann ordinals, it is also consistent with taking the ordinals* to be isomorphic with the von Neumann ordinals, followed by an ω-sequence of additional objects—or two ω-sequences of additional objects, or an additional ω-sequence for each von Neumann ordinal. And so on.

If you give me a definite characterization of 'ordinal*', I can use it to supply a significantly more generous one. (I can say, for instance, 'the ordinals* are isomorphic to the structure you just articulated followed by a copy of the structure you just articulated for every point in the structure you just articulated'.) And, crucially, I am *not* able to say anything definite about what it would mean to continue this sort of process 'all the way up'—anything significantly more illuminating than the original instruction to carry on the process 'indefinitely'.

The upshot is that there is no sense to be made of an absolutely general ordinal*-quantifier. But this is not because of some dark metaphysical thesis about the nature of ordinals*, and it is not because of some mysterious limit on our referential abilities: it is simply that the notion of ordinal* is not well enough defined for the phrase 'absolutely all ordinals*' to have a definite range of application (Parsons 1974).

I think something similar holds for our general notion of linguistic representation. If you give me a definite characterization of 'linguistic representation', I suspect I'll be able to use it to supply a significantly more generous one. If you give me a first-order language, I can give you a second-order language. If you give me an α-level language for some ordinal* α, I can give you an $\alpha + 1$-level language (Linnebo and

Rayo forthcoming). But I'm not able to say anything very informative about what it would mean to iterate this process 'all the way up'—anything significantly more illuminating than the vague idea that it could be carried out 'indefinitely'. And, of course, the order of the quantifiers is not the only dimension along which the expressive power of a language might be expanded. If you give me a definite system of linguistic representation, there may be other ways in which I can use it to build a significantly more generous one.

A light-weight conception of objecthood?   You may be worried that my way of cashing out the carving-metaphor is too light-weight. 'If the only relevant difference between asserting "there are tables" and asserting "some things are arranged tablewise" is to do with the system of compositional representation one chooses to employ'—you might be tempted to complain—'then someone who asserts "there are tables" hasn't *really* committed herself to the existence of tables. For what she says could be true even if there are *really* no tables.'

As far as I'm concerned, all it takes for there to *really* [table thump!] be tables is for an English sentence like 'there are tables' to be strictly and literally true. And all it takes for 'there are tables' to be strictly and literally true is that there be some things arranged tablewise (equivalently: that the property of being a table be instantiated; equivalently: that there be two half-tables put together in the right sort of way; equivalently: that there be tables).

Perhaps you mean something different by 'really'. Perhaps what you have in mind is that in order for something to *really* exist, it must figure in a 'fundamental' description of the world. It must, in other words, be carved out by the world's metaphysical structure. In this sense of real existence, the view defended in this paper is *neutral* on the issue of whether there is anything that exists but doesn't 'really' exist.

Whence the Metaphysicalists?   I have often heard the complaint that the metaphysicalist is a straw man. 'You are attacking a view that nobody believes!', I am told.

The complaint would be unfair. As I emphasized in Section 1.2, metaphysicalism was introduced as a device for elucidating and defending compositionalism. If there are no flesh-and-blood metaphysicalists, that will help rather than hurt, since it will make it that much easier to bring people over to compositionalism, which is my real aim. I suspect, however, that there is no shortage of metaphysicalists amongst contemporary metaphysicians. The purpose of this section is to explain why I think this is so.

Our discussion of absolute generality suggests that the disagreement between metaphysicalists and compositionalists can be recast as a disagreement about the notion of objecthood. The compositionalist should think that the only real grip we have on the notion of objecthood is via the notion of singulartermhood (Dummett 1981: 497). If you ask me what an object is, I can use singular terms, or variables taking singular-term-positions, to give you some examples. Or I can use a quantifier binding such variables to make a more general claim—as it might be, '$\forall x(x$ is an object$)$'. But I can't do much more than that. According to the metaphysicalist, on the other hand, we have an independent grasp on the notion of objechood, one which goes via the notion of metaphysical structure. She will claim that part of what it takes to be an object is to get carved out by the world's metaphysical structure.

The lesson of our discussion of absolute generality is that this distinction matters. For if the compositionalist is right, our notion of objecthood is no more constrained than our notion of singulartermhood. And the compositionalist thinks that the notion of singulartermhood is itself pretty unconstrained: all it takes to successfully introduce a new singular term is to come up with a suitable specification of truth-conditions for sentences in which the term occurs (see Section 1.3). So there is no reason to expect a final answer to the question of what objects exist—not because the world is somehow incomplete, but because our notion of singulartermhood, and therefore our notion of objecthood, is so unconstrained. If the metaphysicalist is right, on the other hand, one should expect the question of what objects exist to be settled by the world's metaphysical structure.

So: whence the metaphysicalists? Many contemporary metaphysicians —perhaps even most—believe that there is a definite answer to the question of what objects exist. (For an extended discussion of this issue and a list of references, see Rayo and Uzquiano 2006.) But, as far as I can tell, there can be no good reason for thinking this in the absence of some version or other of metaphysicalism. So I *supsect* that the views of many contemporary metaphysicians are underwritten by a tacit adherence to some form of metaphysicalism. But few contemporary metaphysicians address the issue explicitly. So it's hard to be sure.

A language-infused world?   'Wait a minute!'—you might be tempted to complain—'Are you setting forth a view according to which the existence of objects is somehow constituted by language?'

Absolutely not. What is 'constituted by language' is the use of *singular terms*. If we had no singular terms (or variables taking singular-term-positions) we wouldn't be able to *describe* the world in a way that made the existence of objects explicit. But there would be objects just the same. Speakers of a language with no singular terms can say things like 'Lo, tableization!'. But for it to tableize *just is* for there to be a table. So even without singular terms, they would be in a position to convey information about tables.

For the anti-metaphysicalist, the existence of tables depends entirely on how the *non-linguistic* world is. If there are things arranged tablewise (equivalently: if it tableizes; equivalently: if there are tables), then there are indeed tables. If no things are arranged tablewise (equivalently: if it fails to tableize; equivalently, if there are no tables), then it is not the case that there are tables. The metaphysicalists' mistake is to conflate form and content. They think there is a difference in *content* (i.e. truth-conditions) between 'there are tables' and 'some things are arranged tablewise', when in fact there is only a difference in form (i.e. syntactic structure). So it is hard to give a final answer to the question of what objects exist, not because the world is somehow incomplete, but because our notion of singulartermhood—and therefore our notion of objecthood—is so unconstrained.

1.6 Conclusion

I have argued that a 'just is'-statement like TABLES or DINOSAURS shouldn't be rejected on general linguistic or metaphysical grounds.

I argued, first, that metaphysicalism is bad philosophy of language, and suggested compositionalism as a promising alternative. Compositionalists are in a position to accept a number of interesting 'just is'-statements. The possibility of accepting such statements can be extremely valuable, because by accepting a 'just is'-statement one eliminates the need to address a certain kind of awkward question. (By accepting DINOSAURS, for instance, one eliminates the need to answer a question that many philosophers have found troubling: 'I can see that there are no dinosaurs, but why is it *also* true that the number of dinosaurs is Zero'?)

I then argued that anti-metaphysicalists—compositionalists who accept metaphysically contentious 'just is'-statements—are not saddled with an unattractive metaphysics. They are not committed to anti-realism, or to the view that the world is a structureless blob, or to the view that the existence of objects is constituted by language. I noted, finally, that anti-metaphysicalists have reasons to be skeptical of the claim that there is a definite answer to the question of which entities the world might get carved into.

2

Logical Space

In the preceding chapter I developed the first component of my overall case for Trivialist Platonism, a form of Mathematical Platonism according to which every instance of the following schema is true:

NUMBERS
> For the number of the Fs to be *n just is* for there to be exactly *n* Fs.

I argued that the acceptance of interesting 'just is'-statements is compatible with an attractive philosophy of language, and an attractive metaphysics. In developing my arguments, however, I relied on a rough-and-ready understanding of the 'just is'-operator. The purpose of the present chapter is to further elucidate the 'just is'-operator by addressing the question of what sorts of considerations might ground the acceptance or rejection a given 'just is'-statement, and by establishing connections between the 'just is'-operator and other notions.

2.1 Accepting a 'Just is'-Statement

I will begin by developing an account of the sorts of considerations that might ground the acceptance or rejection of a 'just is'-statement. I will be developing, in other words, an *epistemology* of 'just is'-statements. The further question of what the truth or falsity of a 'just is'-statement consists in will be taken up in Section 2.3.

2.1.1 The Big Picture

Carnap believed that true sentences can be usefully divided into those that are true in virtue of the meaning of their constituent vocabulary, and those whose truth depends not just on meaning but also on the way the world is. The former—sentences like 'bachelors are unmarried'—were thought of as consequences of 'meaning postulates'. They were described as analytic and said to be knowable *a priori*. The latter—sentences like 'the mass of the Sun is approximately 1.9891×10^{30} kilograms'—were described as synthetic and said to be knowable only *a posteriori*.

Quine objected to Carnap by complaining that our understanding of notions like *meaning postulate* or *analyticity* is not robust enough to do the work demanded by Carnap's project. I think Quine was right about this, but I also think it is easy to overestimate the reach of his criticism. The lesson to take from Quine is that talk of meaning postulates and analyticity is a bad way of characterizing the sort of distinction Carnap was after, not that the project of finding such a distinction is misguided. The right way of making the distinction, it seems to me, is by using 'just is'-statements in place of analyticity.

A simple model of scientific inquiry can be used to illustrate the point. According to the model, logical space can be represented as a set of 'possibilities'. As inquiry progresses, one rules out possibilities one comes to see as unactualized, thereby narrowing the range of possibilities that one regards as candidates for truth.

On a Carnapian implementation of this model, logical space is determined by the analytic truths. Say that a set of sentences is *analytically consistent* if it is logically consistent with the set of analytic truths. Logical space can then be taken to consist of the *maximal* analytically consistent sets: analytically consistent sets with no analytically consistent proper superset. A meaningful sentence is counted as *synthetic* if it is logically entailed by some maximal analytically consistent sets but not others. The story is then that, as scientific inquiry progresses, one comes to see some synthetic statements as true and others as false.

On the alternate picture, we don't have a notion of analyticity robust enough to deliver a useful characterization of logical space. But one can use the set of true 'just is'-statements instead. Say that a set of sentences is *metaphysically* consistent if it is logically consistent with the set of true 'just is'-statements. Logical space can be taken to consist of the *maximal* metaphysically consistent sets: metaphysically consistent sets with no metaphysically consistent proper superset. A meaningful sentence is counted as *non-trivial* if it is logically entailed by some maximal metaphysically consistent sets but not others. The story is then that, as scientific inquiry progresses, one comes to see some non-trivial statements as true and others as false.

The Carnapian picture would be the more desirable of the two, if it were viable. For suppose one's language of inquiry has been fixed. Then, on the assumption that the analytic truths of the language are knowable *a priori*, the Carnapain picture would allow us to factor scientific inquiry into an *a priori* component—the delineation of logical space—and an *a posteriori* component—the ruling out of particular regions of logical space.[1] On the picture I am recommending, in contrast, the project of characterizing logical space cannot be cleanly separated from the rest of one's scientific inquiry because the truth of a 'just is'-statement cannot generally be known *a priori*.

How should one decide which 'just is'-statements to accept? What I suggested in Chapter 1 is that the decision should be the result of a cost-benefit analysis. By accepting a 'just is'-statement one reduces the size of logical space. The *cost* of such a reduction is a decrease in the range of theoretical resources one has at one's disposal. (By accepting 'to experience the sensation of being red *just is* to be in brain state R', for example, one loses the ability to account for Mary's cognitive accomplishment by deploying possibilities whereby Mary's brain is in state R but she is not experiencing the sensation of seeing red.) The *benefit* of the reduction is that one is relieved from the need to answer certain questions. (For instance, 'Why do people in brain state R experience the sensation of seeing red, instead of an "inverted" sensation?') And the relevant questions can be very awkward indeed: they don't lend themselves to satisfying answers from the perspective of one's current theorizing, and extensions of one's theorizing that might deliver better answers seem *ad hoc*.

The resulting picture is one according to which scientific inquiry involves three interrelated tasks. First, one must identify a language that is

---

[1] It is worth keeping in mind that a friend of analyticity will think that different languages yield different sets of analytic truths. And a Carnapian might think that the issue of whether the adoption of a particular language would lead to fruitful theorizing is not something that can be decided *a priori*. (See, for instance, §179 of the *Aufbau*.) So she might think that the the project of choosing a theoretical language cannot be cleanly separated from the rest of one's scientific inquiry. The result is that even if the Carnapian thinks that logical space can be characterized *a priori* once the relevant language has been selected, she may not take the project of characterizing a conception of logical space to be fully independent from the rest of one's scientific theorizing. (This is different from the approach I am recommending because on my proposal logical space cannot be characterized *a priori*, *even after the relevant language has been selected*.)

suitable for one's theoretical needs. Second, one must decide which of the 'just is'-statements that can be expressed in the language to accept, and thereby form a working hypothesis about the contours of logical space. Finally, one must work towards reducing the regions of logical space where one thinks that actualized possibility might be located. Developments in the third of these tasks are more common than developments in the other two. But the tasks are not independent of each other. Movement in any one of them can cause tensions in the other two, and lead to further adjustments. Successful theorizing requires finding a workable balance between all three.

2.1.2 World and Language

A sentence's truth-conditions, as they will be understood here, consist of a *requirement* on the world—the requirement that the world would have to satisfy in order to be as the sentence represents it to be. The truth-conditions of 'snow is white', for example, consist of the requirement that snow be white, since that is how the world would have to be in order to be as 'snow is white' represents it to be.

True 'just is'-statements have trivial truth-conditions; false 'just is'-statements have impossible truth-conditions. Consider 'to be hot *just is* to have high mean kinetic energy' as an example. What is required of the world in order for the truth-conditions of this sentence to be satisfied is that there be no difference between having high mean kinetic energy (i.e. being hot) and being hot. Equivalently: that there be no difference between being hot and being hot—a condition which is satisfied trivially. The result is that controversies surrounding the truth of a 'just is'-statement will never pertain to the following question: concerning the truth-conditions that are actually expressed by the 'just is'-statement, is the world such as to satisfy those truth-conditions? For everyone agrees that trivial truth-conditions are satisfied and impossible truth-conditions are not.

Disagreements concerning 'just is'-statements are, in part, disagreements about the satisfaction-conidtions of the expressions involved in the 'just is'-statement. A caloric-fluid theorist thinks that what it takes to satisfy 'is hot' is to contain sufficient quantities of caloric fluid, and her opponent thinks that what it takes is to have high mean kinetic energy. This is not to say, however, that controversies surrounding a 'just is'-statement are purely terminological.

Disagreements about the truth of 'to be hot is to have high mean kinetic energy' are connected to *empirical* questions (e.g the existence of a substance with particular properties), as well as differences in the lines of research that were regarded as fruitful (e.g. whether the theoretical resources that would be made available by countenancing possibilities whereby a high concentration of caloric would allow a substance to be hot without having high mean kinetic energy would be fruitful enough to earn their keep.)

It will be useful to consider some additional examples.

Example 1: The Zoologists   Consider two zoologists. Neither of them has any false beliefs about questions of lineage, or about who is able to interbreed with whom. But one of them thinks it fruitful to place considerations of lineage at the center of his theorizing whereas another finds it more useful to emphasize the ability of individuals to interbreed and produce fertile offspring.[2] This might lead to disagreement about which 'just is'-statements involving the term 'species' to accept. Whereas the first zoologist might be inclined to accept something along the lines of 'for two individuals to be members of the same species *just is* for them to share the right kind of lineage', the second might prefer something along the lines of 'for two individuals to be members of the same species *just is* for them to be members of a group of organisms that are able to interbreed and produce fertile offspring'.

There is an interesting sense in which this dispute is purely terminological. For even though the two zoologists have accepted different 'just is'-statements, and are therefore working with different conceptions of logical space, the rival conceptions are *isomorphic* to one another, in the following sense. Suppose the first zoologist characterizes a possibility whereby individuals x and y are members of the same species. The second zoologist will be in a position to characterize a corresponding possibility, by specifying that x and y are to share the right kind of lineage. Now suppose the second zoologist characterizes a possibility whereby individuals x and y are members of the same species. The first zoologist will be in a position to characterize a corresponding possibility, by specifying

[2] For a more sophisticated discussion of species concepts, see Claridge *et al.* 1997; for discussion of the surrounding philosophical issues, see Kitcher 1984 and Sober 1984.

that x and y are to be members of a group of organisms that are able to interbreed and produce fertile offspring.

The result is that any substantial theorizing that could be done from the first zoologist's perspective could also be done from the perspective of the second, and vice-versa. This is not to say that the dispute between them is *totally* insignificant: some terminological disputes are worth having. Acceptance of the right 'just is'-statement might be a powerful way of emphasizing that considerations of lineage should play a more central role in one's theorizing than considerations to do with the ability to interbreed, or vice-versa. And it might make it easier to formulate certain theoretical claims. Such advantages might be worth a fight. They are usually not worth a big fight, but sometimes they are (Haslanger 2012).

Example 2: The Chemist and the Crank   A chemistry crank believes that the chemical composition of various substances varies with temperature. Methanol, she thinks, is normally composed of hydrogen, oxygen and carbon; but at a temperature of precisely $\sqrt{2}$ degrees celsius, its chemical composition changes to hydrogen and platinum. Similarly, our crank expects the chemical composition of water to vary with temperature. Her model predicts that at a temperature of precisely π degrees celsius, water is composed of oxygen and gold. Our crank sets out to test this hypothesis by carrying out water-electrolysis at a range of temperatures. What she finds, of course, is that hydrogen and oxygen bubble up, regardless of how closely the temperature approximates π degrees. She concludes that every portion of water on Earth is composed of hydrogen and oxygen. She takes this to be a remarkable fact, in need of explanation. 'Perhaps Earth's gravitational field is getting in the way'—she thinks—'perhaps under low-gravity conditions water is composed of oxygen and gold at π degrees.'

What 'just is'-statements will our crank accept? Her model presupposes that we allow for a theoretical gap between 'x is composed of water' and 'x is composed of H_2O' so that 'why is this portion of water composed of oxygen and hydrogen?' can be treated as a legitimate demand for explanation. So she had better *not* to accept 'part of what it is to be water is to be composed of oxygen and hydrogen'. Perhaps she will instead be inclined to accept 'part of what it is to be water is to be a colorless, odorless liquid' (and therefore reject the idea that, e.g. 'why is this portion of water a liquid?' should be treated as presenting a legitimate demand for explanation).

Now consider a real chemist. She thinks that part of what it is to be water is to be composed of hydrogen and oxygen, so she does not think it at all remarkable that every portion of water on Earth be composed of hydrogen and oxygen. She sees no theoretical gap between 'x is composed of water' and 'x is composed of H_2O', and therefore rejects the idea that 'why is every portion of water on Earth composed of hydrogen and oxygen?' should be treated as a legitimate demand for explanation. But she does think that 'why is water liquid under such-and-such conditions?' presents a legitimate demand for explanation. So she would wish to reject 'part of what it is to be water is to be a liquid'.

There is much more at stake in the disagreement between the crank and the chemist than in the disagreement between the two zoologists. The first thing to note is that each of the zoologists has settled on a package of 'just is'-statements and ordinary theoretical claims that is empirically adequate by his own lights. In contrast, the crank is working with a package of 'just is'-statements and ordinary theoretical claims that is not empirically adequate, even by her own lights. For the view predicts that gold can be extracted from water under the right conditions (e.g. zero-gravity), and this is a result which she would recognize as incorrect if she were in a position to make the requisite observations.

There is, however, an additional difference between the chemistry example and the zoology example. Like the two zoologists, the crank and the chemist favor different scientific methodologies. And the most natural articulations of the different methodologies call for different ranges of 'just is'-statements. But in the zoology example, we noted that each of the two zoologists is in a position to find a satisfactory reformulation of her theory while adhering to the 'just is'-statements that are favored by his rival. In the case of the chemist and the crank, on the other hand, matters are not so simple. In order to accept 'part of what it is to be water is to be composed of oxygen and hydrogen' the crank would be forced to reformulate some of her chemical claims. Rather than saying, e.g. 'under ideal conditions, water is composed of oxygen and gold at π degrees celsius', she will now have to say, e.g. 'under ideal conditions, colorless, odorless liquids with such-and-such additional properties are composed of oxygen and gold at π degrees celsius'. As long as the crank is able to spell out the 'such-and-such' clause, carrying out the reformulations shouldn't be more than an inconvenience. But suppose that the crank isn't able to spell out the 'such-and-such' clause: all she has is a *partial* characterization of what it is to be water.[3] She believes that part of what it is to be water is to be a colorless, odorless liquid, but thinks that there might be more to being water than that. Then she may not be able to reformulate her theory within the framework of the 'just is'-statements that are preferred by the chemist. So—unlike the zoology example—we do *not* get the result that any interesting theorizing claims that could be articulated from the crank's perspective could also be articulated from the perspective of the chemist. (For instance, the crank will be unable to characterize, from the perspective of the chemist, a possibility corresponding to what she would have previously described by saying 'under ideal conditions, water is composed of oxygen and gold at π degrees celsius'.) A change in the 'just is'-statements that the crank accepts would *not* lead to an isomorphic conception of logical space. And, in this sense, the disagreement between the chemist and the crank about which 'just is'-statements to accept is *not* purely terminological.

Example 3: Deciding Between Rival Logics   Our final examples concerns the problem of deciding which sentences to count as *logically* true. When one treats a sentence as logically true, one does more than simply treat it as true. When the classical logician treats $\ulcorner \neg\neg\phi \leftrightarrow \phi \urcorner$ as logically true, for example, she is committed to the claim that the biconditional is true for arbitrary ϕ. But she is also committed to there being *no theoretical space* between $\ulcorner \neg\neg\phi \urcorner$ and ϕ. She will think, in particular, that an understanding of why $\ulcorner \neg\neg\phi \urcorner$'s truth-conditions are satisfied is *already* an understanding of why ϕ's truth-conditions are satisfied. There is no need to add an explanation of why the *transition* from $\ulcorner \neg\neg\phi \urcorner$ to ϕ is valid: that ϕ's truth-conditions be satisfied is *what it is* for $\ulcorner \neg\neg\phi \urcorner$'s truth-conditions to be satisfied.

By treating a sentence as a logical truth, one is, in effect, accepting a 'just is'-statement. Part of what it is to treat the sentence $\ulcorner \phi \leftrightarrow \psi \urcorner$ as a logical truth is to accept $\ulcorner$for it to be the case that ϕ *just is* for it to be the case that $\psi \urcorner$. And part of what it is to treat the sentence ϕ as a

---

[3] The issue of whether it is in principle possible for the crank to spell out the such-and-such clause is closely related to the discussion between friends and foes of two-dimensional semantics. Friends might claim that the crank's language-use determines an answer to the question of how the such-and-such clause should be spelled out, even if the crank is not immediately able to articulate it. Foes might disagree. For one side of the debate, see Jackson 1998 and Chalmers and Jackson 2001; for the other, see Block and Stalnaker 1999 and Stalnaker 2001.

logical truth is to accept ⌜for it to be the case that ϕ *just is* for it to be the case that $\top$⌝ (where $\top$ is a sentence one takes to have trivial truth-conditions).

Generally speaking, there is a delicate balance to be struck in deciding which 'just is'-statements to accept. If one accepts too many, one will be committed to eschewing scenarios that might have been useful in theorizing about the world. If one accepts too few, one opens the door to a larger range of possibilities, all of them candidates for truth; in discriminating amongst these possibilities one will have to explain why one favors the ones one favors, and although the relevant explanations could lead to fruitful theorizing, they could also prove burdensome.

The adoption of a logical system plays an important role in finding the right balance between these competing considerations. Take the decision to treat ⌜$\neg\neg\phi \leftrightarrow \phi$⌝ as a logical truth (and therefore accept every 'just is'-statement of the form 'for $\neg p$ to fail to be the case *just is* for p to be the case'). A friend of intuitionistic logic, who denies the logicality of ⌜$\neg\neg\phi \leftrightarrow \phi$⌝, thinks it might be worthwhile to ask why it is the case that p even if you fully understand why it is not the case that $\neg p$. In the best case scenario, making room for an answer will lead to fruitful theorizing. But things may not go that well. One might come to see the newfound conceptual space between a sentence and its double negation as a pointless distraction, demanding explanations where there is nothing fruitful to be said.

Even if none of the decisions one makes in adopting a family of 'just is'-statements is wholly independent of empirical considerations, some decisions are more closely tied to empirical considerations than others. And when it comes to 'just is'-statements corresponding to logical truths, one would expect the focus to be less on particular empirical matters and more on the question of how to best organize one's methods of inquiry. So there is room for a picture whereby an epistemically responsible subject can accept 'just is'-statements on the basis of considerations that aren't grounded very directly in any sort of empirical investigation.

2.1.3 The Upshot

By changing the 'just is'-statements one accepts, one changes one's conception of logical space. Different conceptions of logical space can be more or less hospitable to one's scientific or philosophical theorizing. So the decision to adopt a particular 'just is'-statement should ultimately be guided by the statement's ability to combine with the rest of one's theorizing to deliver a fruitful tool for scientific or philosophical inquiry.

When one revises one's conception of logical space, it can sometimes happen that the revised conception is isomorphic to the original. The result is that any substantial theorizing that could be done from one of the two perspectives could also be done from the other. In this sense, a debate about which of the relevant 'just is'-statements to accept is a debate about terminology. But it doesn't quite follow that nothing of interest is at stake. The new conception of logical space might supply a better way of calling attention to the right methodology, or make it easier to state the right scientific or philosophical theory. So disagreement about which 'just is'-statements to accept might be working as a surrogate for disagreement about interesting non-linguistic issues. And even if it is a surrogate that could ultimately be dispensed with, it might earn its keep by supplying an economical way of identifying the non-linguistic disagreement.

More interestingly, there are cases in which the revised conception of logical space is *not* isomorphic to the original. Here the issue of which of the rival 'just is'-statements to accept becomes genuinely important because one may be unable to articulate one's original theory in the alternate framework. The decision to adopt a particular 'just is'-statement over its rival will turn on the question of whether the new conception of logical space allows for better theorizing than the old—an issue that cannot be settled independently of the rest of one's scientific or philosophical theorizing. The result is that one's decision to adopt a particular 'just is'-statement won't be cleanly separable from other aspects of one's inquiry.

2.1.4 Objective Naturalness

I would like to mention a possible constraint on the acceptance of 'just is'-statements that has so far been ignored. Suppose one is an objectivist about naturalness: one thinks it makes sense to speak of a property's being *objectively* natural, as something over and above the issue of whether the property would be counted as natural by the lights of some subject or theory (Lewis 1983a). Then one might think that preference should be given to 'just is'-statements that take our predicates to pick out objectively natural properties.

Go back to the two zoologists. They disagree about the referent of the two-place predicate 'x is the same species as y'. The first zoologist takes it to be the property of sharing the right sort of lineage; the second zoologist takes it to be the property of sharing membership in a group of organisms that are able to interbreed and produce fertile offspring. If you think that the property of sharing a lineage is the most objectively natural of the two, you might think that there are metaphysical considerations favoring the first zoologist's position, and that one should therefore accept 'to be members of the same species *just is* to share a lineage of the right kind' in favor of its rival.

On this way of thinking about the zoologists' debate, one gets a guarantee that the disagreement won't be construed as a purely terminological matter. For the debate will be seen as turning on a substantial metaphysical question, and is therefore to be decided on the basis of metaphysical theorizing. Whether you see this as an advantage or a disadvantage might depend on your philosophical temperament. If you were initially inclined to see the debate as concerning a substantial metaphysical issue, you might welcome the newfound subject-matter. If, on the other hand, you were initially inclined to see the debate as less substantial, you might see the move to objective naturalness as muddying the waters.

The account of 'just is'-statements that I have offered here is certainly compatible with the view that in deciding which 'just is'-statements to accept, some weight should be given to the question of whether or not the relevant predicates get paired with objectively natural properties. It is worth mentioning, however, that this sort of approach has a couple of shortcomings.

The first thing to note is that there is a range of cases in which an appeal to objective naturalness won't be very effective. Consider a discussion over whether to accept 'to be hot *just is* to have high mean kinetic energy' or 'to be hot *just is* to contain large amounts of caloric'. If it was agreed on all sides that there is such a thing as the property of containing large amounts of caloric, there might be room for arguing that the debate ought to be resolved by determining whether such a property enjoys greater objective naturalness than the property of having high mean kinetic energy. But someone who thinks that what it is to be hot is to have high mean kinetic energy can be expected to think that there is no such thing as caloric. And there is a case to be made for the view that the property of containing caloric is like the property of being taller than Reginald Triplehorn: if Reginald Tripelhorn doesn't exist, then there is no such thing as the property of being taller than he is; similarly, if there is no such thing as caloric, then there is no such thing as the property of containing it (Kripke, 1980). So we are left with no rival property to compare for naturalness with the property of containing high mean kinetic energy.

Here is a more general way of putting the point. When rival 'just is'-statements generate isomorphic conceptions of logical space—as in the case of the two zoologists—proponents of the rival statements could consider the question of which ways of carving up their shared picture of logical space should be counted as objectively natural, and use their conclusions to reassess the status of the relevant statements. But rival 'just is'-statements don't always generate isomorphic conceptions of logical space, and in most of the interesting cases they do not. So proponents of rival 'just is'-statements might lack a shared conception of logical space on the basis of which to have the requisite debate about objective naturalness.

Consider the debate between intuitionists and classical logicians. Classical logicians think there is no theoretical space between p and $\neg\neg p$. Intuitionists disagree. And it is not just that they wish to allow for theoretical space between, say, the proposition that one can prove that p, on the one hand, and the proposition that one can prove a contradiction from the assumption that one can prove a contradiction from the assumption that p, on the other—*that* is something the classical logician will readily agree to. To the extent that intuitionism is genuinely incompatible with its classical counterpart, the debate is not about provability. In allowing for theoretical space between p and $\neg\neg p$, the intuitionist is allowing for a more generous conception of logical space than her classical counterpert—one according to which there are additional distinctions to be made. Correspondingly, in denying that there is any theoretical space between p and $\neg\neg p$, the classicist is adopting a more restricted conception of logical space—one in which the additional distinctions fail to make sense.

Now suppose that one hopes to construe the debate between intuitionists and classical logicians as a debate about which of intuitionist and classical negation enjoys greater objective naturalness. From the perspective of the classicist's conception of logical space, there is no such thing as intuitionist negation—the intuitionist is attempting to draw a distinction where there is no distinction to be drawn. So someone who, unlike the classicist, presupposes that the intuitionist negation is available to be assessed for objective naturalness has thereby begged the question in favor of the intuitionist.

The second point I would like to make is that the notion of objective naturalness comes at a cost. To see the worry, it is useful to go back to the discussion of objectivism in Section 1.2. Objectivism about fashion is the view that it makes sense to talk about an outfit's being fashionable objectively, as something over and above fashionability by the standards of some community or other. By endorsing such a view, one would, in effect, be rejecting a 'just is'-statement: 'to be fashionable *just is* to be fashionable by the lights of some community or other'. As a result, fashion objectivism delivers an increase in one's stock of theoretical resources. (For instance, it makes room for possibilities whereby an objectively fashionable ascot is universally regarded as tasteless.) But this increase in theoretical resources comes at a cost. Fashion objectivists face the awkward task of elucidating a non-trivial connection between objective fashion and fashion by the lights of a given community. They also have to choose between coming up with an explanation of what it takes for something to be objectively fashionable and burdening their picture of the world with the view that there are brute facts about objective fashion.

Objectivism about naturalness offers a similar tradeoff. By endorsing the view one would, in effect, be rejecting a 'just is'-statement: 'to be a natural property *just is* to be natural by the lights of some person or theory'. As a result, objectivism about naturalness delivers an increase in one's stock of theoretical resources. (For instance, it makes room for possibilities whereby an objectively natural property is universally regarded as unnatural.) But the increase in theoretical resources comes at a cost. Objectivists about naturalness face the awkward task of elucidating a non-trivial connection between objective naturalness and naturalness by the lights of a subject or theory. And they have to choose between coming up with an explanation of what it takes for a property to be objectively natural and burdening their picture of the world with the view that there are brute facts about objective naturalness.

I do not mean to suggest that objectivism about naturalness should be ruled out from the start. Its benefits may well turn out to outweigh its costs (Lewis 1983*a*; Schaffer 2009; Sider 2012). But it is important to be clear that it does come with costs.

2.2 Connections

In this section I will argue for a connection between the 'just is'-operator and four other notions: possibility, inconsistency, sameness of truth-conditions and why-closure.

I will *not* be presupposing that one of these notions is 'fundamental' and the rest are 'derived'. It is no part of the picture that possibility—to pick an arbitrary example—is the fundamental notion, and that the other notions should be understood on the basis of a firm and independent grasp of the distinction between the possible and the impossible. Instead, I will treat each of the five notions as contributing to our understanding of the rest, so that even if our grasp of any one of them is somewhat limited when considered in isolation, they are all better understood when considered in light of the connections with their peers.

2.2.1 Metaphysical Possibility

The use of 'metaphysical' in 'metaphysical possibility' lends itself to two very different readings (Rosen 2006).

On one reading, 'metaphysical' is used as a way of indicating a level of *strictness* that is to be employed when talking about possibility—a level of strictness more demanding than conceptual possibility but less demanding than physical possibility. Kment (2006), for example, suggests that we replace 'the concept of a possible world with the wider, non-modal notion of a world. Worlds [...] comprise both possible and impossible worlds [and] are ordered by their closeness to the actual world [...] [F]or a proposition to be metaphysically necessary is for it to be true in every world that has at least a certain degree of closeness to the actual world' (2006: 6–7). Nomological and conceptual possibility are said to work the same way, but with standards of closeness that are, respectively, more and less strict.[4] (A proponent of this sort of view need not think that metaphysical possibility captures a level of strictness that is philosophically significant; Cameron (2010) and Sider (2012) argue that nothing important would be lost if we chose to work with a different standard of stringency.)

On a second reading—arguably the reading that Kripke had in mind in *Naming and Necessity*—the role of 'metaphysical' in 'metaphysical

---

[4] See also Salmon 1989.

possibility' is to determine a *type* of possibility, rather than a level of strictness. It is meant to distinguish between possibility *de mundo* and possibility *de repraesentatione*.

The difference, informally, is that whereas possibility *de repraesentatione* is a property of *sentences*, possibility *de mundo* is a property of the *truth-conditions* expressed by such sentences. Somewhat more precisely, whereas possibility *de mundo* applies to ways for the world to be *regardless of how they happen to be represented*, possibility *de repraesentatione* is sensitive to how ways for the world to be happen to be represented. Logical consistency, for example, is a notion of possibility *de repraesentatione*. For 'Hesperus ≠ Phosphorus' and 'Hesperus ≠ Hesperus' differ in terms of logical consistency, even though satisfaction of their truth-conditions imposes the same (impossible) requirement on the world.

On this second reading, the role of 'metaphysical' in 'metaphysical possibility' is to clarify that the notion of possibility in question is to be thought of as a form of possibility *de mundo*, rather than a form of possibility *de repraesentatione*. The thought, then, is that metaphysical possibility is the most inclusive form of possibility *de mundo* there is. Going beyond metaphysical possibility is not a matter of going beyond a given limit of strictness: it is a matter of lapsing into *absurdity*.

I would like to suggest that when metaphysical possibility is understood in this way, there is a tight connection between metaphysical possibility and the 'just is'-operator:

> A first-order sentence (or set of first-order sentences) describes a metaphysically possible scenario if and only if it is logically consistent with the set of true 'just is'-statements.

And, relatedly:

> A 'just is'-statement ⌜for it to be the case that ϕ *just is* for it to be the case that ψ⌝ is true just in case the corresponding modal statement ⌜$\Box(\phi \leftrightarrow \psi)$⌝ is true.

So many philosophers have said so many different things about the notion of metaphysical possibility—and so much about the notion is poorly understood—that there are limits to how much light can be shed on the 'just is'-operator by defining it in terms of metaphysical possibility. It is better to think of the above connections as a two-way street: they use the notion of metaphysical possibility to help explain how the 'just is'-operator should be understood, but they also use the 'just is'-operator to help explain how the notion of metaphysical possibility should be understood. Neither of the two notions is being defined in terms of the other, but getting clear about how they are related is a way of shedding light on both.

In Section 2.1.1, I suggested that one can think of logical space as determined by the set of true 'just is'-statements. Regions in logical space correspond to sets of sentences that are logically consistent with the true 'just is'-statements, and a point in logical space corresponds to maximal such set. Now we are in a position to present a richer picture. Each region in logical space can be thought of as a metaphysical possibility: a consistent way for the world to be. A point is a maximally specific such region: a maximally specific possibility; for short: a possible world.

I will have much more to say about metaphysical possibility in Chapter 5.

2.2.2 Metaphysical Inconsistency

In Section 2.1.1, I introduced some terminology to describe sets of sentences that are consistent with the true 'just is'-statments—*metaphysical consistency*. Using this notation, one can describe the main contention of the previous subsection as follows:

> A first-order sentence (or set of first-order sentences) describes a metaphysically possible scenario just in case it is metaphysically consistent.

Here I intend the label 'metaphysical' in 'metaphysical consistency' to be given a Kripkean reading, analogous to the Kripkean reading of 'metaphysical' in 'metaphysical possibility'. It is meant to indicate that we are talking about consistency *de mundo*, rather than consistency *de repraesentatione*. As before, the difference is that whereas consistency *de repraesentatione* is a property of *sentences*, consistency *de mundo* is a property of the *truth-conditions* expressed by such sentences.

For a meaningful sentence to be *de mundo* consistent is for it to not represent the world as satisfying an absurdity. Consistency *de repraesentatione* is a weaker notion, and one for which we will have no use in this book. All it requires is that the sentence not represent the world as satisfying an absurdity *as far as could be ascertained a priori*, by reflecting on the sentence in light of one's mastery of the language.

The following is an example of a sentence which is inconsistent *de mundo* but consistent *de repraesentatione*:

> There is something that is composed of water but is not composed of H_2O.

Here is why. To be composed of water *just is* to be composed of H_2O. So a world in which something composed of water fails to be composed of H_2O is a world in which something composed of water fails to be composed of water, which is absurd.[5] So the sentence is inconsistent *de mundo*. But this is not something that could be discovered *a priori*, simply by reflecting on the sentence in light of one's mastery of the language. So the sentence is *de repraesentatione* consistent.

In contrast, consider:

> There is something that is composed of water but is not composed of water.

This sentence is inconsistent *de mundo*, for the same reason as before: it depicts the world as being such that something composed of water fails to be composed of water, which is absurd. But in this case it is natural to think that this could be discovered *a priori*, by reflecting on the sentence in light of one's mastery of the language. If so, one should say that the sentence is inconsistent *de repraesentatione*, in addition to being inconsistent *de mundo*.

I submit that there is a tight connection between representing an absurdity and the 'just is'-operator:

> A first-order sentence (or set of first-order sentences) represents the world as satisfying an absurdity if and only if it is logically inconsistent with the set of true 'just is'-statements.

Earlier I had claimed that going beyond metaphysical possibility was not a matter of going beyond a given limit of strictness, but a matter of lapsing into absurdity. We now have a different way of putting the point: to go beyond metaphysical possibility is to lapse into inconsistency *de mundo*.

---

[5] Here and throughout, I make the simplifying assumption that dialetheism is false. Dialetheists and paracompletists can be accommodated by the general picture I have been defending, but require a somewhat different diet of examples. For more on dialetheism and paracompletism, see Priest 2006; Field 2008; and Beall 2009.

The decision whether to accept a 'just is'-statement is, in effect, a decision about where to place the limits of absurdity. In accepting 'to be composed of water *just is* to be composed of H_2O', for example, one is committing oneself to the view that it would be absurd for there to be something composed of water but not composed of H_2O. An ordinary sentence like 'snow is white', in contrast, tells us nothing about the limits of absurdity. It merely helps discriminate amongst non-absurd ways for the world to be.

2.2.3 Truth-Conditions

In Section 2.1.2, I suggested that a sentence's truth-conditions consist of a *requirement* on the world—the requirement that the world would have to satisfy in order to be as the sentence represents it to be.

It is important to keep in mind that two sentences might have the same truth-conditions even if they have different meanings, in a pre-thoeretic sense of 'meaning'. Consider 'the Sun is hot' and 'the Sun has high mean kinetic energy'. These two sentences play very different roles in our linguistic practice, so it is appropriate to describe them as meaning different things. But one should still think that the two sentences have the same *truth-conditions*. For to be hot *just is* to have high mean kinetic energy. So there is no difference between what would be required of the world in order to be as 'the Sun is hot' represents it to be and what would be required of the world in order to be as 'the Sun has high mean molecular motion' represents it to be.

I would like to suggest that there is a tight connection between the 'just is'-operator and the notion of sameness of truth-conditions:

> The first-order sentences ϕ and ψ have the same truth-conditions if and only if $\ulcorner$for it to be the case that ϕ *just is* for it to be the case that $\psi\urcorner$ is true.

Suppose, for example, that you think that for A to be composed of water *just is* for A to be composed of H_2O. Then you should think that 'A is composed of water' and 'A is composed of H_2O' have the same truth-conditions. For what the former requires of the world is that A be composed of water. But to be composed of water *just is* to be composed of H_2O, which is what the latter requires of the world. Conversely: suppose you think 'A is composed of water' and 'A is composed of H_2O' have the same truth-conditions. Then you think there is no difference between satisfying the requirement that A be composed of water and satisfying the requirement that A be composed of H_2O. You should think, in other words, that for A to be composed of water *just is* for A to be composed of H_2O.

I shall say that a sentence's truth-conditions are *trivial* when the assumption that they fail to be satisfied would lead to absurdity. (In other words: a sentence has trivial truth-conditions just in case its negation is metaphysically inconsistent.)

Suppose, for example, that you accept 'for A to be composed of water *just is* for A to be composed of H_2O'. Then you should also think that the sentence 'if A exists, it is composed of water if and only if it is composed of H_2O' has *trivial* truth-conditions. For you will take the condition that A, if it exists, be composed of water if and only if it is composed of H_2O to place the same demands on the world as the condition that A, if it exists, be composed of H_2O if and only if it is composed of H_2O. And it would be absurd to suppose that such a condition fails to obtain.

When a sentence has trivial truth-conditions, I will say that *nothing* would be required of the world in order for its truth-conditions to be satisfied. (This involves ignoring absurd scenarios, but absurd scenarios are rightfully ignored.)

In evaluating a 'just is'-statement it is important to keep in mind that the notion of truth-conditions is distinct from our (pre-theoretic) notion of subject-matter. Compare, for example,

> For the world to contain water *just is* for the world to contain H_2O.

and

> For the world to contain water *just is*: (1) for the world to contain H_2O and (2) for it to either contain purple elephants or not contain purple elephants.

If one of these statements is true, then so is the other. For the requirement that the world either contain purple elephants or not is trivial. So there is *no difference* between the requirement that the world contain H_2O and the requirement that the world contain H_2O and either contain purple elephants or not. There is no denying, however, that the first of the 'just is'-statements above sounds more natural than the second. The difference is presumably due to the fact that the second statement appears to introduce a foreign subject-matter: purple elephants. But focusing on subject-matter would be a distraction in the present context. For the shift in subject-matter carries no shift in truth-conditions, and the truth-value of a 'just is'-statement is sensitive only to differences in truth-conditions.

I do not claim that the notion of subject-matter—or notions of meaning more fine-grained than the notion of truth-conditions—have no place in our linguistic theorizing. (In fact, I will introduce one such notion of meaning in Chapter 4.) The point I wish to make is simply that fine-grained notions of meaning are not relevant to the assessment of 'just is'-statements, except to the extent that they supply information about truth-conditions.

2.2.4 Why-Closure

Suppose it is agreed on all sides that Hesperus (and Phosphorus) exist. Someone says: 'I can see as clearly as can be that Hesperus is Phosphorus; what I want to understand is *why*.' It is not just that one wouldn't know how to comply with such a request—one finds oneself unable to make *sense* of it. The natural reaction is to either find a charitable reinterpretation of the question ('why does one planet play both the morning-star and the evening-star roles?') or reject it altogether ('What do you mean *why*? Hesperus *just is* Phosphorus'.)

Contrast this with a case in which someone asserts one of the following:

- I can see that the window is broken; what I want to understand is *why*.
- I can see that the radioactive isotope decayed at time *t* rather than a second later; what I want to understand is *why*.
- I can see that there is something rather than nothing; what I want to understand is *why*.

In all three of these cases one can make sense of the request, taken at face-value. In the first case, one may even have a satisfying reply (e.g. 'The window is broken because it was hit by soccer ball'). In the second case, it is harder to think of a *good* reply, but one can at least think of a bad one (e.g. 'because God willed it so'). Potential replies are even scarcer in the third case (even bad ones), but one can at least state that there is no good answer to be given without refusing to make sense of the question (e.g. 'Well, that's just the way the world turned out.'). Contrast this with the initial Hesperus/Phosphorus case, where it isn't even appropriate to say 'Well, that's just the way the world turned out'.

Say that a sentence ϕ is treated as *why-closed* just in case one is unable to make sense of the question ⌜Why is it the case that ϕ?⌝ when it is understood as follows:

> I can see exactly what it would take to satisfy ϕ's truth-conditions, but I wish to better understand why the world is such as to satisfy them.

I would like to suggest that there is a tight connection between the 'just is'-operator and why-closure:

> A first-order sentence is why-closed if and only if it is a logical consequences of the set of true 'just is'-statements (if and only if it is metaphysically necessary, if and only if its negation is not metaphysically inconsistent).

Suppose, for example, that someone says: 'I can see that things composed of water are composed of H_2O, but I wish to better understand why the world is such as to satisfy this condition.' The natural reaction is to either find a charitable reinterpretation of the question ('why are watery things composed of H_2O?') or reject it altogether ('What do you mean *why*? For something to be composed of water *just is* for it to be composed of H_2O').

It is worth keeping in mind that there are many different ways of reading the question ⌜Why is it the case that ϕ?⌝, and most of them are *not* relevant to why-closure. Here are some unintended readings:

- I wish to understand why ϕ's 'primary intension' holds.

(For instance: 'Why is it the case that Hesperus is Phosphorus?', meaning 'Why is there a single planet playing both the morning-star and the evening-star roles.')

- I wish to better understand what it would take to satisfy ϕ's truth-conditions.

(For instance: 'Why is it the case that the mean score is different from the median score?', meaning 'I don't understand "mean" and "median" well enough to know what it would take for "the mean score is different from the median score" to be true.')

- I wish to better understand why ϕ has the truth-conditions that it in fact has.

(For instance: 'Why is it the case that $(p \supset q) \vee (q \supset p)$?', meaning 'Help me understand how it comes about that the truth-functional operations corresponding of "$\supset$" and "$\vee$" conspire to make it the case that every row in a truth-table for '$(p \supset q) \vee (q \supset p)$' turns out to be true." ')

- Convince me that ϕ is true.

(For instance: 'Why is it the case that Hesperus is Phosphorus?', meaning 'Give me grounds for thinking that Hesperus is Phosphorus.')

The temptation to interpret a why-question in one of these ways is especially great when the reading that is relevant for present purposes is unavailable (as in cases of why-closure). So it is essential to keep in mind that the alternate readings should be ignored when it comes to assessing why-closure.

I have been suggesting that when one accepts a 'just is'-statement one closes a theoretical gap. The connection between why-closure and 'just is'-statements allows me to make this point a little more precisely. For when one accepts ⌜for ϕ to be the case *just is* for ψ to be the case⌝ one comes to see the biconditional ⌜$\phi \leftrightarrow \psi$⌝ as why-closed, and thereby disregards any pressure to explain why it should be the case that ϕ is true given that ψ is the case (or vice versa).

2.3 Truth and Falsity for 'Just is'-Statements

The main objective of this chapter is to shed light on the 'just is'-operator. I have attempted to do so in two different ways. In Section 2.1, I sketched an account of the sorts of considerations whereby one might decide to accept or reject a 'just is'-statement, and, in Section 2.2, I articulated connections between the 'just is'-operator and four other notions.

Now that we have a better understanding of the 'just is'-operator I would like to discuss an issue that is extremely delicate, but has a crucial impact on the way in which the family of philosophical positions that I have been defending should be understood. It is the question of what the truth or falsity of a 'just is'-statement consists in—together with the closely related question of whether there is a conception of logical space that is, in some sense, objectively correct.

2.3.1 Truth and Correctness

On the picture that I have been defending, different conceptions of logical space can be more or less hospitable to one's scientific or philosophical theorizing. I suggested, accordingly, that the decision to adopt a particular conception should be guided by its ability to combine with the rest of one's theorizing to deliver a fruitful tool for scientific or philosophical inquiry. But fruitfulness is a goal-relative notion: a theoretical apparatus that constitutes a fruitful way of pursuing one set of goals may not be a fruitful way of pursuing another. So one might end up with a situation in which one has grounds for accepting a particular conception of logical space relative to one set of goals, and a different conception relative to another.

None of this is incompatible with the idea that there is a conception of logical space that is *objectively* correct: correct independently of whether it is a fruitful way of pursuing the goals that a given community happens to endorse. For one might think that, regardless of whether one's decision to *accept* a conception of logical space should be guided by considerations of fruitfulness, there is a gap between fruitfulness and objective correctness. The point might be pressed by drawing an analogy with Scientific Realism. A Scientific Realist would argue that, regardless of whether one thinks that the theory one should *accept* is the one that delivers the best combination of, say, simplicity and strength, there is a gap between being true and being simple and strong. So even if simplicity and strength are *guides* to the truth, being simple and strong is not the same as being true. In a similar vein, an objectivist about logical space might agree that the fruitfulness of a conception of logical space relative to our present goals could constitute a *guide* to its objective correctness, while insisting that fruitfulness and objective correctness are not the same thing.

But what does it mean to say that a conception of logical space is objectively correct? The most straightforward answer would be to say that for a conception of logical space to be objectively correct is for the 'just is'-statements it is based on to be objectively true. But, as we shall see, this doesn't immediately constitute much progress.

The following, I take it, is a natural way of thinking about truth. To *set forth* a statement is to make a distinction amongst ways for the world to be—to divide logical space into distinct regions—and to single out one side of this distinction; for the statement to be *true* is for the region singled out to include the way the world actually is.

On this way of seeing things, the notion of truth *presupposes* a conception of logical space: the distinction between the true and the untrue is just the distinction between regions of logical space that include the way the world actually is, and those that do not. In the case of a *contingent* statement, truth or falsity will nevertheless be constrained by something other than one's conception of logical space. For one's conception will not, on its own, decide the issue of which point in logical space happens to be actualized. But in the case of 'just is'-statements, truth or falsity will be determined *entirely* by the background conception of logical space. Every conception of logical space will count those 'just is'-statements on which it is based as true, and the rest as false.

So, against the background of which conception of logical space should one assess the question of whether a given 'just is'-statement is true? One would like to respond: 'against the background of the *objectively correct* conception of logical space'. But the notion of objective correctness is precisely what we were trying to get a handle on. It is for this reason that I find it hard to see how one could succeed in elucidating the notion of objective correctness by saying that for a conception of logical space to be objectively correct is for it to be based on the set of objectively true 'just is'-statements.

An analogy might be helpful. Think of contingent sentences as akin to statements about a game's 'score', and of 'just is'-statements as akin to statements about the 'legality' of a move in the game. What counts as a game's score and what counts as a legal move are both *relative* to the game one is playing. But there is an important difference between the two. For even after one has decided what game to play, one has to look to the world to determine what the score is. In contrast, when one decides what game to play, one thereby settles the issue of what the legal moves are. Moreover, it would be wrong-headed to ask what moves are legal in an 'objective' sense, a sense that transcends the game one chooses to play. It is not always wrong-headed to ask the question of what game 'ought' to be played, since one might have *practical* considerations in mind: one might wonder which game would be most enjoyable or most illuminating or best at community-building. But it is not clear that there is good sense to be made of the question of what game 'ought' to be played when practical considerations are set aside—and it certainly wouldn't help to insist that the game one 'ought' to play is the one with 'objectively' legal moves. Similarly, it is not obvious that there is good sense to be made of the question of what conception of logical space 'ought' to be accepted when practical considerations are set aside—and I have tried to argue it isn't much help to insist that one ought to accept the conception of logical space based on the set of objectively true 'just is'-statements.

2.3.2 Deploying the Wrong Distinctions

The crux of the matter, I think, is that it is unhelpful to think of a rival conception of logical space as misdescribing the world *by representing it as being one way when in fact it is another*. It is better to think of a rival conception of logical space as misdescribing the world *by deploying the wrong set of distinctions in trying to represent it*. The purpose of this section is to spell out this idea in further detail.

Let us start by revisiting some of the examples we discussed in Section 2.1.2. Consider, first, the case of the rival logicians. One of them is a classicist, and thinks that for it to be the case that $\neg\neg\phi$ *just is* for it to be the case that ϕ; the other is an intuitionist, and thinks the classicist's 'just is'-statement ought to be rejected. (We may assume, for simplicity, that the intuitionist thinks that every material biconditional of the form '$\neg\neg\phi \leftrightarrow \phi$' is true, not because it has trivial truth-conditions, as the classicist believes, but because its non-trivial truth-conditions happen to be satisfied.)

Each of our two logicians thinks that the other is deploying the wrong set of distinctions to represent the world. The classicist thinks that the intuitionist is making a distinction without a difference, by incorrectly distinguishing between the condition that ϕ and the condition that $\neg\neg\phi$. And the intuitionist thinks that the classicist is conflating two distinct conditions, by mistakenly identifying the condition that ϕ and the condition that $\neg\neg\phi$. One could, if one wanted, describe this disagreement as a disagreement about how the world is 'on the subject of negation', or 'on the subject of what follows from what'. But this way of speaking would gloss over an important difference: the difference between disagreements in which there is no dispute about the distinctions that the rival party uses to describe the world—think of a straightforward dispute about who committed the murder—and disagreements in which a dispute about the distinctions that the rival party uses to describe the world is at the heart of the matter, as in the case at hand. I therefore propose that we refrain from describing the debate about whether to accept 'for it to be the case that $\neg\neg\phi$ *just is* for it to be the case that ϕ' as a debate about *how the world is*. The most perspicuous way to proceed, it seems to me, is to describe it as a debate about *which distinctions to deploy* in representing the world.[6]

The classicist may well find himself unable to make sense of the theoretical space that the intuitionist wishes to open up between $\neg\neg\phi$ and ϕ. He may find that he is unable to form a *conception* of how the world would have to be for it to be the case that $\neg\neg\phi$ without it also being the case that ϕ. If so, the classicist will find it hard to put himself in the intuitionist's shoes—to see the world as she does, by deploying her preferred set of distinctions to represent it. (One way for the classicist to make progress on this issue is by *immersion*: he could try to become fluent in the use of the intuitionist's theoretical machinery, and expose himself to the advantages of deploying it to describe the world.)

It is interesting to contrast this example with another: the case of the chemist and the crank. The chemist, recall, thinks that for something to be composed of water *just is* for it to be composed of H_2O. The crank thinks, instead, that for something to be composed of water *just is* for it to be a colorless, odorless liquid with such-and-such additional properties.

---

[6] One might see things differently if one prefers a different construal of the debate between our rival logicians. Suppose, for example, that one thinks that the world is endowed with 'logical structure', and that the disagreement between classicists and intuitionists is a disagreement about the nature of this structure. Then there would be nothing inappropriate about describing the debate as a disagreement about the way the world is 'on the subject of logical structure'. For—as in the case of a straightforward disagreement about who committed the murder—there would be no dispute about the distinctions that others use to represent the world: the debate would be concerned with a straightforward factual matter. The point that is essential for present purposes, however, is that on this way of construing the debate, classicists and intuitionists should no longer be thought of as endorsing rival conceptions of logical space. For the limits of logical space, as it is understood here, are the limits of *absurdity*: to go beyond logical space is to lapse into metaphysical inconsistency. And there is no reason to think that a mischaracterization of the world's 'logical structure' would lead to *absurdity*: it would be an inaccurate but metaphysically consistent representation of the way the world is 'on the subject of logical structure'. So, on this way of thinking about the debate, there is no reason to think that classicists and intuitionists couldn't share a single conception of logical space.

Unlike the classicist, the chemist is *partially* able to see things from the crank's point of view. She can see that there are supposed to be two different distinctions—one corresponding to the condition that x be composed of H_2O, and the other corresponding to the condition of x being an odorless, colorless liquid with such-and-such additional properties. And she can see that the expression 'x is composed of water' is to be used as a label for the latter. So far so good. There will be trouble, however, if the crank is unable to spell out the 'such-and-such' clause. For in that case the chemist will be left without an adequate grasp of one of the crank's distinctions. And it would be no use for the crank to explain that the missing properties are simply the essential properties of *water*, or to point to a sample and say 'the essential properties of *this* stuff'. For the chemist couldn't use her own views about what being composed of water consists in without thereby failing to do justice to the crank's point of view.

Consider, finally, the debate between the two zoologists. Neither of them has any false beliefs about how organisms are related to one another, or about who is able to interbreed with whom. But whereas one of the zoologists thinks that for two individuals to be members of the same species *just is* for them to share the right kind of lineage, the other thinks that for two individuals to be members of the same species *just is* for them to be members of a group of organisms that are able to produce fertile offspring.

In this case it is reasonable to assume that each zoologist is able to see things from the point of view of the other. For they both agree that there are two different distinctions—that of sharing the right kind of lineage, and that of being members of a group of organisms that are able to produce fertile offspring. They agree, moreover, that the two distinctions are adequately understood—or so I shall assume. But they disagree about which of the distinctions to associate the label 'x and y are members of the same species' with. They might each insist that the other's use of the label is suboptimal—because it is harder to work with, say, or because it emphasizes the wrong set of issues. But neither of them should have much difficulty adopting the other's point of view because they already have the right set of distinctions in place. All they need to do is become accustomed to a new way of using a particular label.

I have been suggesting that someone who adopts a rival set of 'just is'-statements—and thereby adopts a rival conception of logical space—can be thought of as deploying a rival set of distinctions to represent the world. What our examples illustrate is that one's misgivings about a rival set of distinctions can take many different forms. At one end of the spectrum, one might find that one is unable to make sense of the alternate set of distinctions (as in the case of the two logicians). At the other end of the spectrum, one might see the alternate set of distinctions as nothing more than a suboptimal relabeling of one's own (as in the case of the two zoologists). And—as illustrated by the case of the chemist and the crank—there is plenty of room in between.

On this way of seeing things, the question of whether a conception of logical space is 'objectively correct' can be recast as the question whether a given set of distinctions is the 'objectively correct' means for representing the world. But what does it mean to say that a set of distinctions is 'objectively correct' as a means for representing the world? My suspicion—and this is only a suspicion—is that it will be hard to separate the question of which set of distinctions ought to be deployed in representing the world from the aims of the subject who is doing the representing.

Go back to the game analogy. The question of which game one ought to play is ultimately a *practical* matter—it is a question that makes no sense independently of the aims of a particular community—but it is a practical matter that depends, in part, on the way the world is. Suppose one is trying to decide on a game to play after a somewhat awkward Thanksgiving dinner. One's decision should be sensitive to the way the world is. (Has Uncle Brian had too much to drink? Can Granny remember the rules of Contract Bridge?) But it should also be sensitive to one's aims. (Is one hoping for a harmonious end to a difficult evening? Is one hoping to prove that one is smarter than one's brother-in-law?)

Similarly, there is room for thinking that the question of which set of distinctions one ought to deploy in representing the world is ultimately a *practical* matter—it is a question that makes no sense independently of the aims of a particular community. But it is a practical matter that depends, in part, on the way the world is. Suppose one is trying to decide whether to incorporate a particular distinction into one's theorizing—for instance, the distinction between experiencing the sensation of seeing red and being in the right kind of brain state (Section 1.3.1). One's decision should be sensitive to the way the world is. (Would such a distinction lead to fruitful theorizing? Would it help us understand Mary's cognitive accomplishment when she is first exposed to a red tomato?) But it should also be sensitive to one's aims. (Does one find the theoretical resources delivered by the additional distinction fruitful enough to justify the need to explain, for instance, why Mary experiences the sensation of seeing red, rather than an 'inverse' sensation?)

2.3.3 Objective Correctness?

Let us take stock. I have done my best to address the issue of what the correctness of a conception of logical space might consist in. I began by articulating a notion of truth that *presupposes* a conception of logical space. On this way of thinking about truth, a 'just is'-statement will be counted as true relative to those conceptions of logical space that are based on it and as false relative to the rest. The upshot is that it makes good sense to talk about the truth or falsity of a 'just is'-statement, but that it is only interesting to do so to the extent that one has an independent grasp of the 'correctness' or 'incorrectness' of a conception of logical space.

I then went on to describe a suitably independent characterization of correctness. I suggested that a conception of logical space might be regarded as 'correct' to the extent that it delivers a set of distinctions which constitute a fruitful way of describing the world. On this way of seeing things, however, the correctness of a conception of logical space is, in part, a *practical* matter—and therefore an issue that cannot be fully separated from the aims of a particular community.

I have not given an argument that this is the only viable way of thinking about the correctness of a conception of logical space. For all I have said, it may well be possible to characterize an 'objective' notion of correctness, one which is relative neither to a conception of logical space nor to the aims of a particular community. I don't know how to do so myself, but would be delighted if it could be done. The only claim I make on behalf of the understanding of correctness that has been developed here is that it is relatively unmysterious—unmysterious by the standards of the difficult philosophical terrain we find ourselves in.

In any event, it is important to keep in mind that nothing in what follows will depend on how one ends up thinking about the correctness of a conception of logical space. There is no obstacle to embracing an objective notion of correctness, provided that it is adequately understood.

2.3.4 Unity

I would now like to set aside the issue of correctness, and focus on the question of whether one should think that the goals of our current scientific and philosophical communities are best served by a single conception of logical space, or whether different projects might call for different conceptions of logical space.

Nancy Cartwright has famously argued for the view that 'physics, though a powerful tool for predicting and changing the world, is a tool of limited utility' and, more generally, that 'our theories are severely limited in scope' (Cartwright 1999: 9). On this picture, different scientific projects call for different theories, and there is no unified theoretical framework that holds them all together. Even if one is more optimistic than Cartwright about the prospects of a unified science, it seems clear that we are not, at present, in a position to formulate precise connections between different regions of our scientific landscape. We are not, for example, in a position to formulate a reduction of psychology to neuroscience (to say nothing of fundamental physics). And in the absence of such a reduction we are not in a position to characterize a conception of logical space that is suitable across sciences. Let me explain.

If one thinks that psychology is ultimately reducible to neuroscience, one must think that there is some truth of the form 'to experience pain *just is* to be in such-and-such a neural state'. Such a truth should be used in characterizing a unified conception of logical space. For suppose that to experience pain *just is* to instantiate neural property N. Then a scenario in which someone experiences pain without instantiating N is inconsistent. So no point in logical space can be such that a subject experiences pain without instantiating N. But someone who is unable to identify N in neural terms won't know which points to exclude. If, for instance, she is unsure whether N is C-fiber stimulation, she will be unsure whether to exclude points whereby someone is in pain without undergoing C-fiber stimulation.

For analogous reasons, one won't be in a position to characterize a unified conception of logical space until one is able to come up with 'just is'-statements capturing reduction statements between different regions of our theoretical landscape. The good news is that fruitful theorizing does not require a unified conception of logical space. All that is required is that we succeed in identifying a family of 'just is'-statements that is rich enough *for the purposes at hand*. All one needs for the purposes of doing psychology, for example, is a characterization of logical space based on psychological vocabulary. A point in such a space should take a stand on the issue of whether a given subject is in pain, but it need not take a stand on the issue of whether the subject undergoes C-fiber stimulation. The resulting conception of logical space would be useless for neuroscientific theorizing, of course. But that needn't get in the way of fruitful psychological theorizing.

None of this is inconsistent with the idea that ideal science (or ideal philosophy) would deliver the needed reduction statements, and therefore allow for a conception of logical space suitable for all inquiry. But it seems clear that we're stuck with a fragmented conception of logical space in practice, at least for the time being.

It is perhaps worth noting that contextualism about logical space—the view that different projects call for different conceptions of logical space—could also turn out to be a fruitful way of addressing certain philosophical problems. Take, for example, the statue and the clay. Even if they share the exact same region of space throughout their existence, there is some pressure to think that they cannot be the same object, since they appear to have different properties: the statue could have survived the replacement of a part, but not the clay. By borrowing an idea from Lewis (1986a: §4.5), the contextualist about logical space could account for this appearance while holding on to the idea that the statue is identical to the clay. Let the clay (i.e. the statue) be X. One could claim that use of the word 'statue' in connection with X generates a context in which 'part of what it is to be X is to be capable of surviving the replacement of parts' is accepted, but use of the word 'clay' in connection with X generates a context in which that same 'just is'-statement is rejected.

Contextualism about logical space is liberal in one respect, since it allows one's conception of logical space to wax and wane with the task at hand. But it is not a view on which anything goes, since the world places substantial constraints on the fruitfulness of a given conception of logical space for a given purpose. Throughout the remainder of the book, I will remain neutral on the question of whether one should embrace some variety of contextualism, or whether our endeavors would be best served by a unified conception of logical space. (For further discussion, see Price 2009.)

2.4 Formal Constraints

The aim of this section is to further elucidate the 'just is'-operator by giving a fuller description of some of its formal properties.

The 'Just is'-Operator   Let $\ulcorner \phi \equiv \psi \urcorner$ be a formalization of $\ulcorner$for ϕ to be the case *just is* for ψ to be the case$\urcorner$. In light of the connection between 'just is'-statements and sameness of truth-conditions, it is natural to think of '$\equiv$' as an *identity predicate* of sorts: $\ulcorner \phi \equiv \psi \urcorner$ is true if and only if ϕ and ψ have the same truth-conditions.

Someone who thinks that the *proposition* expressed by a sentence consists of the sentence's truth-conditions might wish to say that $\ulcorner \phi \equiv \psi \urcorner$ is true if and only if ϕ and ψ express the same proposition. It is worth keeping in mind, however, that this way of putting the point is potentially misleading. On the one hand, a coarse-grained conception of propositions might suggest that the meaning of a sentence is exhausted by its truth-conditions—and here I assume no such thing. On the other hand, proposition-talk might lead one to think that the truth of a 'just is'-statement presupposes naïve realism about propositions: the view that even though there is no absurdity in the assumption that there are no propositions, we are lucky enough to have them. The truth of 'just is'-statements, as I understand them here, is totally independent of such a view. ('$\phi \equiv \psi$' should be thought of as equivalent to '$\Box(\phi \leftrightarrow \psi)$', and there is no reason to think that the truth of '$\Box(\phi \leftrightarrow \psi)$' presupposes naïve realism about propositions.)

The 'just is'-statements we have considered so far have usually taken *closed* formulas in their argument-places. For instance:

> Susan is a sibling $\equiv$ Susan shares a parent with someone else.
> (*Read:* For Susan to be a sibling *just is* for Susan to share a parent with someone else.)

But the 'just is'-operator can also take *open* formulas in its argument-places. For instance:

x is a sibling $\equiv_x x$ shares a parent with someone else.
(*Read:* To be a sibling *just is* to share a parent with someone else.)

Here the 'x' in '$\equiv_x$' is used to indicate that the occurrences of 'x' in 'x is a sibling' and 'x shares a parent with someone else' are *bound* by '$\equiv$'. Thus, whereas

x is a sibling $\equiv_x x$ shares a parent with someone else.

expresses a complete thought, its index-free correlate

x is a sibling $\equiv x$ shares a parent with someone else.

is read 'for *it* to be a sibling *just is* for *it* to share a parent with someone else' (where 'it' is a pronoun awaiting denotation), and expresses an incomplete thought.

One can index '$\equiv$' with more than one variable. One can say, for instance,

x and y are siblings $\equiv_{x,y} x$ and y share a parent and $x \neq y$.
(*Read:* To be related as siblings *just is* to share a parent and be distinct.)

(As before, the indices are used to indicate that occurrences of 'x' and 'y' in 'x and y are siblings' and 'x and y share a parent and $x \neq y$' are *bound* by '$\equiv$'.)

Semi-Identity   Sometimes one is in a position to endorse something in the vicinity of a 'just is'-statement even though one has only partial information. Suppose you know that the chemical composition of water includes oxygen but don't know what else is involved. You can still say:

Part of what it is to be composed of water is to contain oxygen.
(*In symbols:* 'Composed-of-water$(x) \gg_x$ Contains-Oxygen(x).')

I shall call this a *semi-identity statement*. Think of it as a more idiomatic a way of saying:

To be composed of water *just is* (to contain oxygen and to be composed of water).

In general, I shall treat the semi-identity statement '$\phi(\vec{x}) \gg_{\vec{x}} \psi(\vec{x})$' as a syntactic abbreviation of the identity-statement '$\phi(\vec{x}) \equiv_{\vec{x}} (\psi(\vec{x}) \wedge \phi(\vec{x}))$', where $\vec{x}$ is shorthand for $x_1, \ldots, x_n$. (It is worth noting that '$\equiv$' can also be defined in terms of '$\gg$', since '$F(\vec{x}) \equiv_{\vec{x}} G(\vec{x})$' is equivalent to the conjunction of '$F(\vec{x}) \gg_{\vec{x}} G(\vec{x})$' and '$G(\vec{x}) \gg_{\vec{x}} F(\vec{x})$'.)

It is natural to think of indexed 'just is'-statements as expressing identities amongst *properties* (e.g. 'the property of being a sibling = the property of sharing a parent with someone else'), and it is natural to think of indexed semi-identity statements as expressing the parthood relationship amongst properties (e.g. 'the property of being water has the property of containing oxygen as a part'). There is nothing objectionable about these descriptions when property-talk is understood in a suitably deflationary way. (To have the property of being composed of water *just is* to be composed of water.) But, as in the case of proposition-talk, it is important to be aware that property-talk is potentially misleading. It might be taken to suggest that one should only assert an indexed 'just is'-statement if one is prepared to countenance a naïve realism about properties: the view that even though there is no absurdity in the assumption that there are no properties, we are lucky enough to have them. The truth of indexed 'just is'-statements, as I understand them, is totally independent of such a view.

It is also worth keeping in mind that '$F(x) \gg_x G(x)$' should *not* be understood as entailing that being G is, in some sense, 'metaphysically prior' to being F, or as entailing that something is G 'in virtue' of being F. Notice, in particular, that '$F(x) \gg_x H(x)$' will turn out to be equivalent to the modal statement '$\Box(\forall x(F(x) \to H(x)))$'.

Semi-identity-statements capture an interesting notion of entailment. Suppose $\ulcorner \phi \gg \psi \urcorner$ is true. Because of the connection between the 'just is'-operator and truth-conditionality, the demand imposed on the world by ϕ's truth-conditions must be *strictly stronger* than the demand imposed on the world by ψ's truth-conditions. In other words: *part of what it takes* for ϕ's truth-conditions to be satisfied is that ψ's truth-conditions be satisfied. Accordingly, '$\gg$' might be thought of as expressing *metaphysical entailment*.

First-Order Identity-Statements   There are two different readings of the first-order identity predicate '='. On the weaker (Kripkean) reading 'Hesperus = Phosphorus' is true at all worlds; on the stronger reading, 'Hesperus = Phosphorus' is false at worlds in which Venus fails to exist. On the weaker reading, 'Hesperus = Phosphorus' is equivalent to

'$x = $ Hesperus $\equiv_x x = $ Phosphorus' (regardless of whether '=' takes the weaker reading in the paraphrase). On the stronger reading, 'Hesperus = Phosphorus' is equivalent to the conjunction of '$x = $ Hesperus $\equiv_x x = $ Phosphorus' and '$\exists x$(Hesperus $= x$)'.

One can think of the weaker reading as claiming only that what it takes to satisfy the condition of being identical to Hesperus is precisely what it takes to satisfy the condition of being identical to Phosphorus. If such a claim is true, it will be true even at worlds in which Venus fails to exist (though, of course, the existence of Venus in the actual world is a precondition for our being able to talk about the relevant conditions).

When '=' takes the weaker reading and a and b are proper names, $\ulcorner a = b \urcorner$ can always be paraphrased as $\ulcorner a = x \equiv_x b = x \urcorner$. But this need not hold when we have definite descriptions. 'Obama = the 44th president of the United States', for example, cannot be paraphrased as 'to be Obama *just is* to be the 44th president of the United States'. For even though 'Obama' and 'the 44th president' refer to the same individual, the predicates '$x = $ Obama' and '$x = $ the 44th president' have different satisfaction-conditions: what it takes to satisfy the condition of being identical to Obama is different from what it takes to satisfy the condition of being the 44th president.

Constitutive Properties and Conditional Semi-identity Statements P is a *constitutive* property if the assumption that z has P is enough to license the conclusion that part of what it is to be z is to be P. One might think, for example, that being human is a constitutive property. For one might think that the assumption that Socrates is human is enough to license:

$$x = \text{Socrates} \gg_x \text{Human}(x)$$

(*Read:* part of what it is to be Socrates is to be human.)

Being snub-nosed, on the other hand, is not a constitutive property. For the assumption that Socrates is snub-nosed does not license:

$$x = \text{Socrates} \gg_x \text{Snub-Nosed}(x)$$

(*Read:* part of what it is to be Socrates is to be snub-nosed.)

We shall say that a predicate is *constitutive* just in case it expresses a constitutive property.

The claim that P is a constitutive property can be formulated as a *conditional* semi-identity statement:

$$\frac{P(z)}{x = z \gg_x P(x)}$$

(*Read:* assume z is P; then part of what it is to be z is to be P.)

One might think that having w as a biological parent is a *parameterized* constitutive property. For one might think that the assumption that z has w as a biological parent is enough to warrant the conclusion that part of what it is to be z is to have w as a parent. Parameterized constitutive properties can also be captured by conditional semi-identity statements. One can say, for example:

$$\frac{B(z, w)}{x = z \gg_x B(x, w)}$$

(*Read:* assume z has w as a biological parent; then part of what it is to be z is to have w as a biological parent.)

As usual, there is a connection between semi-identity and metaphysicial possibility. The conditional semi-identity statement above, for example, will be true if and only if the following modal statement is true:

$$\Box(\forall z \forall w B(z, w) \rightarrow \Box(\exists y(y = z) \rightarrow B(z, w))).$$

More generally, $\ulcorner\Box(\forall z \forall \vec{w}(\phi(z, \vec{w}) \rightarrow \Box(\exists y(y = z) \rightarrow \phi(z, \vec{w}))))\urcorner$ is true just in case $\phi(z, \vec{w})$ expresses a constitutive property.

The conditions under which a conditional semi-identity statement of the form exemplified above should be accepted or rejected may be thought of as *derivative* on the conditions under which the consequent semi-identity statement should be accepted or rejected. If knowing of an object that it is human is enough for you to feel warranted in the conclusion that part of what it is to be that object is to be human, then you should accept

$$\frac{\text{Human}(z)}{x = z \gg_x \text{Human}(x)}$$

Otherwise you shouldn't. And, as we saw in Section 2.1, there is a lot to be said about the circumstances under which an (unconditional) 'just is'-statement should be accepted or rejected.

Logical Properties of '≡' I would like to suggest that the logical properties of '≡' should be inferred from the equivalence between '$F(\vec{x}) \equiv_{\vec{x}} G(\vec{x})$' and '$\Box(\forall\vec{x}(F(\vec{x}) \leftrightarrow G(\vec{x})))$'.

More specifically, let $L^{\equiv}$ be the result of enriching a first-order language L with '≡' and characterizing well-formedness and sentencehood in the obvious way. If ϕ is a formula of $L^{\equiv}$, we define the *modal analogue* ϕ^{M} of ϕ as follows:

- if ϕ is $\ulcorner\psi(\vec{x}) \equiv_{\vec{x}} \theta(\vec{x})\urcorner$, then ϕ^{M} is $\ulcorner\Box(\forall\vec{x}(\psi^{M}(\vec{x}) \leftrightarrow \theta^{M}(\vec{x})))\urcorner$;
- if ϕ is $\ulcorner\psi \wedge \theta\urcorner$, then ϕ^{M} is $\ulcorner\psi^{M} \wedge \theta^{M}\urcorner$;
- if ϕ is $\ulcorner\neg\psi\urcorner$, then ϕ^{M} is $\ulcorner\neg(\psi^{M})\urcorner$;
- if ϕ is $\ulcorner\forall x\psi\urcorner$, then ϕ^{M} is $\ulcorner\forall x(\psi^{M})\urcorner$;
- if ϕ is atomic, then $\phi^{M} = \phi$.

If ϕ is a sentence of $L^{\equiv}$ and Γ is a set of sentences of $L^{\equiv}$, we shall say that ϕ is a *logical consequence* of Γ just in case ϕ^{M} is an S5-consequence of $\Gamma^{M} = \{\psi^{M} : \psi \in \Gamma\}$.

From this it follows that '≡' is an equivalence relation, and that a sentence ϕ of L is a logical consequence of the sentence '$F(\vec{x}) \equiv_{\vec{x}} G(\vec{x})$' of $L^{\equiv}$ (where $F(\vec{x})$ and $G(\vec{x})$ are atomic) just in case ϕ is a logical consequence of the material biconditional '$\forall\vec{x}(F(\vec{x}) \leftrightarrow G(\vec{x}))$'.

2.5 Conclusion

The aim of this chapter was to elucidate the 'just is'-operator. I attempted to do so in four different ways.

Firstly, I set forth a view about the sorts of considerations that might ground the acceptance or rejection of a given 'just is'-statement. I argued that by changing the 'just is'-statements one accepts, one changes one's conception of logical space, and that different conceptions of logical space can be more or less hospitable to the rest of one's theorizing. Accordingly, the decision to adopt a particular 'just is'-statement should be guided by the statement's ability to combine with the rest of one's theorizing to deliver a fruitful tool for scientific or philosophical inquiry.

Secondly, I argued that there are important connections between the 'just is'-operator and four other notions: inconsistency, sameness of truth-conditions, metaphysical possibility and why-closure. My claim was not that some of these notions were to be defined on the basis of the rest.

What I suggested is that one can shed light on all five notions by getting clear about the connections between them.

Thirdly, I addressed the question of whether it makes sense to speak of the objective correctness of a conception of logical space, as something over and above the issue of whether the conception delivers a fruitful way of pursuing our goals. Although I am not myself in a position to characterize a suitable notion, nothing in this book presupposes that it can't be done.

Finally, I described the 'just is'-operator from a formal point of view. I generalized the notion of a 'just is'-statement in several different ways, and made a note of some of its logical properties. I also suggested that it can be useful to think of the 'just is'-operator as an identity-predicate of sorts.

3

Mathematics

I suggested in the Introduction that this book might be thought of as an extended argument for Trivialist Platonism, a form of mathematical Platonism according to which every instance of the following schema is true:

NUMBERS

For the number of the Fs to be *n just is* for there to be *n* Fs.

The first two steps of my argument are already in place. I argued in Chapter 1 that there is no general linguistic or metaphysical obstacle for the acceptance of NUMBERS. Trivialist Platonism should therefore not be ruled out from the start—it is a view worth taking seriously.

In Chapter 2, I developed an account of the sorts of considerations that might ground the acceptance or rejection of a 'just is'-statement. On the resulting picture, one's conception of logical space is shaped by the 'just is'-statements one accepts. To accept a 'just is'-statement '$\phi \equiv \psi$' is to treat a scenario in which one of ϕ and ψ holds without the other as *absurd*, and therefore as unavailable for scientific or philosophical inquiry. Accordingly, in accepting a 'just is'-statement one moves to a conception of logical space that makes room for fewer possibilities. Such a move comes with costs and benefits. The benefit is that there are less explanatory demands on one's theorizing because there are fewer possibilities to be ruled out in one's quest for truth; the cost is that one has fewer distinctions to work with, and therefore fewer theoretical resources. Because of these costs and benefits, different conceptions of logical space can be more or less hospitable to one's scientific and philosophical theorizing. I suggested, accordingly, that the decision to accept a particular 'just is'-statement should be determined by the statement's ability to combine with the rest of one's theorizing to deliver a fruitful tool for scientific or philosophical inquiry.

Where does this leave us with respect to NUMBERS? As I argued in Section 1.3.2, it is natural to think that the costs of accepting NUMBERS are far outweighed by the benefits. For by accepting NUMBERS, one eliminates the need to answer questions such as the following:

> I can see that there are no dinosaurs. What I want to know is whether it is *also* true that the number of the dinosaurs is Zero. And I would like to understand how one could ever be justified in taking a stand on the issue, given that we have no causal access to the purported realm of abstract objects.

There is no need to explain how the non-existence of dinosaurs might be correlated with dinosaurs' having Zero as a number because there is *no difference* between the two: for the number of the dinosaurs to be Zero *just is* for there to be no dinosaurs.

It is true that there is also a cost. By accepting NUMBERS one loses access to a certain amount of theoretical space, since one is no longer in a position to work with scenarios in which there are no numbers. But it seems to me that this is not much of a price to pay, since the availability of such scenarios is not very likely to lead to fruitful theorizing.

The upshot is that there is significant theoretical pressure to accept NUMBERS—at least provided that it can be used to construct a viable philosophy of mathematics. The aim of this chapter, and the next, is to make a case for the view that NUMBERS can indeed be used to construct a viable philosophy of mathematics.

3.1 Preliminaries

Mathematical Platonism is the view that mathematical objects exist. *Mathematical Trivialism* is the view that the truths of pure mathematics have trivial truth-conditions, and the falsities of pure mathematics have trivial falsity-conditions.

Platonism is compatible with both trivialism and non-trivialism. The easiest way of getting a handle on *non-trivialist* Platonism is by imagining a creation myth. On the first day God created light; by the sixth day, God had created a large and complex world, including black holes, planets and sea-slugs. But there was still work to be done. On the seventh day God created mathematical objects. Only *then* did She rest.

On this view, it is easy to make sense of a world with no mathematical objects: it is just like the world we are considering, except that God rested on the seventh day, instead of creating mathematical objects. For in the world we are considering, God had to do something *extra* in order to bring about the existence of mathematical objects—something that wasn't already in place by the time She had created black holes, planets and sea-slugs. The existence of numbers is, in this sense, a non-trivial affair.

According to the version of Trivialist Platonism we will be considering here, in contrast, every instance of the following schema is true:

> For the number of the Fs to be *n just is* for there to be *n* Fs.
> (*In symbols:* $\#_x(F(x)) = n \equiv \exists!_n x(F(x))$.)

So when God created the planets, and made sure that there were exactly eight of them, God *thereby* made it the case that the number of the planets was Eight. There was nothing *extra* that She needed to do, or refrain from doing, to bring about the existence of numbers.

On this view, the assumption that there are no numbers is not just false, but *absurd*. (Suppose, for *reductio*, that there are no numbers. According to trivialist Platonism, for the number of numbers to be Zero *just is* for there to be no numbers. So the number Zero must exist, contradicting our assumption.) An immediate consequence of this conclusion is that the sentence 'there are numbers' has *trivial* truth-conditions: truth-conditions whose satisfaction requires *nothing* of the world. (See Section 2.2.3.)

Trivialist Platonism is a form of anti-metaphysicalism, in the sense of Chapter 1. It entails that a single feature of reality—the fact that there are no dinosaurs, for example—can be fully and accurately described by using mathematical vocabulary ('the number of the dinosaurs is Zero'), and also fully and accurately described without using mathematical vocabulary ('there are no dinosaurs').

A defender of trivialist Platonism—or trivialism, for short—faces three main challenges:

SPELLING OUT THE DETAILS

> We have seen what a trivialist thinks would be required of the world in order for the truth-conditions of simple sentences like 'the

number of the dinosaurs is Zero' to be satisfied. But a proper defense of trivialism would need to go beyond that, by explaining what would be required of the world in order for the truth-conditions of an *arbitrary* arithmetical sentence to be satisfied.

GENERALIZING THE PROPOSAL

Attention so far has been focused on the special case of arithmetic. But the proposal would be significantly less interesting if it couldn't be generalized to other branches of mathematics—and to set theory in particular.

DEVELOPING AN EPISTEMOLOGY

If Mathematical Trivialism is to have any plausibility, we need a story to tell about what mathematical knowledge consists in, and how it is possible.

The aim of the present chapter is to address the first two of these challenges. I will address the first by developing a *trivialist semantics*: a compositional specification of truth-conditions that assigns to each sentence in the language of arithmetic the truth-conditions that a trivialist thinks it should have. I will then address the second challenge, by showing that this technique can be extended beyond the language of arithmetic. We will turn to the third challenge in Chapter 4.

3.2 Neo-Fregeanism

Before turning to semantics, I would like to bring the proposal into sharper focus by describing some connections between trivialist and neo-Fregean accounts of mathematics.

3.2.1 *Varieties of Neo-Fregeanism*

Hume's Principle is the following sentence:

$$\forall F \forall G(\#_x(F(x)) = \#_x(G(x)) \leftrightarrow F(x) \approx_x G(x))$$
(*Read:* the number of the Fs equals the number of the Gs just in case the Fs are in one-one correspondence with the Gs)

Neo-Fregeanism is the view that when Hume's Principle is set forth as an implicit definition of '$\#_x(F(x))$', one gets the following two results: (1)

the truth of Hume's Principle is knowable *a priori*, and (2) the referents of number-terms constitute a realm of mind-independent objects.[1]

Just like one can distinguish between trivialist and non-trivialist varieties of mathematical Platonism, one can distinguish between trivialist and non-trivialist varieties of neo-Fregeanism. Both versions of neo-Fregeanism agree that numbers—the referents of numerical-terms—constitute a realm of mind-independent objects. But they disagree about whether the existence of this realm of objects is a trivial affair.

Trivialist neo-Fregeans go beyond mere acceptance of Hume's Principle; they also accept the 'just is'-statement corresponding to Hume's Principle:

$$\#_x(F(x)) = \#_x(G(x)) \equiv_{F,G} F(x) \approx_x G(x)$$

(*Read:* for the number of the Fs to equal the number of the Gs *just is* for the Fs to be in one-one correspondence with the Gs)

A consequence of this 'just is'-statement is that the assumption that there be no numbers is not just false, but *absurd*. Non-trivialist neo-Fregeans, in contrast, accept Hume's Principle, but refrain from accepting the corresponding 'just is'-statement, and in doing so refrain from treating a world with no numbers as an absurdity.

It seems to me that there is some confusion in the literature about which of these two version of neo-Fregeanism is being discussed. Some critics of neo-Fregeanism—the author of Rayo (2003) and Rayo (2005), for example—have interpreted the program as a version of *non*-trivialist neo-Fregeanism.[2] But it is not clear that this is what *proponents* of neo-Fregeanism have had in mind. There are strong indications that trivialist neo-Fregeanism is closer to the mark. One such indication is the use of 'neo-Fregeanism' as a name for the program. For there is good reason to think that Frege himself was a proponent of trivialist Platonism.

As noted in Section 1.4, when Frege claims that the sentence 'there is at least one square root of 4' expresses the same thought as 'the concept *square root of 4* is realized', and adds that 'a thought can be split up in many ways, so that now one thing, now another, appears as subject or predicate'

---

[1] Neo-Fregeanism was first proposed in Wright 1983, and has since been championed by Bob Hale and Crispin Wright, amongst others. For a collection of relevant essays, see Hale and Wright 2001*a*.

[2] For a survey of neo-Fregean literature, see MacBride 2003.

(Frege 1892: 199), it is natural to interpret him as embracing the 'just is'-statement:

> For the concept *square root of 4* to be realized *just is* for there to be at least one square root of 4.

And when he claims, in *Grundlagen* §64, that in treating the judgement 'line *a* is parallel to line *b*' as an identity, so as to obtain 'the direction of line *a* is identical to the direction of line *b*', we 'carve up the content in a way different from the original way', it is natural to interpret him as embracing the 'just is'-statement:

> For the direction of line *a* to equal the direction of line *b just is* for *a* and *b* to be parallel.

In both instances, Frege puts the point in terms of content-recarving, rather than as a 'just is'-statement. But, as emphasized in Section 2.2.3, one's views about truth-conditions are tightly correlated with the 'just is'-statements one accepts.

Neo-Fregeans have been sympathetic towards Frege's views on content-recarving (Wright 1997). And even though talk of content-recarving has become less prevalent in recent years, with more of the emphasis on implicit definitions, a version of neo-Fregeanism rooted in trivialist Platonism is clearly on the cards. In any event, it seems to me that a trivialist form of neo-Fregeanism would constitute the most interesting version of the proposal.

Let me now mention three respects in which the account of mathematics I defend in this book departs from the extant literature on neo-Fregeanism. The first concerns abstraction principles; the second concerns mixed identities; the third concerns the 'Bad Company Problem'.

3.2.2 Abstraction Principles

Neo-Fregeans have tended to assume that only *abstraction principles*—that is, principles of the form '$\forall\alpha\forall\beta(f(\alpha) = f(\beta) \leftrightarrow R(\alpha,\beta))$'—can be used as the basis for a neo-Fregean account of mathematics. This has made it difficult for them to extend the proposal to branches of mathematics such as set-theory, where it is not straightforward to find satisfying axiomatizations that take the form of abstraction principles. (For a selection of relevant literature, see Cook 2007.)

When it comes to neo-Fregeanism of the trivialist variety, I can certainly see the appeal of working with abstraction principles. For every abstraction principle '$\forall\alpha\forall\beta(f(\alpha) = f(\beta) \leftrightarrow R(\alpha, \beta))$' has a correspnding 'just is'-statement:

$f(\alpha) = f(\beta) \equiv_{\alpha,\beta} R(\alpha, \beta)$
(*Read:* for the f of α to equal the f of β *just is* for α to bear R to β)

So one is in a position to make the crucial claim that in setting forth an abstraction principle one is doing more than setting forth a quantified biconditional—one is setting forth the corresponding 'just is'-statement.

But why think that the *only* way of defending a trivialist account of mathematics is by working with axiom systems that take the form of abstraction principles? Perhaps one thinks that a 'just is'-statement can only be true if it satisfies a certain kind of *syntactic* condition: if its left- and right-hand side components have suitably related logical forms. This would make room for the claim that whereas 'just is'-statements corresponding to abstraction principles satisfy the syntactic condition, 'just is'-statements based on other axiom systems do not. One might claim, in particular, that a 'just is'-statement such as the following,

$\mathcal{A} \equiv \top$
(where $\mathcal{A}$ is the conjunction of the second-order Dedekind-Peano Axioms, and $\top$ is a tautology).

fails the syntactic condition, and is therefore unavailable as an implicit definition for the relevant arithmetical vocabulary.

My own view is that this would be a mistake. On the linguistic picture that I defended in Chapter 1, there are no interesting syntactic obstacles to the truth of a 'just is'-statement. So if one joins the neo-Fregean in the project implicitly defining mathematical vocabulary, one should help oneself to whichever 'just is'-statements get the job done, regardless of whether they happen to satisfy a particular syntactic condition.

It is also worth noting that Mathematical Trivialism need not be tied to the neo-Fregean idea that the truth-conditions of arithmetical statements should be fixed by implicit definition. We will see below that the trivialist has a straightforward way of specifying *compositional* semantic theories for a large range of mathematical languages. Such theories deliver just the right results, and the fact that truth-conditions are specified compositionally makes them significantly more illuminating than an implicit definition.

3.2.3 Mixed Identities

Another difference between neo-Fregean accounts of mathematics and the proposal I develop here concerns 'mixed' identities, such as 'Julius Caesar = 7'. I will start by considering the issue from my own perspective, and then come back to neo-Fregeanism.

Compositionalism and metaphysicalism were introduced in Chapter 1. An important feature of compositionalism is that it leaves room for meaninglessness where metaphysicalism does not. Suppose it is agreed on all sides that the singular terms t_1 and t_2 both have referents, each of them figuring meaningfully in sentences with well-defined truth-conditions. A metaphysicalist is committed to the claim that it must be possible to meaningfully ask whether $\ulcorner t_1 = t_2 \urcorner$ is true. For she believes that each of t_1 and t_2 is paired with one of the objects carved out by the metaphysical structure of the world. So the question whether $\ulcorner t_1 = t_2 \urcorner$ is true can be cashed out as the question whether t_1 and t_2 are paired with the same such object.

For a compositionalist, in contrast, there is no tension between thinking that t_1 and t_2 both have referents and denying that one has asked a meaningful question when one asks whether $\ulcorner t_1 = t_2 \urcorner$ is true. For t_1 and t_2 can satisfy the compositionalist's conditions for singulartermhood and reference even if no truth-conditions have been associated with $\ulcorner t_1 = t_2 \urcorner$. (See Section 1.3.) All it takes is a suitable assignment of truth-conditions to whichever sentences involving t_1 and t_2 one wishes to make available for use.

Arithmetic is a case in point. As we will see in Section 3.3, trivialist Platonists have a straightforward way of specifying a compositional assignment of truth-conditions to arithmetical sentences. On this assignment, every arithmetical sentence a non-philosopher would care about gets well-defined truth-conditions, as does every sentence in the non-arithmetical fragment of the language. And any truth of pure arithmetic—including sentences of the form '$\exists x(x = t)$', for t a numeral—is assigned trivial truth-conditions. But no truth-conditions are supplied for mixed identity-statements, such as 'Julius Caesar = 7'.

Metaphysicalists will claim that something important has been left out. For in the absence of well-defined truth-conditions for 'Julius Caesar = 7', it is unclear which of the objects carved out by the metaphysical structure of reality has been paired with 'the number of the planets'.

But the compositionalist will disagree: it is simply a mistake to think that such pairings are necessary to render a singular term meaningful. In fact, one should *expect* there to be mixed identity statements that lack well-defined truth-conditions. For when a sentence has no clear role to play in communication—as is the case of 'Julius Caesar = 7', philosophical discussion aside—our linguistic practice generates no pressure for it to be assigned truth-conditions, even when its constituent terms figure meaningfully in other sentences.

A metaphysicalist might reply that 'Julius Caesar = 7' doesn't need a role to play in communication in order to have well-defined truth-conditions. Its truth-conditions will be determined by whether 'Julius Caesar' and '7' are paired onto a single one of the objects that are carved out by the world's metaphysical structure—an issue which must have a determinate answer if the terms are to figure meaningfully in other sentences. But the compositionalist would disagree. 'Julius Caesar' and '7' are paired onto objects with respect to different ways of carving up the world: they are components of different systems of representation for describing the world. (See Section 1.5.) So the fact that they occur in sentences with well-defined truth-conditions offers no guarantee that their occurrence in 'Julius Caesar = 7' will result in well-defined truth-conditions. (For further discussion of this issue, see Chapter 8.)

Back to neo-Fregeanism. The upshot of our discussion is that, from the point of view of the compositionalist, there is no pressure for thinking that a mixed identity-statement such as 'Julius Caesar = 7' should have well-defined truth-conditions. So there is no reason to think—in spite of what Frege suggests in §66 of the *Grundlagen* and what proponents of neo-Fregeanism have tended to presuppose—that a characterization of the concept of number will be unacceptable unless it settles the truth-value of mixed identity-statements. (For further discussion, see Heck 1997*a* and Hale and Wright 2001*b*.)

3.2.4 Bad Company

Different abstraction principles can impose different constraints on the size of their domain. So—as long as they are all thought of as concerning the *same* domain—they cannot all be true. The Bad Company Problem for neo-Fregean accounts of mathematics is the problem of identifying principled criteria for determining which of these incompatible abstraction principles to count as true. (For discussion, see Linnebo 2009.)

Notice, however, that if different abstraction principles are thought of as corresponding to different ways of carving up the world into objects, there is no reason to think that there is a shared domain of quantification, and therefore no reason to think that the principles are genuinely in conflict.

Someone who thinks there is such a thing as a 'maxi-domain'—a domain consisting of the entities that result from every possible way of carving up the world into objects—might claim that abstraction principles should generally be thought of as quantifying over such a domain, and therefore insist that there must be a conflict. But, as I argued in Section 1.5, the compositionalist has no real reason to believe that there is such a thing as a maxi-domain. When a new piece of mathematical vocabulary is introduced, it might be introduced as part of a new system of compositional representation, and therefore as part of a new way of carving up the world into objects. And there should be no general expectation that the new carving *extends* carvings corresponding to systems of compositional representation that were already in place. The different systems of representation might constitute independent methods for describing a single world.

I offer an extended discussion of these issues in Chapter 8.

3.3 A Semantics for Trivialists

In this section we will see that the trivialist can give a compositional specification of truth-conditions for arithmetical sentences which yields the result that every true sentence of pure arithmetic is assigned trivial truth-conditions and every false sentence of pure arithmetic is assigned trivial falsity-conditions.

The trivialist semantics is also defined for every sentence of applied arithmetic that a non-philosopher would care about, and whenever it is defined it delivers the intuitively correct results. It does not, however, assign truth-conditions to mixed identity-statements, such as 'the number of the planets = Julius Caesar'. As we saw in Section 3.2.3, the compositionalist should see no tension between thinking that the singular terms t_1 and t_2 figure meaningfully in sentences with well-defined truth conditions and denying that one has asked a meaningful question when one asks whether $\ulcorner t_1 = t_2 \urcorner$ is true.

3.3.1 The Semantics

I will now spell out the semantics. Readers uninterested in the details are
welcome to skip ahead to Section 3.3.3. But there is really nothing to fear:
the material is totally straightforward.

We work with a two-sorted first-order language with identity, L.
Besides the identity-symbol '=', L contains *arithmetical* variables
('n_1', 'n_2', ...), individual-constants ('0') and function-letters ('S', '+' and
'×'), and *non-arithmetical* variables ('x_1', 'x_2', ...), constants ('Caesar' and
'Earth') and predicate-letters ('Planet(...)'). In addition, L has been
enriched with the function-letter '$\#_v(...)$' which takes a first-order
predicate in its single argument-place to form a first-order arithmetical term (as in '$\#_{x_1}(\text{Planet}(x_1))$', which is read 'the number of the
planets').

Let σ be a variable assignment and w be a world. $\delta_{\sigma,w}(t)$ will be our
denotation function, which assigns a referent to term t relative to σ and
w; $Sat(\phi, \sigma, w)$ will be our satisfaction predicate, which expresses the
satisfaction of ϕ relative to σ and w; and $[\phi]_w$ will be our true-at-a-world
operator, which expresses the thought that ϕ is true at w. Denotation
and satisfaction are defined simultaneously, by way of the following
clauses:

Denotation of arithmetical terms:

1. $\delta_{\sigma,w}(\ulcorner n_i \urcorner) = \sigma(\ulcorner n_i \urcorner)$
2. $\delta_{\sigma,w}(\text{'0'}) = $ the number Zero
3. $\delta_{\sigma,w}(\ulcorner S(t) \urcorner) = \delta_{\sigma,w}(t) + 1$
4. $\delta_{\sigma,w}(\ulcorner (t_1 + t_2) \urcorner) = \delta_{\sigma,w}(t_1) + \delta_{\sigma,w}(t_2)$
5. $\delta_{\sigma,w}(\ulcorner (t_1 \times t_2) \urcorner) = \delta_{\sigma,w}(t_1) \times \delta_{\sigma,w}(t_2)$
6. $\delta_{\sigma,w}(\ulcorner \#_{x_i}(\phi(x_i)) \urcorner) = $ the number of zs such that $Sat(\ulcorner \phi(x_i) \urcorner, \sigma^{z/\ulcorner x_i \urcorner}, w)$
7. $\delta_{\sigma,w}(\ulcorner \#_{n_i}(\phi(n_i)) \urcorner) = $ the number of ms such that $Sat(\ulcorner \phi(n_i) \urcorner, \sigma^{m/\ulcorner n_i \urcorner}, w)$

Denotation of non-arithmetical terms:

1. $\delta_{\sigma,w}(\ulcorner x_i \urcorner) = \sigma(\ulcorner x_i \urcorner)$
2. $\delta_{\sigma,w}(\text{'Caesar'}) = $ Gaius Julius Caesar
3. $\delta_{\sigma,w}(\text{'Earth'}) = $ the planet Earth

Satisfaction: Where $\ulcorner[\phi]_w\urcorner$ is read $\ulcorner$it is true at w that $\phi\urcorner$,

1. $Sat(\ulcorner\exists n_i\phi\urcorner, \sigma, w) \leftrightarrow$ there is a number m such that $Sat(\phi, \sigma^{m/\ulcorner n_i\urcorner}, w)$

2. $Sat(\ulcorner\exists x_i\,\phi\urcorner, \sigma, w) \leftrightarrow$ there is a z such that $([\exists y(y = z)]_w \wedge Sat(\phi, \sigma^{z/\ulcorner x_i\urcorner}, w))$

3. $Sat(\ulcorner t_1 = t_2\urcorner, \sigma, w) \leftrightarrow \delta_{\sigma,w}(t_1) = \delta_{\sigma,w}(t_2)$

4. $Sat(\ulcorner\mathrm{Planet}(t)\urcorner, \sigma, w) \leftrightarrow [\delta_{\sigma,w}(t)$ is a planet$]_w$ (for t a non-arith-metical term)

5. $Sat(\ulcorner\phi \wedge \psi\urcorner, \sigma, w) \leftrightarrow Sat(\phi, \sigma, w) \wedge Sat(\psi, \sigma, w)$

6. $Sat(\ulcorner\neg\phi\urcorner, \sigma, w) \leftrightarrow \neg Sat(\phi, \sigma, w)$

3.3.2 Technical Commentary

Infinite numbers   I assume throughout that 'number' includes infinite numbers. This is done in order to ensure that there are no empty terms in the language. If one wanted to restrict one's attention to the natural numbers one could do so by working in a free logic.

Truth-Conditions and Possible Worlds   I had promised an assignment of *truth-conditions* to sentences, but what the trivialist semantics actually delivers is an assignment of *sets of worlds* to sentences. To bridge the gap we need the assumption that a sentence's truth-conditions are adequately modeled by a set of worlds. This is a substantial assumption. But I argued in Section 2.2 that the assumption is satisfied when the space of worlds is taken to be the space of metaphysically possible worlds. (As emphasized in Section 2.2.3, it is important to distinguish between the claim that two sentences have the same truth-conditions and the claim that they have the same meaning. To say that they have the same truth-conditions is only to say that there is no difference between *what would be required of the world* to satisfy the constraints determined by one of the meanings and *what would be required of the world* to satisfy the constraints determined by the other.)

Actualism   To simplify the exposition, I have made the tacit assumption that the range of the metalinguistic quantifiers includes merely possible objects. But it is important to keep in mind that non-actualist quantification could be avoided entirely by employing the dot-notation of Chapter 6. (For a development of the trivialist semantics in explicitly actualist terms, see Rayo 2008.)

3.3.3 Philosophical Commentary

Using Arithmetic in the Metatheory   In order for the trivialist semantics to deliver the right results, the theorist must use arithmetical vocabulary in the metalanguage, and help herself to arithmetical axioms in the metatheory.

This means that the trivialist semantics won't help with the project of explaining a trivialist assignment of truth-conditions to someone who doesn't understand arithmetical vocabulary, or doesn't take the axioms to be true. In order to make progress with such a project, one would need a method for *paraphrasing* arbitrary arithmetical sentences as sentences containing no mathematical vocabulary. As I explain in Chapter 7, there are important limits to what can be achieved by way of characterizing suitable paraphrase-methods.

Fortunately, our aim is not to explicate trivialism to someone who doesn't understand mathematics. Our aim is to give a precise statement of trivialism to someone who does understand mathematics, by saying exactly what truth-conditions a trivialist would associate with each arithmetical sentence—and doing so in such a way that the resulting assignment of truth-conditions can be recognized as delivering trivialism regardless of whether one happens to be a trivialist.

A homophonic semantics does not succeed in doing the latter. The trivialist and the non-trivialist can both agree that the homophonic semantics is correct. They can both agree, for example, that what it takes for '$1 + 1 = 2$' to be true is for it to be the case that One plus One equals Two. The point of introducing the trivialist semantics is that it supplies an assignment of truth-conditions that is unequivocally trivialist. It delivers the conclusion that '$1 + 1 = 2$' is trivially true, and does so regardless of whether one presupposes trivialism in the metatheory. I would like to discuss this point in further detail.

How the Semantics Works   What is distinctive about the trivialist semantics is that mathematical vocabulary always occurs outside the scope of '$[\ldots]_w$' (read 'it is true at w that $\ldots$'). Denis Bonnay gave me a nice name for the procedure that gives rise to semantic clauses of this kind: *outscoping*.

In general, the upshot of outscoping is that all one needs to know *about a world w* in order to determine whether a given arithmetical sentence would be true at w is which *non-mathematical* predicates apply to which objects. Consider, for example, the object-language sentence '$\#_x(\text{Planet}(x)) = 0$'. Straightforward application of the trivialist semantic clauses yields the result that this sentence is true at a world w just in case w satisfies the following metalinguistic formula:

$$\text{the number of } z\text{s such that } [z \text{ is a planet}]_w = 0$$

We are assuming arithmetic in the metatheory. So all that is required of w in order for the metalinguistic formula to be satisfied is that it contain no planets. (Keep in mind that I am assuming metalinguistic quantification over merely possible objects for the sake of simplicity. As I noted earlier, it is possible to get the right results in an actualist framework by employing the dot-notation of Chapter 6; the formula above, for example, would be replaced by 'the number of zs such that $[\dot{z} \text{ is a planet}]_w = 0$'.)

Compare this with the result of using a homophonic semantics to specify truth-conditions for '$\#_x(\text{Planet}(x)) = 0$'. What follows from the usual semantic clauses is that the sentence is true at w just in case w satisfies the following metalinguistic formula:

$$[\text{the number of } z\text{s such that } z \text{ is a planet} = 0]_w$$

In this case, arithmetical vocabulary occurs within the scope of '$[\ldots]_w$'. So we get the result that what is required of w in order for the metalinguistic formula to be satisfied is that it contain the number Zero, and that, at w, Zero numbers the planets.

Of course, if it is true that for the number of the planets to be Zero *just is* for there to be no planets, then the two requirements on w will come to the same thing. So it will be true, both according to the trivialist semantics and according to the homophonic semantics, that all that is required of w to verify '$\#_x(\text{Planet}(x)) = 0$' is that it contain no planets. But there is still an important difference. In order for the homophonic semantics to deliver this result, we need the metatheoretic assumption that for the number of the planets to be Zero *just is* for there to be no planets. The trivialist semantics, on the other hand, will deliver the result *with no need for the metatheoretic assumption*. One does need to use arithmetical reasoning in the metatheory, so in proving the result one is, in effect, assuming that arithmetic is *true*. The point is that one needn't assume that arithmetic is *trivially* true. And this is important because the former assumption is common ground, but the latter is not.

Attention so far has been focused on applied arithmetic. Let us now see how outscoping plays out in the pure case. Consider the object-language sentence '1 + 1 = 2' (in primitive notation: '$S(0) + S(0) = S(S(0))$'). Since there is no non-mathematical vocabulary to remain within the scope of '$[\ldots]_w$', application of the semantic clauses yields the result that the sentence is true at a world w just in case w satisfies a metalinguistic formula in which *all* the vocabulary has been outscoped:

$$1 + 1 = 2$$

What one gets, in other words, is a formula in which '$[\ldots]_w$' *does not occur*, and therefore a formula with no free variables. In general, a formula with no free variables is satisfied by all objects if it is true, and no objects if it is false. Since the metalinguistic formula '1 + 1 = 2' is, in fact, true, it will be satisfied by all objects—and in particular by w for arbitrary w. It is, in other words, satisfied by w *independently of what w is like*. The trivialist semantics therefore delivers the conclusion that *nothing* is required of w in order for the object-language sentence '1+1 = 2' to be true at w. And, of course, the point generalizes. The trivialist semantics (plus arithmetic) yields the result that an arbitrary truth of pure arithmetic is true at w independently of what w is like, and that an arbitrary falsehood of pure arithmetic is false at w independently of what w is like. So—on the assumption that truth-conditions are adequately modeled by sets of worlds—the trivialist semantics entails Mathematical Trivialism.

3.4 Beyond Arithmetic

Our discussion of Mathematical Trivialism has so far been focused on the special case of arithmetic. Is it possible to articulate a trivialist understanding of other branches of mathematics?

From the point of view of an compositionalist, it doesn't take much for a trivialist interpretation of an axiomatic mathematical theory to be available. In the case of pure mathematics, all it takes is for the theory to be *internally coherent* (i.e. for it not to have a logical absurdity as a logical consequence); in the case of applied mathematics, all it takes is for the theory to be *conservative* over sentences of the original language.[3] For, as I show in Chapter 8, one can prove the following result:

> If an axiomatic mathematical theory T is internally coherent (or conservative, in the case of applied mathematics), then there is an assignment of truth-conditions to sentences in the language of T such that: (1) the axioms of T are counted as trivially true, and (2) the compositionalist's conditions of singulartermhood and reference are all satisfied.

Unfortunately, the proof of this result does not deliver a *compositional* method for specifying the relevant assignment of truth conditions.

There is a certain sense in which compositional assignments of truth-conditions are cheap. For once an assignment of truth-conditions to sentences of the object language is in place, one could in principle use one's understanding of the object language to produce a *homophonic* compositional semantics. The reason this is uninteresting is that a homophonic semantics suffers from two important limitations. First, it won't teach us anything of interest about the relevant assignment of truth-conditions. The second limitation is that, as emphasized above, nobody but the trivialist will take a homophonic semantics to succeed in delivering a trivialist specification of truth-conditions: only the trivialist will think that it assigns trivially satisfiable truth-conditions to truths of pure mathematics and trivially unsatisfiable truth-conditions to falsehoods.

In the case of arithmetic, we were able to specify a genuinely illuminating compositional semantics that delivers a trivialist specification of truth-conditions by appeal to *outscoping*. But there is no general recipe for emulating this strategy when it comes to languages that mix mathematical and non-mathematical vocabulary.

The reason we were able to outscope in the case of applied arithmetic is that we were able to set forth the following equivalence:

$$[\#_x(\mathrm{F}(x)) = n]_w \leftrightarrow \#_x([\mathrm{F}(x)]_w) = n$$

---

[3] For axiom system $\mathcal{A}$ to be conservative over sentences in the original language is for the following condition to be satisfied: let O be a set of sentences in the original language, and let ϕ be a sentence in the original language; then ϕ is only a (semantic) consequence of O and $\mathcal{A}$ if it is a (semantic) consequence of O. (In the case of systems whose logic fails to be complete—second-order systems, for example—the choice of semantic, rather than syntactic, consequence is significant. For relevant discussion, see Field 1980; Shapiro 1983; and Field 1985.)

(*Read:* at w (the number of the Fs = n) just in case (the number of the xs such that at w (x is an F)) = n)

(As before, keep in mind that I am assuming quantification over merely possible objects for the sake of simplicity, but that it is possible to get the right results in an actualist framework by employing the dot-notation of Chapter 6; the formula above would be replaced by '$[\#_x(F(x)) = n]_w \leftrightarrow \#_x([F(\dot{x})]_w) = n$'.)

It is thanks to this equivalence that we are able to go from the homophonic semantic clause for '$\#_x(F(x)) = n$',

$$\text{'}\#_x(F(x)) = n\text{' is true at } w \leftrightarrow [\#_x(F(x)) = n]_w,$$

to the outscoped semantic clause that the non-trivialist will recognize as satisfying the needs of the trivialist:

$$\text{'}\#_x(F(x)) = n\text{' is true at } w \leftrightarrow \#_x([F(x)]_w) = n.$$

Unfortunately, such equivalences are not guaranteed to be available in general. For instance, I know of no general way of defining a compositional semantics that delivers outscoping for a plural language that has been enriched with non-logical atomic plural predicates.

3.4.1 Set-Theory

Happily, outscoping—and therefore a genuinely illuminating compositional semantics that delivers trivialist truth-conditions—*is* available for the language of set-theory with urelements. It is an easy modification of the trivialist semantics for the language of arithmetic that was described in Section 3.3.1.

Our object-language will be the language of two-sorted set-theory with urelements: Roman variables $(x, y, \ldots)$ range over urelements, Greek variables $(\alpha, \beta, \ldots)$ range over sets. Let σ be a variable assignment, let w be a metalinguistic variable ranging over worlds and let $\ulcorner[\phi]_w\urcorner$ be read $\ulcorner$it is true at w that $\phi\urcorner$. Then satisfaction can be defined as follows:

1. $Sat(\ulcorner\exists x_i\, \phi\urcorner, \sigma, w) \leftrightarrow$ there is a z such that $([\exists y(y = z)]_w \wedge Sat(\phi, \sigma^{z/\ulcorner x_i\urcorner}, w))$

2. $Sat(\ulcorner\exists \alpha_i\, \phi\urcorner, \sigma, w) \leftrightarrow$ there is a set β such that: (*i*) for any urelement z in the transitive closure of β, $[\exists y(y = z)]_w$, and (*ii*) $Sat(\phi, \sigma^{\beta/\ulcorner \alpha_i\urcorner}, w)$

3. $Sat(\ulcorner F(x)\urcorner, \sigma, w) \leftrightarrow [\sigma(x)$ is an F$]_w$

4. $Sat(\ulcorner \alpha \in \beta \urcorner, \sigma, w) \leftrightarrow \sigma(\alpha) \in \sigma(\beta)$
5. $Sat(\ulcorner x \in \beta \urcorner, \sigma, w) \leftrightarrow \sigma(x) \in \sigma(\beta)$
6. $Sat(\ulcorner x = \gamma \urcorner, \sigma, w) \leftrightarrow \sigma(x) = \sigma(\gamma)$
7. $Sat(\ulcorner \phi \wedge \psi \urcorner, \sigma, w) \leftrightarrow Sat(\phi, \sigma, w) \wedge Sat(\psi, \sigma, w)$
8. $Sat(\ulcorner \neg \phi \urcorner, \sigma, w) \leftrightarrow \neg Sat(\phi, \sigma, w)$

As in the case of arithmetic, I simplify the exposition by making the tacit assumption that the range of the metalinguistic quantifiers includes merely possible objects. But, as before, it is worth keeping in mind that non-actualist quantification can be avoided altogether by appeal to the machinery developed in Chapter 6.

Our semantics delivers just the assignment of truth-conditions that a trivialist would hope for. One gets the result that every truth of the pure fragment of set-theory is trivially true and every falsity of the pure fragment of set-theory is trivially false. And one gets the desired truth-conditions for sentences involving urelements. For instance, one gets the result that all that is required of the world in order for '$\exists\alpha\exists x(x \in \alpha \wedge$ Elephant$(x))$' to be true is for there to be an elephant.

As in the case of arithmetic, one usually needs to prove a mathematical result in the metatheory in order to show that a given sentence is trivially true, or to show that it is trivially false. For instance, in order to show that an object-language sentence stating that there is an inaccessible cardinal has trivial truth-conditions one has to show in the metatheory that there is an inaccessible cardinal. The result is that, as before, the semantics entails very little on its own about what an intended model for the object-language should look like. It all depends on what one assumes about set-theory in the metatheory.

3.4.2 The Iterative Conception of Sets

A trivialist semantics for the language of set-theory is a good way of making explicit the truth-conditions of set-theoretic sentences, as understood by the trivialist. But it fails to deliver a *conception* of sets. As mentioned above, it doesn't offer much guidance about what the hierarchy of sets should look like, since any substantial information about the hierarchy is imported from the background metatheory. The purpose of this section is to consider the question of whether the trivialist is in a position to develop a suitable conception of the set-theoretic landscape.

The picture we will discuss is a version of the *Iterative Conception of Sets*.[4] On the version of the proposal we will consider here, the basic idea is that set-talk is to be introduced in *stages*. At Stage Zero, the only quantification we have available is quantification over *urelements*. At Stage One, we introduce the membership-predicate '∈', and the set-theoretic term-forming operator '$\{z : \ldots z \ldots\}$'. We then set forth the following 'just is'-statement, where 'x' and 'z' range over urelements and 'F' is a second-order variable taking first-order urelement-variables as arguments:

STAGE ONE 'JUST IS'-STATEMENT

$$x \in \{z : F(z)\} \equiv_{x,F} F(x)$$

(*Read:* for x to be a member of the set of Fs *just is* for x to be an F)

The result is that we have a new way of carving up the world. Because of the introduction of additional linguistic resources, the feature of reality that was fully and accurately described by means of 'a is F' can now also be fully and accurately described by means of 'a is a member of the set of Fs'. (Does this mean that novel objects have been brought into existence? Absolutely not. For an extended discussion of these issues, see Section 1.4.)

The Stage One 'Just Is'-Statement is, of course, a close cousin of Frege's Basic Law V, which leads to inconsistency. We avoid inconsistency here because the range of 'x' does not include the referents of the newly introduced set-theoretic terms. A metaphysicalist will grant that inconsistency has been avoided, but she will think that it is the result of an *ad hoc* restriction. 'Why restrict the range of "x" to urelements?' she would ask. 'Is there some reason not to treat it as ranging over absolutely everything, beyond the desire to avoid paradox?'

But the compositionalist has a reply. It is true that from a metaphysicalist point of view it makes good sense to speak of an absolutely general domain: it is simply the domain of objects that gets carved out by the world's metaphysical structure. But from a compositionalist point of view, different uses of quantification presuppose different ways of carving up the world into objects.

---

[4] Early discussions include Zermelo 1930 (which builds on Zermelo 1908) and Gödel 1944 (which was partially anticipated in Gödel 1933). More recent discussions include Boolos 1971; Parsons 1974; and Potter 2004. The discussion in Linnebo 2010 and its technical companion (Linnebo typescript) are especially germane to the present discussion. See also Fine 2006.

'I grant that the compositionalist needn't think of every domain as a subdomain of the domain of objects carved out by the world's metaphysical structure'—a skeptic might reply—'but she must still think of every domain as a subdomain of the 'maxi-domain': the domain that results from every possible way of carving the world into objects. So when the trivialist takes "x" to range over the domain of urelements, she is still placing *ad hoc* restrictions on the range of the variables.' As I pointed out in Section 1.5, however, the compositionalist has no reason to think that there is such a thing as a 'maxi-domain'. For a carving of the world is just a compositional system of representation for describing the world, and there is no obvious reason to think that there is a final answer to the question of what counts as a possible system of representation.

The proper response to the skeptic is therefore this. When we introduce the Stage One 'Just Is'-Statement, the situation is *not* one in which a domain that includes sets is available to us, and we choose to restrict it to urelements in order to avoid paradox. Instead, the label 'urelement' is applied to everything we are able to explicitly quantify over at that point. It is only *after* the 'just is'-statement is introduced, and we have a way of fixing truth-conditions for set-theoretic sentences, that our representational resources are rich enough to quantify over sets. (The sets themselves, however, existed all along; for further discussion, see Section 1.4.)

Once Stage One is in place, one can begin to iterate the process. At each stage μ one starts by treating every object one is in a position to explicitly quantify over as a 'μ-urelement'. One then sets forth the following 'just is'-statement, where 'x_μ' and 'z_μ' take μ-urelements as values, and 'F' is a second-order variable taking first-order μ-urelement-variables as arguments:

STAGE μ 'JUST IS'-STATEMENT

$$x_\mu \in \{z_\mu : F(z_\mu)\} \equiv_{x_\mu, F} F(x_\mu)$$

(*Read:* for x_μ to be a member of the set of Fs *just is* for x_μ to be an F)

[Beware: it is potentially misleading to think of μ-urelements as constituting a single domain, since nothing has been done to fix the truth-conditions of mixed identity statements relating set-theoretic and non-set-theoretic terms. It is better to think of set-theoretic variables and non-set-theoretic variables as falling under different sorts—and therefore ranging over separate domains—and to treat mixed identity statements as ill-formed. I avoid doing so here to improve the exposition, but further discussion of these matters can be found in Section 8.1.]

How far could this procedure be iterated? The first thing to note is that no limits are imposed by the way the world is. *Pace* metaphysicalism, we are not operating against the background of a fixed domain, with enough objects for the procedure to be iterated until a particular point and no further. At each stage of the process, we introduce a new family of set-theoretic terms by way of an axiom system that is (semantically) conservative over the second-order language of μ-urelements, and, according to the compositionalist, (semantic) conservativeness is enough to guarantee that the introduction will be successful (see Section 8.2).[5] So the compositionalist will think that the process is limited only by our ability to introduce further and further 'just is'-statements.

Notice, however, that the compositionalist has no obvious reason to think that it would be helpful to insist that the process is to be iterated 'all the way up' or 'as far as it could possibly go'. In order for such pronouncements to have definite content there would have to be a final answer to the question of what counts as a possible system of representation. And, as emphasized above, the compositionalist has no obvious reason to think that there is such an answer. When one insists that the process be iterated 'all the way up', one will only succeed in

---

[5] The conservativeness claim is easily verified in ZFC. It is enough to show that any standard model of the second-order language of μ-urelements can be extended to a model of the expanded language that satisfies the Stage μ 'Just Is'-Statement. One proceeds by letting first-order set-theoretic variables take the same values as second-order μ-urelement-variables, and letting second-order set-theoretic variables take as values sets of values of first-order set-theoretic variables.

The use of semantic, rather than syntactic, conservativeness here is essential. For the second-order theory of μ-level sets with μ-urelements can be used to define a truth-predicate for the second-order language of μ-urelements. And by using such a predicate to generate new instances of the axiom-schemas governing second-order μ-urelement quantification one can prove sentences containing no μ-set-theoretic vocabulary that one couldn't prove before (such as the Gödel-sentence for the second-order language of μ-urelements). So although the Stage μ 'Just Is'-Statement is itself (syntactically and semantically) conservative, it is couched in a language which can be used to formulate additional second-order axioms, and thereby increase the deductive power of one's second-order theory of μ-urelements. (But, of course, the new axioms will be *semantically* conservative over the second-order language of μ-urelements, since they are all true in every full second-order model.) For additional discussion of these issues see Chapter 8.

saying something with definite content to the extent that one has managed to articulate a definite well-ordering, so that the pronouncement can be understood as signaling that the process is to be iterated so as to form a hierarchy that is isomorphic with that well-ordering. Accordingly, someone who has succeeded in characterizing a well-ordering isomorphic to the natural numbers will be able to iterate the process far enough to get the hereditarily finite sets. Someone who has succeeded in characterizing a well-ordering isomorphic to the smallest strongly inaccessible cardinal will be able to iterate the process far enough to get enough sets for second-order ZF to have an intended interpretation. And so forth.

A consequence of this picture is that the project of developing an iterative conception of sets is inextricably linked to the project of doing set-theory. For the canonical way of identifying a large well-ordering is by describing an ordinal in set-theoretic terms, and motivating the idea that its existence wouldn't lead to inconsistency. The result is that it would be a mistake to think of the iterative construction described in this section as a *substitute* for a theory like ZFC. It is more illuminating than ZFC in some respects, and less illuminating in others. It is more illuminating as a way of shedding light on the truth-conditions of a sentence like 'Caesar is a member of the set of Romans', or as a method for understanding the most general constraints on our reasoning about sets. But it does far worse than ZFC as a method for shedding light on set-theoretic questions of the sort that a mathematician might be interested in. The right attitude, it seems to me, is to use both kinds of theories in tandem, as complementary descriptions of a single subject-matter.

3.4.3 Paraphrase

Is it possible to characterize a trivialist *paraphrase function* for the language of set-theory? Is there, in other words, an algorithmic procedure for mapping each set-theoretic sentence ϕ to a sentence whose truth-conditions are agreed on all sides to be the truth-conditions that the trivialist semantics of Section 3.4.1 associates with ϕ?

If the paraphrase-language includes variables of sufficiently high transfinite order—and if a trivialist understanding of higher-order quantification is taken for granted—then the answer is 'yes'.

Let $\mathscr{L}_\in^\alpha$ be a version of the language of set-theory with urelements in which each occurrence of a quantifier is restricted by some V_β ($\beta < \alpha$). One can show that, for arbitrary α, there is a truth-value-preserving paraphrase-function $\phi \mapsto \phi^{(\alpha)}$ that maps every sentence of $\mathscr{L}_\in^\alpha$ onto a sentence in a language of order $\alpha + 2$, or order α, if α is a limit ordinal (Linnebo and Rayo, forthcoming). Moreover, by assuming a suitable reflection principle, one can show that there is a cardinal ξ such that V_ξ satisfies the same $\mathcal{L}_\in$-sentences as the universe (Shapiro, 1987: 323–4). So one can characterize a trivialist paraphrase-function for the language of set-theory with urelements by using the following procedure. First, trans-form every sentence of the language of set-theory into a sentence of $\mathscr{L}_\in^{\xi+1}$ by restricting the quantifiers to V_ξ. Then apply the paraphrase-function $\phi \mapsto \phi^{(\xi+1)}$. The result is a function that paraphrases every set-theoretic sentence as a sentence of order $(\xi + 3)$. (Would such a paraphrase-func-tion count as algorithmic? Yes, assuming one can help oneself to ξ. But, of course, ξ is far beyond the recursively specifiable ordinals.)

Whether or not a paraphrase-function of this kind succeeds in elu-cidating the truth-conditions of set-theoretic sentences will, of course, depend on one's understanding of languages of very high order. If one's grasp of such languages were suitably independent of set-theory, then the elucidation could be very significant indeed. But it is hard to see how one could acquire a clear grasp of transfinite type-theory without making substantial use of set-theory. Conspicuously, one's ability to characterize a language of order α presupposes that one is able to characterize a well-ordering with an αth member. And, when α is sufficiently large, it is hard to see how much progress would be made independently of set-theoretic reasoning.

My own view is that set-theory and transfinite type-theory are best thought of as different presentations of the same theory. For let ϕ be a set-theoretic sentence and let ϕ^τ be the type-theoretic sentence that results from applying the paraphrase-function above. Then I am inclined to think that $\ulcorner \phi \equiv \phi^\tau \urcorner$ is a true 'just is'-statement. If this is right, then neither set-theory nor type-theory should be regarded as 'prior' to the other, or as supplying the other with a 'foundation'. But one can still benefit from working with both because they shed light on different aspects of the same theoretical landscape. (For further discussion of these issues, see Linnebo and Rayo forthcoming.)

3.5 Conclusion

The aim of this chapter was to address two challenges besetting trivialist accounts of arithmetic. The first was to spell out a trivialist account of arithmetic in detail, by explaining what would be required of the world in order for the truth-conditions of an arbitrary arithmetical sentence to be satisfied. I have done so by setting forth a compositional semantic theory: a specification of truth-conditions that assigns to each sentence in the language the truth-conditions that a trivialist thinks it should have.

The second challenge was to explain how the proposal might be extended beyond arithmetic. Since much of contemporary mathematics is reducible to set-theory, I have addressed it by focusing on the special case of set theory. I showed, first, that the semantic theory that had been used for the case of arithmetic can be extended to encompass set-theory. I then argued that the trivialist is in a position to develop a *conception* of the set-theoretic landscape based on the Iterative Conception of Sets.

There is an important challenge that remains unaddressed. The trivialist needs a story about what mathematical knowledge consists in, and how it is possible. That will be the focus of the next chapter.

4

Cognitive Accomplishment in Logic and Mathematics

Most of my argument for Trivialist Platonism is now in place. In Chapters 1 and 2, I defended an account of 'just is'-statements according to which there is significant theoretical pressure for accepting every instance of the following schema:

NUMBERS
> For the number of the Fs to be *n just is* for there to be *n* Fs.

And in Chapter 3 I built the first half of my case that NUMBERS can be used to build a viable philosophy of mathematics. I set forth a trivialist semantics, which assigns to each sentence in the language of arithmetic the truth-conditions that a trivialist thinks it should have, and showed that the technique can be extended to the language of set-theory.

There is, however, an important issue that is yet to be addressed. If Trivialist Platonism is to have any plausibility, we need an epistemology of mathematics. We need to explain what mathematical knowledge consists in, and how it is possible. The aim of the present chapter is to address this issue.

My discussion will borrow heavily from Bob Stalnaker. The fundamental ideas can all be found in Stalnaker 1984 (especially Chapters 1 and 5) and Stalnaker 1999 (especially Chapters 13 and 14). (See also Perry 2001 and Parikh 2009.) My own thinking about these matters has developed in large part as a result of a joint project with Adam Elga. He has contributed to the project at least as much as I have, but shouldn't be burdened with commitment to the idiosyncrasies of the present discussion.

4.1 Benacerraf's Dilemma

A sizable portion of the debate in contemporary philosophy of mathematics has been shaped by Paul Benacerraf's 'Mathematical Truth'. According to Benacerraf, we face an unhappy choice. We must *either* give a non-standard semantics for mathematical discourse, according to which mathematical statements are not really committed to mathematical objects, *or* stick to a straightforward semantics and explain how we could come to have knowledge about the realm of abstract objects, which is causally inert.

As directed towards a *non-trivialist*—someone who thinks that the truths of pure mathematics have non-trivial truth-conditions—Benacerraf's Dilemma has force, at least on a suitably cleaned up version of the argument (such as that in Field 2005). For if the existence of numbers is non-trivial—if God would have had to do something *extra* to make sure they were in place—then there is room for asking how one could ever *check* whether the world does indeed contain numbers—whether God did the extra work. So unless semantic analysis were somehow to reveal that mathematical sentences are not really committed to numbers, it is not entirely clear what an epistemology for mathematics would look like.

As directed towards a *trivialist*, on the other hand, the dilemma has little force. For, according to the trivialist, *nothing* is required of the world in order for the truth-conditions of a truth of pure mathematics to be satisfied. This means, in particular, that there is no need to go to the world to check whether any requirements have been met in order to determine whether the truth-conditions of a truth of pure mathematics are satisfied. Once one gets clear about the sentence's truth conditions—clear enough to know that they are trivial—one has done all that needs to be done to determine that the sentence is true. (It is important to keep in mind that getting clear about the truth-conditions of a given mathematical sentence can be highly non-trivial. So determining whether the sentence is true is not, in general, a trivial affair—more on this below.)

As Øystein Linnebo pointed out to me, the prevalence of Benacerraf's Dilemma in the literature is partly due to a misunderstanding. Philosophers of mathematics tend to be divided into two groups. Members of the first group reject committalism (i.e. the view that a typical mathematical statement carries commitment to mathematical objects) and Platonism (i.e. the view that mathematical objects exist); members of the second group accept both committalism and Platonism. The problem, I suspect, is that members of the two groups are sometimes talking about different positions when they use the term 'Platonism'. It is agreed on all sides that Mathematical Platonism is the view that there are mathematical objects. But members of the first group tend to assume that the only available form of Platonism is *non-trivialist* Platonism, and therefore see Benacerraf's Dilemma as strong evidence against Platonism—and to the extent that they see the standard mathematical axioms as true, they also see the dilemma as evidence against committalism. Members of the second group, in contrast, tend to have some form of *trivialist* Platonism in mind, and are therefore unmoved by Benacerraf's Dilemma. It is hard to mention particular people without failing to do justice to the subtleties of their views, but it seems to me that Parsons (1983), Wright (1983), Frege (1884), and Stalnaker (1996) can all be interpreted as defending versions of trivialist Platonism.

4.2 A New Puzzle

Trivialist Platonism delivers a straightforward answer to Benacerraf's Dilemma, but it does not immediately deliver an epistemology of mathematics.

Learning mathematics is a highly non-trivial affair, and proving a new theorem can be an intellectual triumph. So it should be agreed on all sides that there is such a thing as cognitive accomplishment in mathematics. But according to the mathematical trivialist the truths of pure mathematics are true throughout logical space. So cognitive accomplishments in mathematics cannot generally consist of the ruling out of ways for the world to be. This leaves the trivialist with a new puzzle: how should one model cognitive accomplishment in mathematics?

The trivialist's 'new' puzzle in the philosophy of mathematics is an old puzzle in the philosophy of logic. For everyone should agree that logical truths are true throughout logical space. So, again, cognitive accomplishments cannot generally consist of ruling out ways for the world to be. What do they consist of then?

The main goal of the present chapter is to offer answers to these questions. I will propose a model of cognitive accomplishment in logic and mathematics.

Propositions   The label 'proposition' can be applied to different theoretical notions. On one usage, propositions are regions in logical space: they track *ways for the world to be*. So if there is no difference between being composed of water and being composed of H_2O, one should say that 'the Earth contains water' and 'the Earth contains H_2O' express the same proposition. On a different usage, propositions track *cognitive accomplishment*. So to the extent that transitioning from the belief that the Earth contains water to the belief that the Earth contains H_2O constitutes a non-trivial cognitive accomplishment, 'the Earth contains water' and 'the Earth contains H_2O' should express different propositions. Each of these two theoretical notions is important. So regardless of which of the two one chooses to use the term 'proposition' for, it is important not to neglect the other. And it is important develop an account of the relationship between the two.

This relationship can be highly non-trivial. Suppose, first, that we use propositions to track cognitive accomplishment. Then knowing which propositions are believed by a subject will not immediately tell us how the world is according to the subject. Take a farmer who believes that her square piece of land has a side-length of 8 meters, and an area of 81 (rather than 64) square meters. But this is not because she thinks she lives in an inconsistent world: she has simply made a computational error. What is the world like, according to our farmer? Where does she locate herself in logical space? To see that this is a non-trivial problem, imagine that God sets out to create a world which is to be exactly the way our farmer thinks the actual world is. It is not clear that knowledge of the propositions believed by the farmer is enough for God to complete her task. An inconsistent world is not an option: even God could not create a square piece of land with a side-length of 8 meters and an area of 81 square meters—not, at any rate, in Euclidean space. Perhaps the farmer measured her piece of land by counting the number of square-meter tiles that cover it, and made a mistake calculating the square root of 81. If so, it is tempting to say that God should construct a piece of land with a side-length of 9 meters. Perhaps the farmer proceeded by measuring the side-length and made a mistake calculating the square of 8. It is then tempting to say instead that God should construct a piece of land with a side-length of 8 meters.

Now suppose that we use propositions to track ways for the world to be. Then knowing which propositions are compatible with a subject's beliefs will not tell us the whole story about her cognitive accomplishments. Suppose we are told that our farmer would locate herself in a region of logical space whereby there is a square plot of land with a side-length of 8 meters. This tells us nothing about the *modes of presentation* of the farmer's beliefs. We don't know, for example, whether she would be in a position to articulate her beliefs by saying 'the land has a side-length of 8 meters', or by saying 'the land has an area of 689 feet'. Maybe she can't articulate the belief verbally at all, but would be disposed to buy just the right amount of fencing should she decide to build a fence around the relevant parcel of land.

One lesson of all this is that there is more to cognitive accomplishment than ruling out regions of logical space. Cognitive accomplishment also occurs when one acquires the ability to *transition* from one mode of presentation of a given region to another. This suggests a way of answering our puzzle: cognitive accomplishment in logic and mathematics can be modeled, in part, as the ability to transition between different modes of presentation of a given region in logical space.

Modes of Presentation   For all that has been said so far, the notion of a mode of presentation is not much more than a placeholder for a genuine theoretical notion. If it is to do real work, we need to know what it means to say that a region of logical space—or, as I shall sometimes say, a piece of information—is believed under a particular mode of presentation. (Here and throughout, I use 'information' in its non-factive sense.)

This is what I propose. When a subject possesses a piece of information, she may have the ability to access that information for some purposes but not others. To say that a piece of information is believed under a particular *mode of presentation* is to say that it can be accessed by the subject *for the purposes of a particular task*. Consider, for example, the region of logical space whereby the farmer's square piece of land has a side-length of 8 meters (equivalently: an area of 64 square meters). There are different tasks in the service of which such information might be deployed. It might be used to decide how much fencing to buy if one wants to build a fence around the land, or how many tiles to buy if one wants to cover the land, or what to say if one wants to answer the question 'What is the area of that piece of land, in square feet?'. Someone might be in a position to access the relevant information for the purposes of carrying out one of these tasks without being in a position to access it for the purposes of the others. A subject who is unable to perform multiplications, for example, might have the ability to buy the right amount of fencing—and therefore have access to information about the size of the piece of land relative to one mode of presentation—without having the ability to buy the right number of tiles—therefore lacking access to the information relative to a different mode of presentation.

My proposal can now be stated a little more precisely. The claim is that cognitive accomplishment in logic and mathematics can be modeled, in part, as the acquisition of *information transfer abilities*: abilities whereby information that was available for the purposes of one set of tasks becomes available for the purposes of a different set of tasks.

An Example   Consider a subject who knows that $\sqrt{81} = 9$. What sorts of abilities is she thereby endowed with? There are three that immediately come to mind:

ASSENT
> The subject is able to give a correct answer to the question 'Is it the case that $\sqrt{81} = 9$?' (or to some analogue of this question in a language she understands).

DEDUCTIVE BASIS
> The subject is able to perform certain kinds of deductions on the basis of '$\sqrt{81} = 9$'. For instance, she might be able to derive '$\sqrt{81}$ is divisible by 3' from '9 is divisible by 3'.

APPLICATION
> The subject is able to use a piece of information about the natural world for a new kind of purpose. For instance, upon discovering that it takes 81 one-square-meter tiles to cover a plot of land which is known to be perfectly square-shaped, the subject might acquire the ability to predict how many meters of fencing would be needed to build a perimeter.

Each of these abilities can be usefully modeled as an information-transfer ability.

Let us begin with ASSENT. Suppose our subject has known all along that the arithmetical vocabulary is understood in such a way that the Dedekind Axioms are true, and in such a way that classical inference preserves truth. But suppose she is nonetheless unable to answer the question 'Is it the case that $\sqrt{81} = 9$?'. All the information that is needed to answer the question is stored in the subject's cognitive system. For any region of logical space in which arithmetical vocabulary is used in such a way that the axioms are true, and in such a way that classical inference preserves truth, is a region of logical space in which '$\sqrt{81} = 9$' is true. So the subject's inability to answer the question was not to do with lack of information. It is a problem of *access*: different parts of the relevant information are accessible for different purposes, and not enough of it is accessible for the purposes of answering the question 'Is it the case that $\sqrt{81} = 9$?'.

Now suppose that the subject comes to see that '$\sqrt{81} = 9$' is true by deriving it from the axioms. The deduction gives our subject the ability to deploy information she already possessed in the service of new tasks—and in particular the task of answering the question 'Is it the case that $\sqrt{81} = 9$?'. So her cognitive accomplishment should be construed, at least in part, as the acquisition of an information-transfer ability: she has broadened the range of tasks with respect to which she is able to deploy a certain piece of information.

The case of DEDUCTIVE BASIS is similar. Suppose that when our subject learns that $\sqrt{81} = 9$, she thereby acquires the ability to derive '$\sqrt{81}$ is divisible by 3' from '9 is divisible by 3'. This can be modeled as the claim that when our subject learns that $\sqrt{81} = 9$ she acquires a *conditional* information-transfer ability: should information become available for the purposes of answering the question 'Is 9 divisible by 3?', it will automatically become available for the purposes of answering the question 'Is $\sqrt{81}$ divisible by 3?'.

Finally, consider APPLICATION. So far we have focused on the deployment of *linguistic* information—for instance, information to the effect that arithmetical vocabulary is used in such a way that the axioms turn out to be true—in the service of an essentially *linguistic* task: the task of answering a linguistically-posed question. But when we describe a subject as knowing that $\sqrt{81} = 9$ we sometimes expect this knowledge to be manifested in her non-linguistic behavior as well. Recall our farmer and her square piece of land. Suppose she knows that it takes 81 one-square-meter tiles to cover her land. She therefore possesses the information that the land is 81 square meters in area, and is able to deploy it for the purposes of tiling. But the farmer might nonetheless lack the ability to deploy such information for the purposes of, say, buying just the right amount of fence to build a perimeter. By doing mathematics she can acquire an information-transfer ability: the ability to deploy the relevant information—information about the size of the piece of land that was previously available only for the purposes of tiling—in the service of new tasks, such as perimeter-building.

4.3 Fragmentation

A subject who has access to a piece of information for some purposes but not others is usefully thought of as being in a *fragmented* cognitive state. An advantage of describing a subject as fragmented is that it gives us an attractive way of modeling her information-transfer abilities. One can model an information-transfer ability as the instantiation of a relation of *accessibility* amongst different fragments within the subject's cognitive state.

Recall our farmer, and her coming to know that $\sqrt{81} = 9$. A cognitive accomplishment of this kind will typically involve the acquisition of a family of information-transfer abilities. Say it involves acquiring the ability to deploy information that was previously available only for the purposes of buying tiles, in the service of new tasks, such as buying fencing. On a fragmentation model, this can be captured by saying that the fragment corresponding to the task of buying tiles becomes *accessible* to the fragment corresponding to the task of buying fencing.

When a given fragment gains access to another, there is pressure for it to absorb the newly accessible information. Say that our farmer is confused: she believes that her piece of land has a side-length of 8 meters (i.e. an area of 64 square meteres) for the purposes of buying fencing, but she believes that the land has a side-length of 9 meters (i.e. an area of 81 square meters) for the purposes of buying tiles. Then the farmer learns that $\sqrt{81} = 9$. As a result, the two fragments become accessible to one another, and the farmer comes to see that she has been proceeding on different assumptions relative to different purposes. This realization generates pressure for the conflict to be resolved by bringing the fragments into sync. If the subject isn't sure which of the two fragments to revise, however, she may not be in a position to resolve the conflict, and the fragments will remain out of sync.

Fragment-synchronization need not consist in the resolution of an internal tension, however. Consider a farmer who is able to deploy the information that her piece of land is 81 square meters in area for the purposes of buying tiles, but not for the purposes of buying fencing: if she were to be faced with the project of building a perimeter around her land, she would simply have no idea how much fencing to buy. When the farmer learns that $\sqrt{81} = 9$, the fragment corresponding to the task of fencing-purchase gains access to the fragment corresponding to the task of tile-purchase, so there is pressure for the newly accessible information to be absorbed. But in this case it is easy to bring the fragments into sync: it is simply a matter of transferring information from one fragment to another.

A Formal Model   A fragmented cognitive state can be modeled as an ordered-triple $\langle T, b, \alpha \rangle$:

- The set T consists of *tasks* that the subject might be engaged in; each task in T will correspond to a different fragment in the subject's cognitive state. (T should be chosen so as to deliver a happy medium between recognizing too many tasks to allow for systematic theorizing and recognizing too few tasks to do justice to the subject's behavior.)
- The belief-function b maps each element in T to a 'belief-state'. To keep things simple, I shall assume that a belief-state can be modeled as a (partial) function from regions of logical space to truth-values. A more sophisticated version of the proposal would model a belief-state as a (partial) assignment of credences to regions of logical space, or some variation thereof.
- The relation α expresses *accessibility* amongst members of T. More specifically, $\alpha(t_1, t_2)$ is meant to capture the fact that the belief-state corresponding to task t_1 is accessible for the purposes of carrying out task t_2.

Many of the cognitive accomplishments of a subject whose cognitive state is represented by $\langle T, b, \alpha \rangle$ can be modeled as updates of the belief-function b, or of the accessibility relation α. Changes in b represent changes in the information that the subject has available for the purposes of a given task; changes in α represent changes in the subject's information-transfer abilities.

Suppose that my cognitive state is modeled by $\langle T, b, \alpha \rangle$, and that I have no idea when the Great Fire of London took place. Then b might assign an *empty* belief-state to the task of answering the question 'What year did the Great Fire of London take place?'. In other words, if t_{GFL} is the task of answering the relevant question, $b(t_{GFL})$ is undefined for every region in logical space. Now suppose I am told that the Great Fire of London took place in 1666. This might be represented by updating b so that $b(t_{GFL})$ assigns 'true' to regions of logical space whereby the Great Fire of London took place in 1666, and 'false' to regions of logical space whereby it did not.

Perhaps I am only in a position to deploy the newly acquired information for the purposes of answering the relevant question. If so, the model will treat the belief-state corresponding to t_{GFL} as inaccessible to every other task; in other words, $\alpha(t_{GFL}, t)$ will be false whenever $t \neq t_{GFL}$. In all probability, however, I will acquire the ability to deploy the relevant information for other purposes. I might, for example, acquire the ability to deploy it for the purposes of answering the question 'Did London exist in 1666?' Even though this is an easy inference, it constitutes a cognitive accomplishment. Our model can represent such an accomplishment as an update of α whereby the belief-state corresponding to t_{GFL} becomes accessible to the task of answering the question 'Did London exist in 1666?' In other words, we treat $\alpha(t_{GFL}, t_{LE})$ as true, where t_{LE} is the task of answering the new question.

I suggested above that there is pressure for accessible information to be taken into account. In this case, the pressure can be resolved by tansferring information from $b(t_{GFL})$ to $b(t_{LE})$. Suppose I start out having no idea whether London existed in 1666, so that b starts out assigning an *empty* belief-state to the task t_{LE}. When the belief-state corresponding to t_{GFL} becomes accessible to t_{LE}, b is updated so that $b(t_{LE})$ assigns 'true' to regions of logical space whereby the London exists in 1666, and 'false' to regions of logical space whereby it did not.

It is worth keeping in mind that when I describe a cognitive state as fragmented, I do *not* claim that a physical system which is in that state must be *modular*—I do *not* claim that the system must be made up of different components (or modules) which operate with some degree of independence from one another. All I claim is that the best way to model the *information* contained in the system is by relativizing different pieces of information to different purposes. Whether or not this relativization is in some sense mirrored by the system's physical realization is a separate issue, about which the present proposal remains totally neutral.

Modeling Logic and Mathematics Our formal model allows us to represent a significant range of cognitive accomplishments in logic and mathematics. Certainly not everything—it does not give us the resources to capture the capacity for mathematical creativity, for example. But it does allow us to represent the main pillar of accomplishment in logic and mathematics: deduction.

Deductions are modeled as the acquisition of information-transfer abilities, that is, as increases in the range of the accessibility relation, α. In the case of pure logic and pure mathematics, deductions will usually be modeled as increases of accessibility between tasks aimed at answering linguistically posed question concerning the truth of a particular sentence. So, for example, the deduction of '$\sqrt{81} = 9$' from the Dedekind Axioms, might be modeled by letting the belief-states corresponding to the tasks of answering the question 'Are the Axioms true?' and the question 'Are thus-and-such inferences truth-preserving?' become accessible to the task of answering the question 'Is it the case that $\sqrt{81} = 9$?' (or the question 'Is '$\sqrt{81} = 9$' true?'; it makes no difference for present purposes whether questions are put in the formal or the material mode). If the deduction takes several steps, the model will generate an accessibility chain. Suppose the nth step in a proof consists in deriving ϕ from ψ_1 and ψ_2. Then the model will let the belief-states corresponding to t_{ψ_1} and t_{ψ_2} become accessible to t_ϕ (where t_ϕ, t_{ψ_1} and t_{ψ_2} are the tasks of answering the question 'Is ϕ true?', 'Is ψ_1 true?' and 'Is ψ_2 true?', respectively).

In the case of applied mathematics, deduction will usually be modeled as an increase in accessibility between tasks not all of which are language-related. Suppose our farmer uses her knowledge that $\sqrt{81} = 9$, together with her knowledge that 81 square-meter tiles would be needed to tile her land, to deduce that 9 meters of fencing would be needed to fence each side of her land. Our model will capture this inference by letting the belief-state corresponding to the (non-linguistic) task of choosing the right number of tiles become accessible to the (non-linguistic) task of choosing the right amount of fencing.

In order to capture this inference in detail, however, the model may need to postulate accessibility between linguistic and non-linguistic tasks, since the farmer's inference may have relied on her linguistic abilities. Suppose she proceeded in several steps. She first used information about the number of tiles needed to tile her land to conclude that the sentence 'the area is 81 square meters' is true. She then relied on her knowledge of the fact that '$\sqrt{81} = 9$' and 'the side-length-in-meters of a square piece of land is the square root of its area-in-square-meters' are both true to conclude that 'the side-length is 9 meters' is true. Finally, she used this conclusion to determine that 9 meters of fencing would be needed to fence each side of her land. Our model would represent this inference by first letting the belief-state corresponding to the non-linguistic task of choosing the right number of tiles become accessible to the linguistic task of answering the question 'Is the land 81 square meters in area?'. After that, the model will postulate accessibility between linguistic tasks, as in the previous example. Finally, the model will let the belief state corresponding to the linguistic task of answering the question 'Does the land have a side-length of 9 meters?' become accessible to the non-linguistic task of choosing the right amount of fencing.

Is the Model Overly Linguistic?   On the proposal I have been defending, deduction in pure logic and pure mathematics will frequently be modeled as an increase in accessibility between language-related tasks—and, more specifically, linguistically posed questions. Moreover, the *information* that gets transferred between fragments will often concern language: as it might be, information to the effect that the arithmetical vocabulary is understood in such a way as to make the Dedekind Axioms true. This might lead to the worry that our model is overly reliant on linguistic information.

There is no denying that mathematical practice doesn't usually *feel* like a linguistic endeavor. When one is trying to prove a theorem, or trying to understand why a theorem is true, one's experience is usually more akin to the exploration of an abstract realm than to an analysis of the workings of language. To see why the reliance on language is nonetheless appropriate, it is useful to begin with a non-mathematical example. Suppose you are asked 'Are there any tapirs in the area?'. In order to answer this question, you need two pieces of information. First, you need some non-linguistic information: you need to know whether there are any tapirs in the area. Second, you need some linguistic information: in particular, you need to know what 'tapir' means. This linguistic information is not part of the *content* of the question: whether or not there are tapirs in the area does not depend on what 'tapir' means, or, indeed, on whether there is such a thing as language use. But it is nonetheless true that you will only succeed in understanding the question—and therefore in supplying an appropriate answer—if you know what 'tapir' means.

This is not to say that language users are usually attending to the relevant linguistic processing. Quite the contrary: when an English speaker who understands the word 'tapir' is asked 'Are there any tapirs in the area?', she will usually focus exclusively on the question's subject-matter, regardless of the linguistic processing that is required to understand the question. Linguistic processing can nonetheless take up a substantial portion of the work. Suppose you are asked 'Are there any tapirs who are not such that it is not the case that they are not non-mammals?' You may need a moment to figure out what, exactly, is being asked. But once you've figured it out, you'll see that answering the question correctly requires only basic knowledge about tapirs.

The task of answering ⌜Is it the case that ϕ?⌝, for ϕ a *logical truth*, is an extreme example of this sort of phenomenon. Such questions can be very difficult to answer. But the difficulty is *not* that it is hard to figure out how things stand regarding the question's subject-matter: the truth-conditions of a logical truth are satisfied *trivially*. The difficulty is all to do with linguistic processing—it can be extremely hard to determine whether the particular arrangement of vocabulary in ϕ results in trivial truth-conditions. And even though figuring out the answer would constitute a feat of linguistic processing, it need not *feel* like a feat of linguistic processing.

Now suppose ϕ is a truth of pure *mathematics*. According to the mathematical trivialist, the truths of pure mathematics have truth-conditions which are no less trivial than the truth-conditions of logical truths. So, as before, the difficulty in answering the question is *not* that it is hard to figure out how things stand regarding the question's subject matter. It is all to do with linguistic processing: it is a matter of determining whether the particular arrangement of vocabulary in ϕ results in trivial truth-conditions. But, as before, the subject needn't experience this as linguistic processing. The nature of the experience is more likely to be determined by the cognitive tools that are used to aid the processing in question; mathematical visualization, for instance, whereby mental images are associated with mathematical objects.

Consistency Work in the foundations of mathematics is often concerned with consistency. An important problem in the foundations of set-theory, for example, is to identify a unified conception of sets that is both consistent and strong enough to be interesting.

Acquiring a warrant for the internal coherence of an axiom system is a tricky affair. One can sometimes prove the consistency of one formal system in another. But it is a consequence of Gödel's Second Theorem that (when the systems in question are consistent and sufficiently strong) the system in which the proof is carried out cannot be a subsystem of the system the proof is about. There is therefore reason to expect that one's warrant for the internal coherence of a formal system will turn on more than just consistency proofs. It might turn on whether one has a good feel for the sorts of things that can be proved in the system, or on whether one has a good feel for the sorts of things that can be proved in formal systems within which one has been able to produce a consistency proof. It might also turn on whether one has a good feel for what a *model* for the system would look like.

In spite of all this, the problem of assessing the consistency of an axiom system is largely a problem of *deduction*. One's ability to 'get a feel' for a system will ultimately turn on the sorts of deductions one is able to produce within the system, and on the sorts of deductions one is able to produce within theories where the system might be described. So insofar as our model is able to capture deduction, it will have the resources to capture an important component of our ability to assess the consistency of an axiom system. The aim of the present section is to consider this point in further detail.

It will be useful to start with an example. Let us consider Frege's cognitive state, just before he received Russell's letter revealing the inconsistency of Basic Law V. On the proposal I have been defending, Frege's cognitive system should be modeled as being in a fragmented state. It contained the information that Basic Law V is inconsistent with the other axioms all along, but the information had yet to be *consolidated*: different components of the information were restricted to fragments corresponding to different tasks.

One component of the relevant information is the datum that, on an interpretation of the relevant vocabulary that respects all of the constraints that Frege set forth in the *Grundgesetze*, the sentence expressing Basic Law V should be counted as true. But this datum was only accessible for a limited range of purposes; it was accessible for the purposes of answering the question 'Is Basic Law V true?' (or its German equivalent), but perhaps not for the purposes of answering the question 'Does the concept of being the extension of a concept one doesn't fall under have an extension?'

Another component of the overall information is the datum that, on an interpretation satisfying Frege's constraints, every classically valid inference should preserve truth. Yet another is the datum that a certain string of symbols—which turns out to involve the concept of being the extension of a concept one doesn't fall under—should be allowed as an instance of Basic Law V. But, as before, these data were only accessible for limited sets of purposes. It was not until Frege was able to access these different pieces of information *together*—for the purposes of a *single* task—that the contradiction became apparent to him. Russell's letter made the consolidation possible. In reading through the proof, Frege was able to render the disparate pieces of information salient in a single context, enabling them to become available together and deploy them for the purposes of revealing the inconsistency of the system.

When Frege worked through Russell's proof he attained a cognitive accomplishment. The accomplishment was largely a feat of deduction: he improved his information-transfer abilities. But the deductive feat was, at the same time, a linguistic feat. For in coming to see the consequences of his axiom system, Frege attained a better grasp of what a standard interpretation for his system would look like: an interpretation satisfying all of the constraints that he had set forth in the *Grundgesetze*. This linguistic information was in Frege's cognitive system from the start: it was, after all, Frege himself who laid down the principles constraining interpretation. But the information was fragmented: for the purposes of any given task, only partially constrained interpretations of the system were available. Russell's proof allowed for consolidation, enabling Frege to access enough of the components of a standard interpretation of his system in the context of a single task to recognize it as inconsistent.

A normal subject's grasp of *logic* is deeply fragmented. Even in the case of a system like first-order logic, whose workings can be finitely specified, one won't enjoy unrestricted access to information about which inferences are counted as truth-preserving. A logically competent subject will be able to 'see' some of the consequences of a given sentence, if information concerning the validity of such inferences is accessible in the relevant context. But going beyond this range of immediately accessible inferences will require a non-trivial operation of information-transfer. Even one's grasp of simple rules such as *modus ponens* or universal instantiation is not unrestrictedly accessible. Someone who knows that a system is to be interpreted classically possesses the information that a universal generalization will only be counted as true if each of its instances is counted as true. Such information is readily available for the purposes of answering the question 'Is Universal Instantiation valid?' But suppose one is struggling to understand a proof, and that a particular instance of Universal Instantiation is just beyond the range of sentences one is able to 'see' as consequences of the present stage of the proof. Then the information that the relevant instance of Universal Instantiation is counted as truth-preserving is not immediately available to the subject, for the purpose of advancing in the proof.

I suggested earlier that one's ability to assess the consistency of a mathematical system will turn on the sorts of deductions one is able to produce within the system (and within theories describing the system). On the proposal I have been defending, this can be restated as the claim that one's ability to assess the consistency of a system turns on one's ability to consolidate fragmented information about the workings of the system. The better one's consolidation, the better one's grasp of the system's standard interpretation, and the more one will be in a position to deploy such a grasp for the purposes of answering questions about the system, including questions of consistency.

4.4 Belief Reports

I have been defending a model of cognitive accomplishment in logic and mathematics, but I haven't said much about how the model is supposed to relate to everyday belief-ascriptions.

One way to elucidate the relationship would be to use our model to characterize a regimented notion of belief—belief*, say—and argue that the following is true:

SIMPLE PICTURE
> For an ordinary belief-report of $\ulcorner S$ believes that $\phi \urcorner$ to be correct is for S to believe* the proposition expressed by ϕ.

It is not immediately clear, however, that we have a notion of proposition with the right sorts of properties. Notice, first, that it wouldn't do to think of propositions as tracking regions of logical space, or ways for the world to be. For the truths of pure logic and pure mathematics are all necessarily true, and therefore have truth-conditions that are satisfied throughout logical space. This means that the SIMPLE PICTURE would deliver the result that $\ulcorner S$ believes that $\phi \urcorner$ can only be correct for some truth of pure logic or pure mathematics ϕ if it is correct for *any* truth of pure logic or pure mathematics ϕ.

Notice, moreover, that the SIMPLE PICTURE can't be saved by thinking of propositions as tracking regions of logical space *under a mode of presentation*—at least not if modes of presentation are understood in accordance with the present proposal, as corresponding to *purposes* in the service of which a piece of information might be deployed. For, as we have seen, logical and mathematical accomplishment will often involve the acquisition of *information-transfer* abilities, rather than just an ability to deploy a particular piece of information for a particular purpose.

It is also worth noting that a single belief-statement can be used to ascribe different sets of abilities in different contexts. When one describes the cognitive state of our farmer with an assertion of the form '*S* believes that $\sqrt{81} = 9$', for example, one may be ascribing her the ability to transfer land-size information between different fragments of her cognitive state: some fragments corresponding to purposes whereby side-length is paramount and others corresponding to purposes whereby area is paramount. But, in the right sort of context—a context in which the farmer is known to be linguistically-impoverished, say—one may wish to refrain from ascribing her certain linguistically-focused abilities: for instance, the ability to deploy the information that the axioms are true for the purposes of answering the question 'Is '$\sqrt{81} = 9$' true?' And this may be so even if just such an ability would be reported by asserting '*S* believes that $\sqrt{81} = 9$' in a different context—for instance, when describing the cognitive state of a student who has learned to derive '$\sqrt{81} = 9$' from the axioms but knows nothing about applied arithmetic.

A proponent of the SIMPLE PICTURE could try to accommodate these difficulties by setting forth a new notion of proposition. She could claim that a 'proposition' corresponds to a hybrid of information-under-a-mode-of-presentation and information-transfer abilities, and that different sentences of pure logic or pure mathematics express different 'propositions' in different contexts. It seems to me, however, that there is not much to be gained by making this sort of move. I think it is more perspicuous to proceed by using a different approach—one which does not require a complex notion of proposition.

Here is what I propose, in very rough outline. Think of the sentence ϕ in the everyday belief-attribution $\ulcorner S$ believes that $\phi\urcorner$ as performing *double-duty*. First, ϕ is used to specify a region of logical space: a piece of information about the world. The belief-attribution tells us that S represents the world as being such as to satisfy this piece of information.

But this is only half the story. The *second* job of φ is to supply hints as to the purposes with respect to which S might be able to *deploy* this information, or as to the information-transfer abilities that S might be capable of in connection with the stored information.

In the case of belief-reports concerning empirical matters, it is often the first of these duties—that of specifying a piece of information—that does most of the work. Consider, for example, a belief-report such as 'S believes that snow is white'. Once the embedded sentence has been used to identify an appropriate piece of information—as it might be, the information that snow is white—the belief-report will have succeeded in telling us most of what we needed to know about S. For we have learned that S represents the world as being such that snow is white. And as long as S's cognitive system is not too different from our own, it will be easy enough for us to make educated guesses about the sorts of tasks that S might be in a position to use such information in the service of.

In the case of belief-reports concerning logic and mathematics, on the other hand, it tends to be the second duty—that of supplying hints about the purposes to which information might be deployed, or about information-transfer abilities—that does most of the work. Consider, for example, a belief-report $\ulcorner S$ believes that $\phi\urcorner$, where φ is a theorem of pure arithmetic. What sort of information might φ be used to pick out in such a report? Depending on context, it might be the region of logical space that verifies φ—that is, the *trivial* information consisting of the set of all worlds. Or it might be the *diagonal* proposition corresponding to φ—that is, the non-trivial information that we use arithmetical vocabulary in such a way as to make φ true. (See Stalnaker 1979 and Stalnaker 1984; for criticism, see Nuffer 2009.) In neither case do we learn much about S by being told that S represents the world as being such as to satisfy the relevant information. (In the first case, we learn nothing at all. In the second case we learn something non-trivial. But as emphasized by Field (1986), it is not enough to give us what we want. For the truth of φ is *entailed* by the truth of the axioms, in a classical setting. So *any* cognitive system that represents the world as being such that the relevant vocabulary is used in a way that renders the axioms true and the logic classical will *thereby* represent the world as being such that the relevant vocabulary is used in a way that renders φ true.) In spite of all this, the belief-report might succeed in conveying useful information about S. For it might tell us something new about the *purposes* with respect to which the relevant information is accessible to the subject. The use of ϕ in the belief-report might be used to hint that the information is accessible for a particular purpose—as it might be, the purpose of answering the question $\ulcorner$Is it the case that ϕ?$\urcorner$.

On this way of seeing of things, belief-reports in ordinary language turn out to be a messy affair. There are no precise rules for going from the sentence embedded in the belief-report to the information the report would succeed in conveying to the right kind of audience in the right kind of context. But this is just what one should expect if natural language belief-reports use a single catch-all notion—belief—to convey information about three essentially distinct forms of cognitive accomplishment: information possession, information access and information transfer.

I have tried to explain how I think the model of cognitive accomplishment that has been defended in this chapter relates to our ordinary practice of belief-attribution. I have not, however, attempted to give a *semantics* for English sentences of the form 'S believes that ϕ'. (An analogy: one can explain how the concept of wavelength relates to our ordinary practice of color-attribution without giving a semantics for the English word 'blue'.) This chapter is concerned with the philosophical project of explaining what cognitive accomplishment in logic and mathematics consists in, not the linguistic project of modelling the linguistic resources that are used to communicate such accomplishment in ordinary discourse.

4.5 Independent Motivation

The postulation of fragmented belief-states is not an *ad hoc* maneuver. It can be motivated independently of the project of giving an account of cognitive accomplishment in logic and mathematics.

It should be agreed on all sides that a subject might possess information that she is able to deploy in the service of some tasks but not others. Consider, for example, the expert gymnast, who is able to perform a perfect back salto but is unable to explain how she does it. The gymnast possesses a piece of information—information to the effect that such-and-such bodily movements are an effective way of producing a back salto—that she is able to deploy for certain practical purposes (i.e. the task of performing a back salto) but not for theoretical purposes (e.g. the task of explaining how to perform a back salto). Such differential access to information is naturally accounted for on a fragmentation model.

It should also be agreed on all sides that a subject's beliefs can be *incoherent*. I once saw my friend Pedro eating an enormous breakfast while reporting that he never eats big breakfasts. He suddenly realized the inconsistency, and laughed. Incoherent belief states of this kind are naturally accounted for on a fragmented model. Before the crucial realization, Pedro can be described by saying that for the purposes of articulating a general description of his eating habits he represents the world as being such that his breakfasts are always light, and for the purposes of reporting how much he is currently eating he represents the world as being such that he is eating a very substantial breakfast. Pedro's realization can then be modeled by saying that the two fragments become accessible to each other, and that the former is updated so as to represent the world as being such that he has a light breakfast *almost* always. (For additional discussion, see Lewis 1982.)

By modeling a cognitive state as fragmented one can give a unified treatment of three phenomena that might have initially seemed unrelated: imperfectly accessible information, incoherence and cognitive accomplishment in mathematics.

Mary and the Tomato   Actually, there is an additional kind of cognitive accomplishment that can be accounted for by appeal to fragmentation. Here is Frank Jackson's *Knowledge Argument*:

> Mary is confined to a black-and-white room, is educated through black-and-white books and through lectures relayed on black-and-white television. In this way she learns everything there is to know about the physical nature of the world... If physicalism is true, she knows all there is to know. For to suppose otherwise is to suppose that there is more to know than every physical fact, and that is just what physicalism denies... It seems, however, that Mary does not know all there is to know. For when she is let out of the black-and-white room or given a color television, she will learn what it is like to see something red, say. (Jackson 1986: 29)

What the argument brings out is that physicalists face a challenge. They must somehow accommodate the fact that it seems like Mary acquires information about the world—information she did not already have—when she first experiences the sensation of seeing red, even though physicalism appears to entail that she does not.

Suppose that, before her release, Mary is informed that she will be presented with a red tomato at noon. Suppose, moreover, that physicalism is true, and, in particular, that for a normal human to experience the sensation of seeing red *just is* for her to be in brain-state R. Mary knows this. So any world compatible with what Mary knows is a world in which her brain enters state R at noon. Accordingly, Mary possesses a certain piece of information—the information that her brain will be in state R at noon—and is able to deploy it for the purposes of certain tasks (for instance, the task of answering the question 'Will your brain be in state R at noon?')

She does not, however, have the ability to deploy this information in the service of certain other tasks. Suppose, for example, that before seeing the tomato Mary is shown a red ball, but is not told the color of the ball. Any world in which Mary has a sensation with the same kind of phenomenal character as the sensation she experiences when she sees the ball is a world in which she is in brain-state R. So every world in which Mary is in brain-state R at noon and has an experience with the relevant phenomenal character before noon is a world in which Mary has two experiences with the same kind of phenomenal character. It follows that two pieces of information that are already in Mary's possession—the information that she will be in brain-state R at noon, and the information that, while seeing the ball, she experiences a sensation with *this* phenomenal character—are enough to determine that the experience of seeing the tomato at noon will have the same kind of phenomenal character as the experience of seeing the ball. And yet Mary is unable to deploy the information in her possession for the purposes of answering the question 'Is this what it will be like to see the tomato?' when she is still looking at the ball.

There is an attractive way of modeling Mary's predicament in a fragmented system. Whereas she is able to deploy the information that her brain will enter state R at noon for the purposes of answering the question 'Will your brain be in state R at noon?' (or the question 'Will you see something red at noon?'), she is not able to deploy this information for the purposes of answering the question 'Is this what it will be like to see the tomato?' while looking at the ball. What she lacks, in other words, is a certain information-transfer ability.

When Mary is finally shown the tomato, she accomplishes a cognitive feat. For she is now able to deploy the information that her brain enters state R at noon for the purposes of answering the question 'Is this what it will be like to see the tomato?' while looking at the ball. This shouldn't be modeled as a feat of information acquisition, since Mary had all the relevant information to begin with. It should be modeled by treating certain of the fragments of Mary's cognitive state as accessible to one another.

4.6 Conclusion

I have offered an account of cognitive accomplishment in logic and mathematics. I argued that many such accomplishments should be thought of as *information-transfer abilities*: abilities whereby information that was available for the purposes of one set of tasks becomes available for the purposes of a different set of tasks. I went on to argue that the cognitive state of a normal subject is best thought of as *fragmented*, and that an information-transfer ability can be modeled as the ability to make the information that is stored in one fragment *accessible* for the purposes of another.

PART II
Detours

5

Possibility

In Section 2.2.1, we focused on a Kripkean reading of metaphysical possibility, according to which 'metaphysical' is used to single out a *type* of possibility, rather than a *level of strictness* that might be used to discriminate between more or less restrictive notions of possibility. The type of possibility in question is possibility *de mundo*, which applies to ways for the world to be regardless of how they happen to be represented (as opposed to possibility *de repraesentatione*, which is sensitive to how ways for the world to be happen to be represented). On this reading of 'metaphysical', metaphysical possibility is to be thought of as the most inclusive form of possibility *de mundo* there is. Going beyond metaphysical possibility it not a matter of exceeding a given level of strictness: it is a matter of lapsing into *absurdity*.

I also suggested that there is a tight connection between 'just is'-statements and the notion of metaphysical possibility:

> A first-order sentence (or set of first-order sentences) describes a metaphysically possible scenario just in case it is logically consistent with the set of true 'just is'-statements.

The aim of the present chapter is to explore this connection further.

5.1 A Sketch of the Proposal

Suppose one is working within a first-order language enriched with boxes and diamonds—for short, a first-order *modal* language. How should one determine which sentences of the language to accept? The main objective of this chapter is to offer an answer to this question. I will give a rough sketch of the proposal in the present section, and spell out the details in Section 5.3.

I will start by putting the point very informally, and add precision in stages. Let us start with the observation that all it takes to determine whether an interpreted first-order sentence is true is a specification of which objects exist and which properties and relations they instantiate. So we may think of a 'scenario', for present purposes, as a domain of objects together with an assignment of properties and relations to those objects. The question of which scenarios to count as metaphysically possible can therefore be recast as the question of which domain/assignment pairs to count as metaphysically possible. The answer I will be exploring in this chapter is roughly this: *any* domain/assignment pair should be counted as metaphysically possible, provided that no *property identifications* are violated, and provided that all *essences* are respected.[1] Let me explain what each of these provisos consists in.

To violate a property identification is to claim that an object has property P but not property Q when, in fact, P and Q are the same property. One would violate a property identification if, for instance, one claimed that something has the property of being composed of water but not the property of being composed of H_2O. For being composed of water and being composed of H_2O are one and the same: to be composed of water *just is* to be composed of H_2O.

To fail to respect an essence is to count two scenarios as metaphysically possible even though they assign different *constitutive properties* to the same object (or different constitutive relations to the same sequence of objects). A constitutive property, recall, is a property P such that if you have P then part of what it is to be you is to have P. The property of being human, for example, counts as constitutive if the following conditional 'just is'-statement is true:

$$\frac{\text{Human}(z)}{x = z \gg_x \text{Human}(x)}$$

(*Read:* Assume z is human; then part of what it is to be z is to be human.)

---

[1] Kit Fine has also explored the idea that essences might be used to fix the limits of metaphysical possibility. (See, for instance, Fine 1994.) One important difference between the two proposals is that Fine thinks that essence-statements are too fine-grained to be captured using an operator that expresses metaphysical possibility. I, on the other hand, work on the assumption that for F to be part of a's essence *just is* for it to be the case that, necessarily, if a exists, it has F.

So one would fail to respect an object's essence if one counted as metaphysically possible a scenario whereby an object is assigned the property of being human and a scenario whereby that same object fails to be assigned the property of being human.

The provisos are important because—assuming that the discussion of Section 2.2 is along the right lines—one would be landed in *absurdity* by violating a property identification, or by failing to respect an essence. The truth of the claim that something is composed of water but not H_2O, for example, would require of the world that something that is composed of water (i.e. H_2O) fail to be composed of H_2O—which is absurd. And the truth of the claim that a human might have failed to be human would require the non-absurdity of a scenario in which something fails to be human even though being human is part of what it is to be that thing—which is absurd.

Our proposal might therefore be thought of as based on a *Principle of Maximality*, according to which metaphysical possibility is to be construed as liberally as possible—but not so liberally that one is landed in absurdity. The meat of the proposal is the hypothesis that the *only* way of being landed in absurdity—at least within the confines of a first-order modal language—is by violating a property identification, or by failing to respect an essence.

Because 'just is'-statements can be used to capture property identifications and constitutive properties, our Principle of Maximality might be put as follows: count as many scenarios as metaphysically possible as you can—just make sure you always verify the 'just is'-statements in a particular class. Which class? Our hypothesis is that attention can be restricted to 'just is'-statements of the following two kinds: (1) simple 'just is'-statements like 'to be composed of water is to be composed of H_2O' in which there are no iterated applications of the 'just is'-operator; and (2) simple conditional 'just is'-statements such as

$$\frac{\text{Human}(z)}{x = z \gg_x \text{Human}(x)}$$

in which the consequent contains no iterated applications of the 'just is'-operator and the antecedent contains no occurrences of the 'just is'-operator. I shall refer to the statements in this limited class as *basic statements*. (As emphasized in Section 2.4, a semi-identity statement like 'part of what it is to be composed of water is to contain hydrogen' can be cashed out as 'just is'-statements with no iterated applications of the 'just is'-operator. And so can a simple first-order identity-statement like 'Hesperus = Phosphorus', as long as it is understood according to its Kripkean reading. So they will both be counted as basic statements in the present sense.)

The suggestion, then, is that an assignment of truth-values to *basic* statements can be used to determine the truth-values of arbitrary sentences in a first-order modal language. To see that this is a substantial claim, note that each basic statement has a modal correlate. I argued in Chapter 2 that a 'just is'-statement of the form $\ulcorner\phi(x) \equiv_x \psi(x)\urcorner$ should be thought of as having the same truth-conditions as the modal statement $\ulcorner\Box(\forall x(\phi(x) \leftrightarrow \psi(x)))\urcorner$, and that a conditional 'just is'-statement of the form

$$\frac{\phi(x)}{x = z \gg_x \phi(x)}$$

should be thought of as having the same truth-conditions as the modal statement $\ulcorner\Box(\forall z(\phi(z) \rightarrow \Box(\exists x(x = z) \rightarrow \phi(x))))\urcorner$.[2] So in claiming that an assignment of truth-values to basic statements can be used to settle the truth-value of every sentence in a first-order modal language, I am, in effect, claiming that an assignment of truth-values to the members of a restricted class of first-order modal sentences can be used to settle the truth-value of *every* first-order modal sentence. And the restriction in question is non-trivial because there are sentences outside the restricted class such that neither they nor their negations are entailed by sentences within the restricted class. As an example, take a simple possibility-statement like '$\Diamond\exists x(\text{Human}(x) \wedge 9\text{-feet-tall}(x))$', which falls outside of the restricted class. It will be counted as true on the present

---

[2] In fact, by allowing iterated applications of the 'just is'-operator, one can find a 'just is'-correlate for any first-order modal sentence. Let ϕ be an arbitrary sentence in a first-order language enriched with '$\Box$', and define $\phi^\star$ as follows:

- if $\phi = \ulcorner\Box\psi\urcorner$, then $\phi^\star = \ulcorner\psi^\star \equiv \top\urcorner$ (where $\top$ is a tautology);
- if $\phi = \ulcorner\psi \wedge \theta\urcorner$, then $\phi^\star = \ulcorner\psi^\star \wedge \theta^\star\urcorner$;
- if $\phi = \ulcorner\neg\psi\urcorner$, then $\phi^\star = \ulcorner\neg\psi^\star\urcorner$;
- if $\phi = \ulcorner\exists x\psi\urcorner$, then $\phi^\star = \ulcorner\exists x\psi^\star\urcorner$;
- if ϕ is atomic, then $\phi^\star = \phi$.

The suggestion is then that for any first-order modal sentence ϕ, $\phi \equiv \phi^\star$. So ϕ and $\phi^\star$ have the same truth-conditions.

proposal, given reasonable assumptions. But neither it nor its negation is a logical consequence of sentences in the restricted class.

The official characterization of our Principle of Maximality will have to wait until Section 5.3.2, but we are now in a position to articulate it as follows:

PRINCIPLE OF MAXIMALITY (Informal Version)

Metaphysical possibility—insofar as it is expressible in a first-order modal language—is to be limited only by the condition that the modal correlates of true basic 'just is'-statements should all be satisfied.

(It is worth keeping in mind that although the Principle of Maximality is a thesis about the limits of metaphysical possibility, it is also a thesis about the expressive limitations of first-order modal languages. It presupposes that a first-order language cannot be used to express modal truths that transcend what is already implicit in the class of basic 'just is'-statements that can be built from the language's non-logical vocabulary. We will come back to this point in Section 5.5.1.)

Embracing the Principle of Maximality has an important advantage. In Chapters 1 and 2 I set forth a view about the sorts of considerations that might ground the acceptance of a basic 'just is'-statement. I suggested that different 'just is'-statements are more or less hospitable to different kinds of scientific or philosophical theories, and argued that one can decide between them on the basis of whether the package that results from combining them with the rest of one's theorizing delivers a fruitful tool for scientific or philosophical inquiry. If this is right, there is no special mystery about how one might come to be justified in accepting or rejecting a basic 'just is'-statement.

The big advantage of a conception of metaphysical possibility based on the Principle of Maximality is that it allows the epistemic tractability of basic 'just is'-statements to carry over to arbitrary first-order modal statements. For one can decide which first-order modal statements to accept by using the following two-step process:

STEP 1

Assign a truth-value to every basic statement by gauging the statement's ability to accommodate fruitful theorizing, as discussed in Chapters 1 and 2.

STEP 2

Extend this assignment of truth-values to an assignment of truth-values to arbitrary sentences in a first-order modal language by implementing (a formal version of) the Principle of Maximality.

The possibility of carrying out Step 2 is a non-trivial assumption. But it is underwritten by a technical result, which is proved in Appendix C and will be further discussed in Section 5.3. Namely,

THE EXTENSION THEOREM

Informally: an assignment of truth-values to basic statements can be extended to arbitrary sentences in a first-order modal language by implementing (a formal version of) the Principle of Maximality.

And, as we shall see, the construction on which the proof of the Extension Theorem is based has an unexpected consequence. It allows us to prove a second result:

THE REDUCTION THEOREM

Informally: the truth-conditions of any sentence in a modal language can be specified using a (possibly infinite) sentence containing no boxes or diamonds (and no occurrences of the 'just is'-operator).

This is an attractive result. It tells us that there is a certain sense in which boxes and diamonds are unnecessary—or at least would be unnecessary if we were prepared to countenance infinitely long sentences.

All of this is, of course, premised on the claim that metaphysical possibility is limited only by the condition that set of true basic 'just is'-statements be satisfied. But how did we decide which particular class of statements to treat as basic? The class we have chosen has two desirable properties:

TRACTABILITY

The discussion in Chapters 1 and 2 gives us a relatively clear understanding of the sorts of considerations that might ground the acceptance or rejection of statements in the relevant class.

SUFFICIENCY

By using that class as input for the Extension Theorem, we get a plausible assignment of truth-values to modal statements—one which is roughly in line with the literature on metaphysical possibility. (See Section 5.3.3.)

I do *not* claim, however, that the particular class of statements we have chosen to treat as basic is the only class with these properties, or that it forms anything like a natural kind. We use it here because it gets the job done: it allows us to develop a conception of the modal landscape that allows for a sensible epistemology while respecting the truth-values of the modal statements that philosophers tend to have firm opinions about. If we were to choose a different range of sentences as our input class, we might get somewhat different results. But the differences are likely to lie mostly beyond the region with respect to which the notion of metaphysical possibility is robustly understood. As our understanding of modal notions develops—and as the applications of these notions demand that we take a stance on more complex issues—we might find it fruitful to treat a different class of statements as basic in a way that reflects our improved theoretical outlook. For now, however, it seems to me that our understanding of metaphysical possibility is not robust enough to mandate any particular choice of basic statements. All I claim on behalf of the choice that has been made here is that it is a sensible one, given the extent to which we have a firm grasp on the notion of metaphysical possibility.

5.2 An Unlewisian Account of Possibility

Before describing the proposal in further detail, it will be useful to explain how it differs from the conception of metaphysical possibility that David Lewis developed in *On the Plurality of Worlds*. I will focus on two central elements of Lewis's proposal: his Principle of Recombination, and his account of possible worlds.

5.2.1 The Principle of Recombination

According to Lewis's Principle of Recombination, any two non-overlapping things are such that (a duplicate of) one can coexist with (a duplicate of) the other, and such that (a duplicate of) one can exist without (a distinct duplicate of) the other (Lewis 1986a: §1.8).

Like our Principle of Maximality, Lewis's Principle of Recombination is intended to capture the informal idea that the notion of metaphysical possibility should be understood as broadly as possible: 'there are no gaps in logical space'. And, like our Principle, Lewis's is intended to play a pivotal role in explaining how one might come to form views about the truth or falsity of modal statements (Lewis 1986a: §2.4). There are, however, significant differences.

First, there is a methodological difference: we are primarily engaged in the *linguistic* project of assigning truth-conditions to modal sentences; Lewis is primarily engaged in the *metaphysical* project of characterizing a space of Lewisian worlds (which are maximal spatiotemporally connected objects). The two projects are interrelated, of course, since a space of Lewisian worlds can be used, in the presence of a suitable counterpart relation, to assign truth-conditions to modal sentences, and an assignment of truth-conditions to modal sentences imposes significant constraints on the space of Lewisian worlds.

Second, because of Lewis's emphasis on metaphysics, his Principle of Recombination focuses on one particular level of description of ways the world might be. Lewisian worlds are to be described by specifying which regions of space-time are occupied and which intrinsic properties are instantiated by the relevant occupiers. But now consider the question of whether there is a Lewisian world according to which there is a *husband* with such-and-such properties. The Principle of Recombination offers no direct guidance on the issue because 'husband' does not express an intrinsic property. In order to apply the Principle, one first needs to transform the question about husbands into a question about the spatiotemporal distribution of intrinsic properties. Ideally, one would come up with a family of bridge principles along the following lines:

1. The property of being a husband can be analyzed as the property of being male and married.
2. The property of being male can be analyzed as the property of having thus-and-such ... (body type? genetic properties? reproductive capabilities? social role?)
3. the property of being married can be analyzed as the property of ... (having been involved in a ceremony of such-and-such a kind? playing thus-and-such a role in a society of such-and-such a type?)

But there is no reason to suppose that we are in a position to fill in the blanks in 2 and 3. So, in practice, one may have to settle for a less precise way of transforming the question about husbands into something that the Principle of Recombination can be applied to, and hope it is enough to address the issue at hand.

From our perspective, the issue looks significantly different. We are no better placed than the Lewisian to analyze 'husband'. But proper application of the Principle of Maximality does not require that our question about husbands be recast as a question about spatiotemporal distributions of intrinsic properties. All that is required is that we succeed in identifying a family of basic statements that is rich enough for the purposes of the language under consideration. If, for example, we were to work with a language whose non-logical vocabulary is limited to genealogical terms ('husband', 'parent', 'marriage', 'male', etc.), then genealogical 'just is'-statements along the lines of 1 above will suffice for the Extension Theorem to deliver a suitable assignment of truth-values to modal sentences.

We might run into difficulties if we turn to a language containing both genealogical vocabulary and vocabulary expressing purely intrinsic properties, since in that case proper application of the Principle of Maximality would require a family of basic statements linking the two. The point I wish to make is that the Principle of Maximality, unlike Lewis's Principle of Recombination, allows for a piecemeal approach. It allows us to settle the truth-values of sentences in the language of modal genealogy even if we are not in a position to transform genealogical questions into questions about the spatiotemporal distribution of intrinsic properties.

A third difference between Lewis's Principle of Recombination and our Principle of Maximality is that Lewis's principle is tied up with a particular kind of foundationalist project. The most natural way of motivating a principle of plentitude based on spatiotemporal distributions of intrinsic properties is by presupposing a Humean metaphysics whereby all global matters are determined by the spatiotemporal distribution of local matters. But, as emphasized by Maudlin (1998), there is no real reason to believe that we live in such a world. There is no real reason to believe, for example, that a system consisting of two entangled particles could be fully described by specifying the location and intrinsic properties of each particle. Our Principle of Maximality, on the other hand, is independent of any such assumptions.

5.2.2 Lewisian Worlds

In addition to the Principle of Recombination, Lewis endorses a strong form of realism about possible worlds. His view can be divided into two distinct components. The first establishes a connection between possibility and possible worlds:

POSSIBILITY

> For it to be possible that *p just is* for there to be a world at which it is true that *p*.

The second component elucidates the true-at-a-world relation:

REPRESENTATION

> For it to be true that *p* at a world *just is* for the world to represent that *p* (relative to a suitable counterpart relation).

But what does it take for a world to represent that *p*? Here is Lewis:

How does a world ... represent, concerning Humphrey, that he exists?...A genuine world might do it by having Humphrey himself as a part. That is how our own world represents, concerning Humphrey, that he exists. But for other worlds to represent in the same way that Humphrey exists, Humphrey would have to be a common part of many overlapping worlds ... I reject such overlap ... There is a better way for a genuine world to represent, concerning Humphrey, that he exists ... it can have a Humphrey of its own, a flesh-and-blood counterpart of our Humphrey, a man very much like Humphrey in his origins, in his intrinsic character, or in his historical role. By having such a part, a world represents *de re*, concerning Humphrey—that is, the Humphrey of our world, whom we as his worldmates may call simply Humphrey—that he exists and does thus-and-so. (Lewis 1986a: 194)

From this it follows that Lewisian worlds cannot be abstract objects. For Humphrey might have won the election. But, by POSSIBILITY, for it it to be possible that Humphrey win the election is for there to be a world at which Humphrey wins the election. So there is a world at which Humphrey wins the election. But, by Lewis's spelling out of REPRESENTATION, for it to be true at a world that Humphrey wins the election is for the world to have a flesh-and-blood counterpart of Humphrey as a part, and for that individual to win a counterpart of our election. So there is a world which has a flesh-and-blood counterpart of Humphrey as a part (and is therefore not an abstract object).

It is also worth noting there is not a one-one correlation between Lewisian worlds and maximally specific ways for the world to be: the same Lewisian world will correspond to different ways for the world to be depending on one's choice of counterpart relation. When the mustachioed man in a Lewisian world is taken to be my counterpart, it represents the possibility that I have a mustache; when it is taken to be my twin brother's counterpart, it represents the possibility that *he* has a mustache.[3]

An important difference between Lewis's project and ours is that the present treatment of modality presupposes neither POSSIBILITY nor REPRESENTATION. I would like to say a few words about each of these principles, and conclude by commenting on Lewis's use of counterparts.

Possibility In making the Principle of Maximality precise, I shall indulge in possible-worlds-talk. But worlds will be introduced as mere technical devices: their job is to help specify an assignment of truth-values to modal sentences, and nothing more. In fact, there is an interesting sense in which I don't appeal to worlds at all. In the proof of the Extension Theorem, the role of possible worlds is played by *a*-worlds, which are set-thereotic constructs similar to the logician's models.[4]

As a result, nothing in this chapter presupposes POSSIBILITY. It seems to me, however, that POSSIBILITY is an attractive thesis, and that there is no reason to refrain from accepting it. The metaphysicalist would disagree (Chapter 1). She would argue that POSSIBILITY can be rejected on purely linguistic grounds, since the left- and right-hand side of the 'just is'-statement carve-up the world in very different ways. I argued in Section 1.2 that metaphysicalism is bad philosophy of language, and that there is no real reason to take it seriously. I suggested, instead, that the

---

[3] See Lewis 1986*a*: §4.4. Thanks here to Damien Rochford.

[4] A thorough discussion of *a*-worlds is supplied in Chapter 6, but the main thing to know about them is that one needn't worry. One can pretend that one is working with genuine possible worlds and rest assured that—as far as semantics is concerned—one will always get the right results. (I mean this in a very precise sense: I prove in Section 6.8 that anything that can be expressed by quantifying over Lewisian possibilia can also be expressed by quantifying over objects in the domains of the relevant *a*-worlds.) One can also rest assured that *a*-worlds won't offend one's philosophical sensibilities. They are designed to be acceptable to a modal actualist—'*a*-world' is short for 'actualist-world'—and presuppose very little by way of ontology: they use a bit of set-theory, but do not assume a specialized modal ontology, or an ontology of properties, or anything else that might be controversial. And they do not presuppose potentially controversial expressive resources such as infinitary languages or non-standard modal operators.

decision whether to accept a 'just is'-statement such as POSSIBILITY should be based on a cost-benefit analysis—one which weighs the decrease in theoretical resources that would result from accepting the statement against the increase in potentially awkward theoretical questions that would result from rejecting it.

In the case of POSSIBILITY, it seems to me that the cost-benefit analysis comes strongly in favor of acceptance. By rejecting POSSIBILITY, one is forced to make room for the following line of inquiry:

> I can see that Humphrey might have won the election. What I want to know is whether it is *also* true that there is a *world* at which Humphrey wins the election. And I would like to understand how one could ever be justified in taking a stand on the issue, given that we have no causal access to non-actualized possible worlds.

Someone who accepts POSSIBILITY will see such queries as resting on a false presupposition. They presuppose that there is a *gap* between the possibility that Humphrey win the election and the existence of a possible world at which Humphrey wins the election—a gap that would need to be plugged with a piece of modal metaphysics. POSSIBILITY entails that the gap is illusory. There is no need to explain how the existence of a world at which Humphrey wins is correlated with the possibility that he win because there is no difference between the two: for there to be a world at which Humphrey wins the election *just is* for it to be possible that Humphrey win the election.

It is true that by accepting POSSIBILITY one would lose access to a certain amount of theoretical space. For instance, one is no longer in a position to work with scenarios in which it is possible that Humphrey win the election even though there is no such thing as a world at which Humphrey wins. It seems to me, however, that this is not much of a price to pay because the availability of such scenarios is unlikely to lead to fruitful theorizing.

Representation   I have just argued that POSSIBILITY is an attractive thesis, which everyone should embrace. In contrast, it seems to me that Lewis's version of REPRESENTATION is potentially problematic. Much has been made of the fact that Lewis is committed to thinking of worlds as concrete spatiotemporal manifolds. But this is not the issue I wish to focus on here—at least not directly. The point I wish to make is that

Lewis's version of REPRESENTATION requires a non-trivial foundationalist assumption.

To get the problem into focus, it is useful to compare Lewis's version of REPRESENTATION with another: the view that worlds are sets of sentences, and that a world w represents that p just in case p is, in some suitable sense, 'entailed' by the propositions expressed by sentences in w. Now consider the following question: what condition would a world have to satisfy, on each of these views, in order for it to represent that Humphrey won the election?

For the linguistic representationist, the answer is straightforward: all it takes is for the world in question to contain the sentence 'Hubert Humphrey wins the 1968 United States presidential election' (or for it to contain other sentences that express propositions which together entail that Humphrey won the election). For the Lewisian, the answer is less straightforward. The difficulty is that a Lewisian world cannot *directly* represent the existence of Humphrey. It can only do so in coordination with the counterpart relation. More specifically, Lewis thinks that representing the existence of Humphrey requires two distinct components. First, the Lewisian world must contain, as it might be, 'a man very much like Humphrey in his origins, in his intrinsic character, or in his historical role'. Second, context must determine a counterpart relation according to which a man with the relevant features counts as a counterpart of Humphrey.

Let us say, in general, that a claim ϕ is *directly representable* if: (1) a Lewisian world represents that ϕ simply by being such that ϕ, and (2) whether or not a world is such that ϕ is independent of which counterpart relation is determined by context. Lewis thinks that claims about spatio-temporal distributions of perfectly natural properties are always directly representable. But, as we have seen, the claim that Hubert Humphrey exists is not directly representable, since one doesn't generally represent that Humphrey exists by containing Humphrey. Nor is the claim that there is something that might have been a poached egg, since it's truth is highly dependent on the counterpart relation.

I am now in a position to state what I think is problematic about Lewis's version of REPRESENTATION. Let ϕ be a claim that is not directly representable: the claim that Humphrey exists, say. Then the claim that ϕ can be represented at all (relative to a given counterpart relation) is non-trivial. It presupposes that ϕ lends itself to a certain kind of *analysis.* There must be a condition ϕ^*—as it might be, the condition that there be an individual with certain origins, intrinsic character and historical role—such that: (*a*) *w* satisfies ϕ^*, and (*b*) context determines that the counterpart relation is such that what it takes for a world *w* to represent ϕ—in our example, the claim that Humphrey exists—is that *w* satisfy ϕ^*.

Not any ϕ^* satisfying (*a*) and (*b*) will do, however. As before, let ϕ be the claim that Humphrey exists. One could easily satisfy conditions (*a*) and (*b*) by letting ϕ^* be the condition of representing, concerning Humphrey, that he exists. But this would leave us with a mystery. It would fail to elucidate the question of how the relevant notion of representation is supposed to work, since all we are being told is that *w* represents, concerning Humphrey, that he exists, and does so in virtue of satisfying the condition ϕ^* of representing, concerning Humphrey, that he exists. Lewis solves the problem by making a strong assumption. He assumes that, for any claim ϕ that a Lewisian world can represent, there is a condition ϕ^* which not only satisfies (*a*) and (*b*) but is also analyzable as a distribution of perfectly natural (and therefore directly representable) properties. For present purposes, however, it will be sufficient to focus on a slightly weaker assumption:

> For any claim ϕ that a Lewisian world can represent, there is a condition ϕ^* which not only satisfies (*a*) and (*b*) but is also directly representable.

This assumption is enough to make clear how Lewis's notion of representation is supposed to work. It entails that which claims a Lewisian world represents will be a function of the contextually determined counterpart relation, and of directly representable features of the relevant world. But the assumption is also a substantial claim.

Let us supose, as before, that ϕ is the claim that Humphrey exists, and try to find a condition ϕ^* which not only satisfies (*a*) and (*b*) but is also directly representable. Note first, that, ϕ^* cannot include the requirement that the relevant world contain an individual who was born in South Dakota, since being born in South Dakota is not directly representable: a world represents someone as born in South Dakota by containing an individual born in a *counterpart* of our South Dakota. More generally, ϕ^* cannot include the requirement that *non-qualitative* properties—properties concerning specific individuals—be instantiated. Nor can ϕ^* include the requirement that the relevant world contain an individual who is, say, *shrewd*, since whether or not one counts as shrewd depends on the behavior of one's counterparts at other worlds, and is therefore not directly representable. More generally, ϕ^* cannot include the requirement that *dispositional* properties—properties whose instantiation depends on the behavior of one's counterparts—be instantiated.

The inadmissibility of non-qualitative and dispositional properties makes it unlikely that a suitable ϕ^* will be statable in plain English, which is seeped in non-qualitative and dispositional vocabulary. It is unlikely, in particular, that one could use English to spell out the claim that something is to count as Humphrey's counterpart (in a suitable context) if it is like Humphrey in its 'origins, intrinsic character or historical role'. For how is one to specify the relevant origins and historical role without appealing non-qualitative properties—properties like *being born in South Dakota*, or *being a Democratic Party nominee*? And how is one to specify the relevant intrinsic character, when so many of the descriptors that suggest themselves—descriptions using psychological predicates, say, or descriptions of an individual's physical appearance—are dispositional?

Couldn't one get the needed vocabulary by *subtraction*? Couldn't one define a directly representable analogue of the property of being born in South Dakota by *subtracting away* its non-qualitative features, or a directly representable analogue of the property of being shrewd by *subtracting away* its dispositional features? The problem is that the needed subtraction operation is not always well defined. Wittgenstein illustrates the point in the *Philosophical Investigations* by asking: 'what is left over if I subtract the fact that my arm goes up from the fact that I raise my arm?' (§621) Here is a more contemporary example. A friend of narrow content might think that one can get to the narrow content of a mental state by subtracting away 'environmental factors'. (Perhaps one can get to the narrow concept *watery* by subtracting environmental factors from the ordinary concept of water.) But foes of narrow content will protest that the needed subtractions are not generally well defined. (See Yablo forthcoming for further discussion.)

Notice, moreover, that it is not obvious that appeal to the properties of fundamental physics would be any help. For it is not obvious that the instantiation of such properties is directly representable. One might think, for example, that part of what it is to be an electron is to be *disposed* to repel other electrons, and that part of what it is to have mass is to be *disposed* to resist acceleration.

Suppose it's true that neither ordinary language nor fundamental physics supplies us with the expressive resources to articulate the directly representable basis on which a world's ability to represent the existence of Humphrey (relative to a suitable conterpart relation) is supposed to be based. This certainly wouldn't *entail* that there is no such basis, since there might be a suitable condition ϕ^* even if we lack the resources to express it. But it does highlight the fact that in presupposing that such a basis exists, one is making a substantial philosophical claim.

Directly representable claims might be thought of as 'non-modal'. Accordingly, Lewis's version of REPRESENTATION might be thought of as presupposing an analysis of modal claims into non-modal components, plus a counterpart relation. The conception of modality I will be defending in this chapter has the advantages of making no such presupposition. It is compatible with the view that there are claims which are modal 'all the way down'—and, indeed, with the view that there is no useful distinction to be drawn between the modal and the non-modal. (At the same time, the present proposal gives us a way of articulating the truth-conditions of arbitrary modal statements without using modal operators, in virtue of the Reduction Theorem; see Section 5.4.)

Contextualism   Lewis's appeal to counterparts allows him to be a contextualist about possibility. For even though the space of *Lewisian worlds* is not context-dependent, which *possibilities* get represented by these worlds depends on the counterpart relation, and Lewis thinks the counterpart relation can vary from context to context (Lewis 1986a: §4.5).

As Lewis notes, modal contextualism has theoretical advantages. Take a statue and the lump of clay it is composed of. Even if they are exactly co-located throughout their existence, there is some pressure to think the statue and the clay must be distinct objects, since they appear to have different modal properties: the statue can survive the replacement of parts; the clay cannot. Lewis's contextualism allows him to respect this apparent divergence while holding on the view that the statue is identical to the clay. For he can claim that use of the word 'statue' and use of the word 'clay' give rise to different counterpart relations, and that the different counterpart relations can generate different possibilities regarding a single object.

As Steve Yablo pointed out to me, the account of modality that is defended in the present chapter allows one to enjoy the advantages of modal contextualism without being married to the idea that the modal can be reduced to the non-modal. For, as noted in Section 2.3.4, the view is consistent with contextualism about logical space, and therefore contextualism about the 'just is'-statements one accepts.

It is worth noting, moreover, that the view need not be committed to the assumption that there is a clean distinction between 'just is'-statements that can shift with context and those that can't. If one wanted to follow Lewis in thinking that some possibility statements are subject to contextual variations (e.g. possibility statements concerning Humphrey) but others are not (e.g. possibility statements concerning distributions of perfectly natural properties), one could do so by insisting that whereas certain 'just is'-statements can vary from context to context, others will always remain constant. The point is that one *needn't* go this route. One can enjoy the advantages of contextualism without committing oneself to Lewis's brand of foundationalism.

5.2.3 The Upshot

The conception of modality I will develop in this chapter might be captured by the slogan: 'Lewis, without the foundationalist metaphysics'. Like Lewis, I will articulate a principle of plentitude. But unlike Lewis, my principle is not tied up with the idea that modally rich claims can be analyzed into non-modal components, plus a counterpart relation. Like Lewis, I will attempt a reduction of modal vocabulary. But unlike Lewis, my reduction does not aspire to have non-modal properties at its base. What is interesting about the reduction is that it does away with modal operators.

5.3 The Details

I would now like to spell out some of the details of the conception of metaphysical possibility that was sketched in Section 5.1.

Let L be an arbitrary first-order language and let $L^\Diamond$ be the modal language that results from adding '$\Diamond$' to L. Our objective is to show that one can use an assignment of truth-values to the set of basic 'just is'-statements built out of vocabulary in L to specify an assignment of truth-values to arbitrary sentences in $L^\Diamond$.

5.3.1 Basic Statements

Although I offered an informal characterization of basic statements in Section 5.1, it is worth being a little more precise. Let a *basic statement* (built from vocabulary in the first-order language L) be one of the following:

1. A 'just is'-statement of the form

$$\phi(\vec{x}) \equiv_{\vec{x}} \psi(\vec{x})$$

where $\vec{x}$ is a sequence of variables $x_1, \ldots, x_k$, and ϕ and ψ are formulas in L.

[As noted earlier, this includes semi-identity statements of the form '$\phi(\vec{x}) \gg_{\vec{x}} \psi(\vec{x})$' (which can be re-written as 'just is'-statements of the form '$\phi(\vec{x}) \equiv_{\vec{x}} (\psi(\vec{x}) \wedge \phi(\vec{x}))$') and weak first-order identity-statements of the form '$a = b$' for a and b proper names (which can be re-written as 'just is'-statements of the form '$x = a \equiv_x x = b$'). See Section 2.4.]

2. A conditional 'just is'-statement of the form

$$\frac{\phi(z_1, \ldots, z_m, \vec{v})}{x_1 = z_1 \wedge \ldots \wedge x_m = z_m \gg_{x_1, \ldots, x_m} \phi(x_1, \ldots, x_m, \vec{v})}$$

where $\vec{v}$ is a sequence of variables $v_1, \ldots, v_k$, and ϕ is a formula in L.

5.3.2 The Extension Theorem

Intuitively, the Principle of Maximality is the claim that possibility—insofar as it is expressible in a first-order modal language—is to be limited only by the condition of verifying the true basic statements.

It is tempting to think that there is a straightforward way of making this informal idea precise. Start with a space of *logically* consistent 'worlds'. Go on to eliminate all and only worlds that fail to verify the modal correlate of some true basic statement. The worlds you're left with are the worlds that depict genuine possibilities.

When one restricts one's attention to the special case of *unconditional* 'just is'-statements, this procedure is well-defined. But things get messy when conditional 'just is'-statements are brought into the picture. To see this, consider a conditional statement to the effect that F-ness is constitutive, and suppose the plan is to eliminate worlds until we get the corresponding sentence of $L^\lozenge$ (i.e. '$\Box(\forall z(F(x)) \to \Box(\exists y(y = x) \to$

F(x)))') to count as true. The plan, in other words, is to secure the result that F-ness is *essential* to its bearers. Assume that our original space of worlds contains a *counterexample* to the essentiality of F-ness: there are worlds w and w' in W such that according to w there is something that is an F, and according to w' that very individual is not an F. The problem is that there is more than one way to get rid of the counterexample. One could do so either by eliminating w or by eliminating w'. As a result, it is not immediately clear how one should go about the project of ensuring that metaphysical possibility 'is limited only by the condition of verifying the true basic statements', as the Principle of Maximality demands.

My best effort to do so proceeds by constructing a space of worlds in stages. At the first stage, we introduce the actual world, and at each succeeding stage we introduce as diverse an assortment of additional worlds as the true basic statements allow. This construction allows us to prove the following result:

EXTENSION THEOREM

Let A be an assignment of truth-values to sentences in our first-order language L and basic 'just is'-statements built up from vocabulary in L. Then one can specify (up to isomorphism) a Kripke Model M_A for $L^\Diamond$ which is such that:

1. M_A *respects unconditional basic statements.*
   More precisely: if the basic statement $\phi(\vec{x}) \equiv_{\vec{x}} \psi(\vec{x})$ is true according to A, then $M_A \models \Box(\forall \vec{x}(\phi(\vec{x}) \leftrightarrow \psi(\vec{x})))$.

2. M_A *respects conditional 'just is'-statements.*
   More precisely: if the basic statement
   $$\frac{\phi(z_1, \ldots, z_m, \vec{v})}{x_1 = z_1 \wedge \ldots \wedge x_m = z_m \gg_{x_1, \ldots, x_m} \phi(x_1, \ldots, x_m, \vec{w})}$$
   is true according to A, then
   $$M_A \models \Box(\forall z_1, \ldots, z_m, \vec{v}(\phi(z_1 \ldots, z_m, \vec{v})$$
   $$\rightarrow \Box(\exists y_1, \ldots, y_m(y_1 = z_1 \wedge \ldots \wedge y_m = z_m)$$
   $$\rightarrow \phi(z_1, \ldots, z_m, \vec{v})))).$$

3. M_A *construes metaphysical possibility as liberally as possible.*
   In particular:

$$M_A \models \exists \vec{x_1}(\phi_1(\vec{x_1}) \wedge \Diamond(\exists \vec{x_2}(\phi_2(\vec{x_1}, \vec{x_2}) \wedge$$

$$\Diamond(\exists \vec{x_3}(\phi_3(\vec{x_1}, \vec{x_2}, \vec{x_3}) \wedge \ldots))))$$

will hold whenever the relevant sentence meets certain minimal constraints: (1) '$\phi_1(\vec{x_1})$' is satisfied by the actual world of M_A, (2) each of the '$\phi_i(\vec{x_1}, \ldots, \vec{x_i})$ is consistent with the basic statements that A counts as true, and (3) there are no clashes amongst the ϕ_i regarding the constitutive properties demanded of the referents of the relevant variables.

(For proofs and details, see Appendix C.)

I would like to suggest that we think of the construction implicit in the Extension Theorem as a formal implementation of the Principle of Maximality. In other words, the vague claim that possibility—insofar as it is expressible in a first-order modal language—should be limited only be the condition of verifying the true basic statements is to be regimented as the precise claim that a first-order modal sentence ϕ is true if and only if $M_A \models \phi$.

Have we succeeded in doing justice to the informal version of the Principle of Maximality that we started with? To a significant extent, we have. But it is difficult to give a more precise answer because the informal statement of the Principle is so incredibly rough. (It is far from obvious, for example, that we have a clear sense of which modal statements should be counted as expressing 'possibilities'.) In any case, it seems to me that it would be a mistake to put too much weight on any particular way of making the Principle of Maximality precise. It is useful to have an existence proof: it is useful to know that there is at least one reasonable way of using the true basic statements to fix the truth-values of arbitrary sentences in $L^\Diamond$. And there may well be value in the project of comparing the virtues of different such proposals. But one shouldn't be too bent on finding the one true way of formalizing the Principle of Maximality when the discussion turns on issues that go beyond the region with respect to which the notion of possibility is robustly understood.

5.3.3 The List of Modal Truths

Say we adopt the proposed formalization of the Principle of Maximality. Which modal sentences turn out to be true?

1. The 'actual' world of the Kripke-semantics is chosen so as to ensure that every true sentence of our base first-order language L turns out to be true.

2. The use of a Kripke-semantics guarantees that one gets a normal modal system, and therefore that every sentence of $L^{\Diamond}$ that is theorem of classical logic will count as true.

   In the version of the construction that is described in Appendix C, I presuppose a trivial accessibility relation—on the grounds that it is the simplest—with the result that every theorem of $S5$ turns out to be true. (The use of non-trivial accessibility relations is also possible; for relevant discussion, see Salmon 1995.)

3. One gets the modal correlate of every basic 'just is'-statement that is counted as true. For instance, by assuming that 'Elephant$(x) \gg_x$ Mammal(x)' is true one gets the result that '$\Box(\forall x(\text{Elephant}(x) \rightarrow \text{Mammal}(x)))$' is true, and by assuming that 'Elephant(x)' is constitutive one gets the result that (an $L^{\Diamond}$ rendering of) 'necessarily, elephants are essentially elephants' is true.

   As far as I can tell, any first-order modal sentence that constitutes a relatively uncontroversial example of a metaphysical necessity can be recovered from suitable 'just is'-statements in this sort of way. Table 5.1 lists some examples.

4. Every possibility statement of the form

$$\exists \vec{x}_1(\phi_1(\vec{x}_1) \wedge \Diamond(\exists \vec{x}_2(\phi_2(\vec{x}_1, \vec{x}_2) \wedge \Diamond(\exists \vec{x}_3(\phi_3(\vec{x}_1, \vec{x}_2, \vec{x}_3) \wedge \ldots)))))$$

   subject to the constraints described in the statement of the Extension Theorem.

   Assuming a reasonable assignment of truth-values to the basic 'just is'-statements, this ensures that one gets $L^{\Diamond}$-renderings of sentences like 'I might have had a sister' and 'I might have had a sister who was a cellist but might have been a philosopher'.

   If e is an egg and s is a sperm, one also gets an $L^{\Diamond}$-rendering of 'e and s might have given rise to different people in different worlds':

$$\exists x \exists y (x = e \wedge y = s \wedge \Diamond(\exists z(\text{GiveRise}(x, y, z) \wedge$$

$$\Diamond(\exists w(w \neq z \wedge \text{GiveRise}(x, y, w)))))))$$

   This seems reasonable. For if a single egg and sperm can give rise to monozygotic twins, why not think that it could give rise to one of the twins without the other? But now suppose that h is a particular dagger-handle and b is a particular dagger-blade. Could h and b be used to build different daggers in different worlds? I myself find it hard to answer this question because I'm not sure I understand what is supposed to be at stake. But if one thinks that the question should be answered in the negative, one can get the desired results by accepting suitable basic statements.[5]

There is no official catalogue of recognized modal truths. But I hope this section lends some plausibility to the claim that, by starting with a suitable class of basic statements, one can get the Principle of Maximality that is implemented by the Extension Theorem to deliver a list of modal truths that is roughly in line with the standard literature on metaphysical possibility.

5.4 Reduction

The Extension Theorem has an interesting corollary. One gets the result that the truth-conditions of arbitrary sentences in $L^\Diamond$ can be specified using only vocabulary in L.

---

[5] One way of doing so is by basing the claim that h and b couldn't have given rise to different daggers in different worlds on the assumption that daggers are unlike embryos in an important respect: whereas it would be a mistake to think of an embryo as a mereological fusion of its originating egg and sperm, a dagger can be thought of as a fusion of its handle and blade. If this is how one thinks of the matter, one can get the desired result by setting forth the following 'just is'-statements, where 'Dagger(x, y, z)' is read 'dagger z is built from handle x and blade y' and 'Fusion(x, y, z)' is read 'z is the mereological fusion of x and y':

$$\text{Handle}(x) \wedge \text{Blade}(y) \gg_{x,y} \exists z\, \text{Fusion}(x, y, z)$$

$$\text{Fusion}(x, y, z) \gg_{x,y,z} \forall v (\text{Fusion}(x, y, v) \rightarrow v = z)$$

$$\text{Dagger}(x, y, z) \gg_{x,y,z} \text{Fusion}(x, y, z)$$

An alternative is to think that the fact that no dagger-handle and dagger-blade could give rise to different daggers in different worlds is a brute fact about daggers. If so, one will need a conditional 'just is'-statement such as the following to get the right results:

$$\frac{\text{Dagger}(x, y, z)}{\exists v\, \text{Dagger}(x, y, v) \gg_{x,y} \text{Dagger}(x, y, z)}$$

Unfortunately, this is not a basic 'just is'-statement. So it cannot be used as input for the Extension Theorem, on its current formulation. It is, however, straightforward to modify the construction on which the proof of the theorem is based so as to accommodate 'just is'-statements of this kind.

To see what I have in mind, it is useful to begin with an example. Ask yourself: what is required of the world in order for the truth-conditions of the following sentence to be satisfied?

MODAL
$\exists x(\text{Mammal}(x) \wedge \Diamond(\text{Human}(x)))$
(*Read:* something is a mammal and might have been a human.)

A perfectly accurate way of specifying truth-conditions for MODAL is by stating that what is required of the world in order of MODAL's truth-conditions to be satisfied is that there be something that is a mammal and might have been a human. But suppose one is aiming for more than mere accuracy. One wants one's specification to take the following form:

> What is required of the world in order for MODAL's truth-conditions to be satisfied is that it be such that p.

where 'p' is replaced by a sentence containing no modal operators. Then one might reason as follows:

> Being a non-human is a constitutive property: if you're a non-human, part of what it is to be you is to be a non-human. So the requirement that the world be such that there is a mammal that might have been a human boils down to the requirement that the world be such that there is a mammal that is also a human. But part of what it is to be a human is to be a mammal. So the requirement that the world be such that there is a mammal that is also a human boils down to the requirement that the world be such that there are humans.

> Accordingly, all that it is required in order for MODAL's truth-conditions to be satisfied is for the world to be such that there are humans—and this gives us what we want, since 'there are humans' contains no modal operators.

The proof of the Extension Theorem can be used to show that an analogous result holds for arbitrary modal sentences. More specifically:

REDUCTION THEOREM
For ϕ an arbitrary sentence of $L^{\Diamond}$, the truth-conditions of ϕ are correctly specified by some clause of the form:

> What is required of the world in order for ϕ's truth-conditions to be satisfied is that it be such that p.

where 'p' is replaced by a (possibly infinite) sentence built out of the vocabulary of L. (See Appendix C for proof.)

It is worth emphasizing that not every sentence of $L^\Diamond$ will turn out to have truth-conditions as interesting as MODAL. Consider, for example,

$$\Box(\forall x(x \text{ is composed of water} \rightarrow x \text{ is composed of } H_2O))$$

If you accept 'To be composed of water *just is* to be composed of H_2O', you should believe that *nothing* is required of the world in order for the truth-conditions of this sentence to be satisfied. For consider an arbitrary scenario σ, and assume that, at σ, some object x is composed of water. Since there is no difference between being composed of water and being composed of H_2O, x is *thereby* composed of H_2O. There is no such thing as a *transition* from x's being composed of water to x's being composed of H_2O, and therefore no requirement that σ would have to satisfy for the transition to be valid. So the truth-conditions of '$\forall x(x$ is composed of water $\rightarrow x$ is composed of $H_2O)$' are trivially satisfied at σ. But σ was arbitrarily chosen. So the truth-conditions of '$\Box(\forall x(x$ is composed of water $\rightarrow x$ is composed of $H_2O))$' are trivially satisfied.

One might be tempted to describe the Reduction Theorem as a reduction of the modal to the non-modal. But that would be a tendentious way of putting the point. It ignores the fact that a predicate such as 'is human' might be thought to be modally rich. (You might think, in particular, that part of what it is to be human is to be essentially human.) What the theorem gives us is a reduction of $L^\Diamond$-vocabulary to L-vocabulary: it tells us that the truth-conditions of sentences in $L^\Diamond$ can be specified using only vocabulary in L.

5.5 Limitations

The purpose of this section is to describe some limitations of the techniques described earlier in the chapter.

5.5.1 Modal Language and Modal Fact

The Extension Theorem is a result about *language*: it shows that the set of identity statements can be used to fix the truth-values of every *sentence* in $L^\Diamond$.

It is worth keeping in mind that the Extension Theorem will only deliver the right results if L has a suitably rich stock of non-logical predicates. Suppose, for example, that you think that there might have been an essentially lonely object:

LONELY

$$\Diamond(\exists x \wedge \Box(\exists y(y = x) \rightarrow (\forall y(y = x))))$$

Since Lonely contains no non-logical predicates, it will be stable in $L^\Diamond$ regardless of which non-logical predicates are in L. But—on reasonable assumptions—one won't be able to express the 'just is'-statements necessary to ensure that Lonely gets counted as true unless some non-logical predicate of L is available, and one is able to say something along the following lines:

$$\frac{P(z)}{z = x \gg_x P(x)} \qquad P(x) \gg_x \forall y(y = x)$$

(*Read:* 'being P is constitutive of its bearers', and 'part of what it is to be a P is to be lonely')

Similarly, one won't be able to state the 'just is'-statements necessary to make the following sentence of $L^\Diamond$ true:

NEMESES

$$\Diamond(\exists x \Diamond(\exists y \Box(x \neq x \vee y \neq y)))$$

(*Read:* There might have been *incompossible* objects: objects each of which might have existed but such that they couldn't have existed together.[6])

unless L contains non-logical predicates, and one is able to say something along the following lines:

$$\frac{A(z)}{z = x \gg_x A(x)} \qquad \frac{B(z)}{z = x \gg_x B(x)} \qquad A(x) \gg_x \neg \exists y B(y)$$

(*Read:* 'being A is constitutive of its bearers', 'being B is constitutive of its bearers' and 'part of what it is to be an A is for there to be no Bs')

---

[6] For more on incompossibles, see Williamson 2010.

Moral: If you want to fix the truth-values of modal statements by using the Extension Theorem, make sure you start off with a rich enough stock of non-logical predicates.

5.5.2 Higher-Order Languages

An interesting project, which I do not develop here, is that of proving a version of the Extension Theorem for languages with higher-order variables. 'Just is'-statements of the form '$\phi(X) \equiv_X \psi(X)$', in which '$\equiv$' binds second-order variables, are particularly interesting. For instance, the higher-order predicate '$\equiv_X$' can be used to capture the difference between Hume's Principle,[7]

$$\forall F \forall G (\#_x(F(x)) = \#_x(G(x)) \leftrightarrow F(x) \approx_x G(x))$$

> (*Read:* the number of the Fs equals the number of the Gs just in case the Fs are in one-one correspondence with the Gs.)

and the 'just is'-statement corresponding to Hume's Principle,

$$\#_x(F(x)) = \#_x(G(x)) \equiv_{F,G} F(x) \approx_x G(x)$$

> (*Read:* for the number of the Fs to equal the number of the Gs *just is* for the Fs to be in one-one correspondence with the Gs.)

The higher-order predicate '$\equiv_X$' can also be used to define an analogue of Kit Fine's '$\Box_F A$' ('*A* is true in virtue of the nature of the objects which *F*'). Namely: '$\forall z(Xz \leftrightarrow Fz) \gg_X A[X/F]$', where second-order quantification is cashed out in plural terms.[8]

Unfortunately, the technique I use in Appendix C to generate a space of worlds won't automatically carry over to a higher-order setting. My guess is that one would need a somewhat different set of tools to prove a higher-order version of the Extension Theorem.

---

[7] For further discussion of Hume's Principle, see Chapter 3; for more on Neo-Fregeanism, see Wright 1983 and Hale and Wright 2001*a*.

[8] See Fine 1995*a*, 2000; see also Fine 1994, 1995*b*; for an important caveat, see footnote 1 of the present chapter.

5.6 Conclusion

I have defended an account of metaphysical possibility. I proceeded by characterizing a class of *basic* 'just is'-statements, and showing that they can be used to fix a truth-value for every sentence in a corresponding modal language. This is the Extension Theorem.

I also showed that the truth-conditions of arbitrary sentences in a modal language can be specified using only the fragment of the language that does not contain modal operators. This is the Reduction Theorem.

Table 5.1 Examples of Metaphysical Necessities

In order to get the result that ... is a true sentence of $L^{\Diamond}$	it is enough to count ... as a true 'just is'-statement.
Analyticity $\Box(\forall x(V(x) \to F(x)))$ (necessarily, every vixen is female)	$V(x) \gg_x F(x)$ (part of what it is to be a vixen is to be female)
Determinates and determinables $\Box(\forall x(E(x) \to M(x)))$ (necessarily, every elephant is a mammal)	$E(x) \gg_x M(x)$ (part of what it is to be an elephant is to be a mammal)
Cross-category prohibitions $\Box(\forall x(E(x) \to \neg O(x)))$ (necessarily, every elephant is not an octopus)	$E(x) \gg_x \neg O(x)$ (part of what it is to be an elephant is to not be an octopus)
Supervenience $\Box(\forall x(\Phi(x) \to \Psi(x)))$ (necessarily, if you have physical property Φ, you have psychological property Ψ)	$\Phi(x) \gg_x \Psi(x)$ (part of what it is to have physical property Φ is to have psychological property Ψ)
Supervenience $\Box(\Phi \to M)$ (necessarily, if physical fact Φ obtains, moral fact M obtains)	$\Phi \gg M$ (part of what it is for physical fact Φ to obtain is for moral fact M to obtain)
Identity $\Box(\exists y(y = h) \to h = p)$ (necessarily, if Hesperus exists, it is identical to Phosphorus)	$h = p$ (Hesperus is Phosphorus)

(continued)

Table 5.1 Continued

In order to get the result that ... is a true sentence of $L^{\Diamond}$	it is enough to count ... as a true 'just is'-statement.
Kind identity $\Box(\forall x(\text{Water}(x) \leftrightarrow \text{H}_2\text{O}(x))$ (necessarily, water is H_2O)	$\text{Water}(x) \equiv_x \text{H}_2\text{O}(x)$ (what it is to be water is to be H_2O)
Essentiality of kind $\Box(\forall z(\text{H}(z) \rightarrow \Box(\exists y(y = z) \rightarrow \text{H}(z)))$ (necessarily, if you're human, you couldn't have failed to be human)	$\dfrac{\text{H}(z)}{x = z \gg_x \text{H}(x)}$ (assume z is human; then part of what it is to be z is to be human)
Essentiality of kind $\Box(\forall z(\text{M}(z) \rightarrow \Box(\exists y(y = z) \rightarrow \text{H}(z)))$ (necessarily, if you're a man, you couldn't have failed to be human)	$\text{M}(x) \gg_x \text{H}(x);\ \dfrac{\text{H}(z)}{x = z \gg_x \text{H}(x)}$ (part of what it is to be a man is to be human; moreover: assume z is human; then part of what it is to be z is to be human)
Essentiality of origin $\Box(\forall w \forall z(\text{B}(w, z) \rightarrow \Box(\exists y(y = z) \rightarrow \text{B}(w, z)))$ (necessarily, if z has w as a biological parent, then z couldn't have failed to have w as biological parent)	$\dfrac{\text{B}(w, z)}{x = z \gg_x \text{B}(w, x)}$ (assume z has w as a biological parent; then part of what it is to be z is to have w as a biological parent)
Essentiality of constitution $\Box(\forall z(\text{W}(z) \rightarrow \Box(\neg\text{I}(z)))$ (necessarily, if you're made of wood, you couldn't have been made of ice)	$\dfrac{\text{W}(z)}{x = z \gg_x \text{W}(x)};\ \text{W}(x) \gg_x \neg\text{I}(x)$ (assume z is made of wood; then part of what it is to be z is to be made of wood; moreover, part of what it is to be made of wood is to not be made of ice)
Essentiality of constitution $\Box(\forall x \forall z((\text{C}(z) \wedge \text{C}(w) \wedge \text{P}(w, z)) \rightarrow \Box(\exists y(y = z) \rightarrow \text{P}(w, z)))$ (necessarily, if z and w are portions of clay and w is part of z, then z couldn't have failed to have w as a part)	$\dfrac{\text{C}(z) \wedge \text{C}(w) \wedge \text{P}(w, z)}{x = z \gg_x \text{C}(x) \wedge \text{C}(w) \wedge \text{P}(w, x)}$ (assume z and w are portions of clay and w is part of z; then part of what it is to be z is to be made of clay, to have w as a part and for w to be made of clay)
Reflexivity $\Box(\forall x(x < x))$ (necessarily, anything is part of itself)	$x = x \gg_x x < x$ (part of what it is to be self-identical is to be a part of oneself)

Antisymmetry

$\Box(\forall x \forall y((x < y \land y < x) \rightarrow x = y))$
(necessarily, if x is part of y and y is part of x, then x is identical to y)

$(x < y \land y < x) \gg_{x,y} x = y$
(part of what it is for x and y to be such that x is part of y and y is part of x is for x and y to be identical)

Transitivity

$\Box(\forall x \forall y \forall z((x < y \land y < z) \rightarrow x < z))$
(necessarily, if x is part of y and y is part of z, then x is part of z)

$(x < y \land y < z) \gg_{x,y,z} x < z$
(part of what it is for x, y and z to be such that x is part of y and y is part of z is for x to be part of z)

Strong Supplementation

$\Box(\forall x \forall y(\neg(y < x) \rightarrow \exists z(z < y \land \neg O(z, x))))$
(necessarily, if y is not a part of x, then y has a part that does not overlap with z)

$\neg(y < x) \gg_{x,y} \exists z(z < y \land \neg O(z, x))$
(part of what it is for x and y to be such that y is not a part of x is for y to have a part that does not overlap with x)

Unrestricted Fusions

$\Box(\exists x(\phi(x)) \rightarrow \exists z \forall x(O(x, z) \leftrightarrow \exists y(\phi(y) \land O(x, y))))$
(necessarily, if there are any ϕs, then there is a sum of the ϕs: a z such that the things that overlap with z are precisely the things that overlap with some ϕ)

$\exists x(\phi(x)) \gg \exists z \forall x(O(x, z) \leftrightarrow \exists y(\phi(y) \land O(x, y))))$
(part of what it is for there to be a ϕ is for there to be a sum of the ϕs: a z such that the things that overlap with z are precisely the things that overlap with some ϕ)

6

A-worlds and the Dot-Notation

The aim of this chapter is to develop a device for simulating quantification over merely possible objects from the perspective of a modal actualist—someone who thinks that everything that exists actually exists.

6.1 Introduction

Philosophers call on possible worlds to perform different kinds of jobs. One of these jobs is that of explaining what the truth of modal truths and the falsity of modal falsities consist in. 'What does the possibility that p consist in?', you ask. 'It consists in the existence of a possible world at which p', someone might reply.

Possible worlds are also used as *semantic machinery*. The semanticist needs entities for her quantifiers to range over, and possible worlds—or, more generally, possibilia—can be used to construct them. One might take a proposition to be a set of possible worlds (structured or not); one might take the intension of a predicate to be a function that assigns each world a set of objects in that world (or some complication thereof); one might use possible worlds to characterize the semantic values of modal operators; and so forth.

The main objective of this chapter is to defend the claim that a specialized modal ontology is not needed *as semantic machinery*. (I argued in Chapter 5 that the project of explaining what modal truth consists in can be carried out without making use of a specialized modal ontology: one can appeal to identity statements instead.) Some philosophers might be interested in this sort of project because of ontological scruples. Not me—I argued in Chapter 1 that such scruples would be misguided. I am interested in the project because I think it helps clarify the role of possible worlds in our philosophical theorizing.

My proposal is an instance of what David Lewis called 'ersatzism'. I will argue that the needs of the semanticist can be fulfilled by using *representatives* for possibilia in place of possibilia. Although there are other ersatzist proposals in the literature,[1] I hope the machinery developed here will earn its keep by delivering an attractive combination of frugality and strength.

The proposal is frugal in two different respects. First, it is metaphysically frugal: it is designed to be acceptable to modal actualists, and presupposes very little by way of ontology. (I help myself to set-theory, but do not assume a specialized modal ontology, or an ontology of properties.) Second, the proposal is ideologically frugal: it does not presuppose potentially controversial expressive resources such as infinitary languages or non-standard modal operators. The point of developing machinery that presupposes so little is that philosophers of different persuasions can put it to work without having to take a stance on difficult philosophical issues.

As far as strength is concerned, one gets a qualified version of the following claim: anything that can be said by quantifying over Lewisian possibilia can also be said by using the machinery developed here. The result is that the proposal can be used quite freely in the context of semantic theorizing, without having to worry too much about running into expressive limitations. An especially useful feature of the proposal is that it allows one to enjoy the benefits of quantification over *sets* of possibilia, which are often appealed to in the course of semantic theorizing.[2]

---

[1] See, for instance, Plantinga 1976 and chapter 3 of Lewis 1986*a*. A recent ersatzist proposal is discussed in Sider 2002 and Fine 2003 (but embraced only by Sider). The sort of proposal that Fine and Sider discuss has a more ambitious objective than the proposal developed here, since it is intended to capture finer-grained distinctions amongst possibilities. It also relies on more substantial expressive and ontological resources. (It relies, in particular, on an infinitary language and an ontology of properties.)

[2] By emulating the benefits of quantification over sets of possibilia the proposal also allows us to go some way towards addressing the expressive limitations identified in Section 7 of Williamson 2010. In particular, one can use the dot-notation introduced in Section 6.6 of the present chapter to express a version of the claim that incompossible objects form a set:

$$\exists\alpha\exists x\exists y(\alpha = \{x, y\} \land \Diamond(\exists z(z = \dot{x})) \land \Diamond(\exists z(z = \dot{y})) \land \neg\Diamond(\exists z\exists v(z = \dot{x} \land v = \dot{y}))).$$

Possible-words-theorists sometimes claim that the same individual exists according to distinct possible worlds. (There is a world according to which I have a sister who is a philosopher, and a world at which that very individual is a cellist rather than a philosopher.) Ersatzist representatives for such worlds might be said to be *linked*. Much of the chapter will be devoted to the phenomenon of linking. An effective treatment of linking is crucial to the success of the ersazist program.

6.2 Possibility

Sadly, I don't have a sister. But I might have had a sister. In fact, I might have had a sister who was a philosopher. And, of course, had I had a sister who was a philosopher, she wouldn't have been a philosopher essentially: she might have been a cellist instead (McMichael 1983). The following is therefore true:

SISTER

$\Diamond(\exists x(\text{Sister}(x, \text{AR}) \wedge \text{Phil}(x) \wedge \Diamond(\text{Cellist}(x) \wedge \neg\text{Phil}(x))))$
(*Read*: I might have had a sister who was a philosopher and might have been a cellist rather than a philosopher.)

On the most straightforward possible-worlds semantics for first-order modal languages, SISTER will only be counted as true if there are worlds w_1 and w_2 with the following properties: according to w_1, there is an individual who is my sister and a philosopher; according to w_2, that very individual—as one is inclined to put it—is a cellist rather than a philosopher. It is therefore tempting to say the following:

$\exists x([\text{Sister}(x, \text{AR}) \wedge \text{Phil}(x)]_{w_1} \wedge [\text{Cellist}(x) \wedge \neg\text{Phil}(x)]_{w_2})$

(*Read:* There is an x such that: (*i*) according to w_1, x is my sister and a philosopher, and (*ii*) according to w_2, x is a cellist rather than a philosopher.)

But is there anything to make this existential quantification true? A merely possible sister could do the job. But modal actualists believe there is no such thing. The job could also be done by an actually existing object who is not my sister but might have been my sister (Williamson 2010). But the claim that such objects exist would be a substantial metaphysical assumption—an assumption that it would be best to avoid, if at all possible.

6.3 A Kripke–Semantics for Actualists

There is a certain sense in which it is straightforward for the actualist to give an adequate Kripke-semantics for modal sentences. The trick is to have one's semantics quantify over *representations* of possibilities, rather than over the possibilities themselves. In this section I will describe one such semantics. It is an elaboration of an idea introduced by Roy (1995) and further developed by Melia (2001).

Let L be a first-order language, and let $L^\Diamond$ be the result of enriching L with the sentential operator '$\Diamond$'. An a-world (short for 'actualist-world') for $L^\Diamond$ is an ordered pair $\langle D, I \rangle$, consisting of a domain and an interpretation function, such that:

- The domain D is a set containing of two kinds of entities. First, it contains every ordered pair of the form $\langle x, \text{'actual'} \rangle$, for x an individual in the domain of L. (These pairs will be used to represent actually existing objects.) Second, it may contain ordered pairs of the form $\langle x, \text{'nonactual'} \rangle$, where x is some *actually existing* individual, set-theoretic or otherwise. (These pairs will be used to represent merely possible objects.)
- If C is an individual constant of L, and x is its intended interpretation, the interpretation-function I assigns the pair $\langle x, \text{'actual'} \rangle$ to C. (Accordingly, if 'SOCRATES' is an individual constant referring to Socrates, I assigns the pair $\langle \text{Socrates, 'actual'} \rangle$ to 'SOCRATES'.)
- I assigns a subset of D^n to each n-place predicate-letter of L, and a function from D^n to D to each n-place function-letter of L.

The notions of truth and satisfaction at an a-world are characterized along standard lines, with the proviso that '$x = x$' is only satisfied at an a-world by objects in the domain of a-world, with the result that '$x = x$' can be used as an existence predicate. (See Appendix A for details.)

The best way to see how a-worlds are supposed to work is by considering a simple example. Take the a-world $\langle D_1, I_1 \rangle$ from Fig. 6.1. The domain of $\langle D_1, I_1 \rangle$ consists of the pairs $\langle \text{Agustín, 'actual'} \rangle$ (which represents me) and $\langle \text{Socrates, 'nonactual'} \rangle$ (which represents *not* Socrates, but a merely possible object), and I_1 assigns 'Sister' a set containing the pair $\langle \langle \text{Socrates, 'nonactual'} \rangle, \langle \text{Agustín, 'actual'} \rangle \rangle$. The result is that $\langle D_1, I_1 \rangle$ makes '$\exists x (\text{Sister}(x, \text{AR}))$' true, and therefore

$\langle D_1, I_1 \rangle$

$\quad D_1 = \{\langle$Agustín, 'actual'$\rangle, \langle$Socrates, 'nonactual'$\rangle\}$

$\quad I_1($'Philosopher'$) = \{\langle$Socrates, 'nonactual'$\rangle\}$

$\quad I_1($'Cellist'$) = \{\}$

$\quad I_1($'Sister'$) = \{\langle\langle$Socrates, 'nonactual'$\rangle, \langle$Agustín, 'actual'$\rangle\rangle\}$

$\quad I_1($'AR'$) = \langle$Agustín, 'actual'$\rangle$

$\langle D_2, I_2 \rangle$

$\quad D_2 = \{\langle$Socrates, 'nonactual'$\rangle\}$

$\quad I_2($'Philosopher'$) = \{\}$

$\quad I_2($'Cellist'$) = \{\langle$Socrates, 'nonactual'$\rangle\}$

$\quad I_2($'Sister'$) = \{\}$

$\quad I_2($'AR'$) = \langle$Agustín, 'actual'$\rangle$

$\langle D_3, I_3 \rangle$

$\quad D_3 = \{\langle$Plato, 'nonactual'$\rangle\}$

$\quad I_3($'Philosopher'$) = \{\}$

$\quad I_3($'Cellist'$) = \{\langle$Plato, 'nonactual'$\rangle\}$

$\quad I_3($'Sister'$) = \{\}$

$\quad I_3($'AR'$) = \langle$Agustín, 'actual'$\rangle$

$\langle D_4, I_4 \rangle$

$\quad D_4 = \{\langle$Agustín, 'actual'$\rangle, \langle$Plato, 'nonactual'$\rangle\}$

$\quad I_4($'Philosopher'$) = \{\langle$Plato, 'nonactual'$\rangle\}$

$\quad I_4($'Cellist'$) = \{\}$

$\quad I_4($'Sister'$) = \{\langle\langle$Plato, 'nonactual'$\rangle, \langle$Agustín, 'actual'$\rangle\rangle\}$

$\quad I_4($'AR'$) = \langle$Agustín, 'actual'$\rangle$

Figure 6.1 Examples of a-worlds.

These examples assume that the only non-logical expressions in L are 'Philosopher', 'Cellist', 'Sister', and 'AR', and that the domain of L is {Agustín}.

represents a possibility whereby I have a sister. (Why use the pair $\langle$Socrates, 'nonactual'$\rangle$ to represent my merely possible sister rather than some other pair—$\langle$Plato, 'nonactual'$\rangle$, say? No good reason. Just like one can write a story according to which I have a sister using any font one likes, so one can define an a-world according to which I have a sister using any pair $\langle z,$ 'nonactual'$\rangle$ one likes.)

It is useful to compare a-worlds to Lewisian worlds. Like a-worlds, Lewisian worlds can be thought of as representing possibilities. Here is a passage from Lewis, which I also quoted in Chapter 5:

> How does a world, [Lewisian] or ersatz, represent, concerning Humphrey, that he exists?... A [Lewisian] world might do it by having Humphrey himself as a part. That is how our own world represents, concerning Humphrey, that he exists. But for other worlds to represent in the same way that Humphrey exists, Humphrey would have to be a common part of many overlapping worlds... I reject such overlap... There is a better way for a [Lewisian] world to represent, concerning Humphrey, that he exists... it can have a Humphrey of its own, a flesh-and-blood counterpart of our Humphrey, a man very much like Humphrey in his origins, in his intrinsic character, or in his historical role. By having such a part, a world represents *de re*, concerning Humphrey—that is, the Humphrey of our world, whom we as his worldmates may call simply Humphrey—that he exists and does thus-and-so.[3]

Whereas Lewisian worlds represent by analogy, a-worlds represent by satisfaction. A Lewisian world represents the possibility that I have a sister by containing a person who is similar to me in certain respects, and has a sister. An a-world, on the other hand, represents the possibility that I have a sister by being such as to satisfy the formula '$\exists x(\text{Sister}(x, \text{AR}))$'.

From the perspective of the Lewisian, an individual with a counterpart in the actual world represents its actual-word counterpart, and an individual with no counterpart in the actual world represents a merely possible object. From the present perspective, a pair of the form '$\langle x, \text{"actual"}\rangle$' represents its first component, and a pair of the form '$\langle x, \text{"nonactual"}\rangle$' represents a merely possible object (even though the pair itself, and both of its components, are actually existing objects).

Two representations are *linked* if—as one is inclined to put it—they concern the same individual, even if the individual in question doesn't exist. In order for a Kripke-semantics based on a-worlds to verify SISTER, there must be linking amongst a-worlds. In particular, some a-world must represent a possibility whereby I have a sister who is a philosopher and another must represent a possibility whereby—as one is inclined to put it—*that very same individual* is a cellist rather than a philosopher.

---

[3] (Lewis 1986a: 194; I have substituted 'Lewisian' where Lewis writes 'genuine'.) Lewis takes the counterpart relation to be context-dependent, but here I shall treat it as constant for the sake of simplicity. Also for the sake of simplicity, I shall assume that the counterpart relation is an equivalence.

Let us first see how linking gets addressed from a Lewisian perspective. l_1 and l_2 are Lewisian worlds: l_1 contains an individual a_1 who bears the right sort of similarity to me and an individual s_1 who is a_1's sister and a philosopher; l_2 contains an individual s_2 who is a cellist. Accordingly, l_1 represents a possibility whereby my sister is a philosopher, and l_2 represents a possibility whereby someone is a cellist. But nothing so far guarantees linking. Nothing so far guarantees that—as one is inclined to put it—the individual l_1 represents as my sister is *the very individual* that l_2 represents as a cellist. What is needed for linking is that s_1 and s_2 be counterparts: that they be similar in the right sorts of respects.

The same maneuver can be used when it comes to a-worlds. Like the Lewisian, we shall use counterparthood amongst representations to capture linking. For Lewis, representations are counterparts just in case they are similar in the right sorts of respects. From the present perspective, we shall say that representations are counterparts just in case they are *identical* (though other ways of defining the counterpart relation could be used as well). Here is an example. The a-world $\langle D_1, I_1 \rangle$ represents a possibility whereby I have a sister who is a philosopher. Now consider a-worlds $\langle D_2, I_2 \rangle$ and $\langle D_3, I_3 \rangle$ from Fig. 6.1. Each of them represents a possibility whereby someone is a cellist rather than a philosopher. But only $\langle D_2, I_2 \rangle$ is linked to $\langle D_1, I_1 \rangle$. For $\langle D_1, I_1 \rangle$ and $\langle D_2, I_2 \rangle$ both employ $\langle$Socrates, 'nonactual'$\rangle$ as a representation, and it is this that guarantees that—as one is inclined to put it—the individual who $\langle D_1, I_1 \rangle$ represents as my sister is *the very individual* that $\langle D_2, I_2 \rangle$ represents as a cellist. On the other hand, since $\langle D_3, I_3 \rangle$ represents a possibility whereby someone is a cellist by using $\langle$Plato, 'nonactual'$\rangle$ rather than $\langle$Socrates, 'nonactual'$\rangle$, what one gets is that—as one is inclined to put it—the individual who $\langle D_1, I_1 \rangle$ represents as my sister is *distinct* from the individual that $\langle D_2, I_2 \rangle$ represents as a cellist.

It is important to keep in mind that an a-worlds-semantics is *not* a way of improving on the informal characterization of linking that I supplied a few paragraphs back. (Representations are linked if—as one is inclined to put it—they concern the same individual, even if the individual in question doesn't exist.) In particular, it is *not* a way of dispensing with the qualifying phrase 'as one is inclined to put it'.[4] What

---

[4] It is worth emphasizing that by availing oneself of an ontology of Lewisian worlds and a Lewisian counterpart relation one does not immediately do any better. What one gets is a way

an *a*-worlds-semantics delivers is an (actualistically acceptable) device for *representing* possibilities, which enjoys the following feature: it is clear when two representations are to be counted as linked. The reason this is helpful is that, as we shall see below, much of the theoretical work that can be carried out by quantifying over possibilities can be carried out by quantifying over representations of possibilities instead. So an *a*-worlds-semantics puts the actualist in a position to get on with certain kinds of theoretical work without having to worry about giving a proper characterization of linking.

6.4 Admissibility

There are *a*-worlds according to which someone is a married bachelor, and *a*-worlds according to which there might have been a human who wasn't essentially human. Such representations need to be excluded from our semantics, on pain of getting the result that '$\Diamond(\exists x(\text{Married}(x) \land \text{Bachelor}(x)))$' or '$\Diamond(\exists x(\text{Human}(x) \land \Diamond(\exists y(y = x \land \neg\text{Human}(x)))))$' are true. What we need is a notion of *admissibility*. Armed with such a notion, one can say that $\ulcorner \Diamond\phi \urcorner$ is true just in case ϕ is true at some admissible *a*-world, and that $\ulcorner \Box\phi \urcorner$ is true just in case ϕ is true at every admissible *a*-world. (I assume, for simplicity, that the accessibility relation is trivial.)

It is important to keep in mind the distinction between the *semantic* project of developing a Kripke-semantics for modal languages, on the one hand, and the project of accounting for the limits of metaphysical possibility, on the other. A semantics based on *a*-worlds is meant to address the former, but not the latter of these projects. Accordingly, the notion of admissibility that is presupposed by the semantic project should be thought of as a placeholder for whatever limits on the metaphysically possible turn out to be uncovered by a separate investigation. (On reasonable assumptions, however, one can show that a suitable notion of admissibility

---

of making clear when two Lewisian worlds are to be counted as linked, not a characterization of linking. A friend of the Lewisian ontology can, however, give a proper characterization of linking by making an additional *reductionist* claim; namely, that there is no more to possibility than the existence of the relevant representation. There is, for example, no more to the fact that I might have had a sister than the fact that someone who is like me in certain respects has a sister.

is guaranteed to exist wherever the limits turn out to lie.[5]) A semantics based on a-words is compatible with different views about how to fix the limits of metaphysical possibility. One might appeal to a Principle of Recombination, for example, or to a set of 'basic modal truths'.[6] (My own account is spelled out in Chapter 5.)

Even if one appeals to an ontology of possible worlds in fixing the limits of metaphysical possibility, one might have good reasons for using a-worlds rather than possible worlds for the purposes of semantic theorizing. The easiest way to see this is by distinguishing between *sparse* and *abundant* conceptions of possible worlds.[7] A sparse conception countenances worlds according to which there are objects that don't actually exist, but not worlds according to which it is true of *specific* non-existent objects that they exist. There is, for example, a possible world w_1 according to which I have a sister who is a philosopher and might have been a cellist rather than a philosopher, but no possible world according to which it is true of the specific individual who would have been my sister had w_1 obtained that she exists. (Not even w_1 is such a world, for even though w_1 is a world according to which I have a sister, it is not a world according to which it is true of some specific individual that she is my sister.) On an abundant conception of possible worlds, on the other hand, there are possible worlds according to which it is true of specific non-existent objects that they exist.

---

[5] More precisely, what one can show is this: provided there is a determinate fact of the matter about which sentences of $L^{\lozenge}$ are true, there is a notion of admissibility relative to which an a-worlds semantics assigns the right truth-value to every sentence in $L^{\lozenge}$. (I assume that the first-order language L on which $L^{\lozenge}$ is based has a set-sized domain, and a name for every object in this domain.) *Proof:* Where S is the set of true sentences in $L^{\lozenge}$, use Kripke's completeness theorem for modal languages to construct a Kripke-model for S in which the domain consists of equivalence-classes of terms. Then transform the Kripke-model into an a-world semantics by substituting the pair $\langle x, \text{'actual'} \rangle$ for each equivalence class in the domain of the actual world of the Kripke-semantics containing a name for x, and the pair $\langle x, \text{'nonactual'} \rangle$ for each object x in the domain of some non-actual world of the Kripke-semantics but not in the domain of the actual world of the Kripke-semantics. (The proof relies on the reasonable assumption that S is consistent relative to a normal logic. To avoid talking about accessibility relations, I have also assumed that S is consistent relative to S5. It is worth noting that—unless one assumes that the language is countable—the Completeness Theorem assumes a weak version of the Axiom of Choice, so the resulting characterization of admissibility will be non-constructive.)

[6] On the Principle of Recombination, see Lewis 1986a: §1.8. For other approaches to grounding admissibility, see Fine 1994 and chapter 4 of Peacocke 1999.

[7] For a sparse conception of possible worlds, see Stalnaker's 'On what there isn't (but might have been)'. Stalnaker makes clear that he does not see sparseness as an obstacle for doing Kripke-semantics.

There is, for instance, a possible world w_2 according to which it is true of the very individual who would have been my sister had w_1 been actualized that she is a cellist rather than a philosopher.

On the sparse conception of possible worlds, the existence of a world is conditional on the existence of the objects the world represents as existing, in the same sort of way that the existence of a set is conditional on the existence of its members. Had w_1 been actualized, I would have had a sister, and all manner of sets containing that very individual would have existed. But as things stand, my sister doesn't exist, and neither do sets having her as a member. Similarly—the story would go—had w_1 been actualized, I would have had a sister, and a world according to which that very individual is a cellist would have existed. But as things stand, my sister doesn't exist, and neither do possible worlds according to which she herself exists.

The absence of w_2 does not prevent a defender of the sparse conception from using possible worlds to determine a truth-value for SISTER. For, on the assumption that possible worlds track metaphysical possibility, the existence of w_1 is enough to guarantee that SISTER is true. But the absence of w_2 does mean that the sparse worlds do not by themselves deliver the ontology that would be needed to give a Kripke-semantics for a sentence like SISTER. For, as emphasized above, a Kripke-semantics will only count SISTER as true if the range of one's metalinguistic quantifiers contains both w_1 and w_2.

Fortunately, a sparse ontology of possible worlds is enough to guarantee the existence of a notion of admissibility relative to which an a-worlds semantics assigns the right truth-value to every sentence in the language (see footnote 5 in this chapter). So it is open to the sparse theorist to use admissible a-worlds, rather than possible worlds, for the purposes of semantic theorizing. The upshot is not, of course, that one has done away with one's specialized modal ontology, since possible worlds may be needed for the project of pinning down the crucial notion of admissibility (or for the project of explaining what modal truth consists in). But by using a-worlds as the basis of one's semantics, the requirements on one's modal ontology are confined to needs of these non-semantic projects.

A related point can be made with respect to mere possibilia. The availability of a-worlds means that there is no need to postulate mere possibilia (or specialized surrogates, such as Plantinga's individual essences) as far as the project of developing a Kripke-semantics for modal languages is concerned.[8]

6.5 Interlude: The Principle of Representation

In previous sections I have made informal remarks about the ways in which a-worlds represent possibilities. The purpose of this interlude is to be more precise. (Uninterested readers may skip ahead to Section 6.6.)

When $\langle D, I \rangle$ is considered in isolation from other a-worlds, anything that can be said about the possibility represented by $\langle D, I \rangle$ is a consequence of the following principle:

PRINCIPLE OF REPRESENTATION (Isolated-World Version)
   According to the possibility represented by <D, I>, p
   if and only if
   There is a sentence s of L such that s says the p and s is true at <D, I>.

Accordingly, when considered in isolation from other a-worlds, $\langle D_2, I_2 \rangle$ and $\langle D_3, I_3 \rangle$ represent the *same* possibility. It is the possibility that there be exactly one thing and that it be a cellist but not a philosopher.

We shall normally assume that L (and therefore $L^\Diamond$) contains a name for every object in the domain of L. With this assumption in place, the following is a consequence of the Principle of Representation:

   Suppose z is in the domain of L. Then z exists according to the possibility represented by $\langle D, I \rangle$ just in case $\langle z, \text{'actual'} \rangle$ is in D.

In particular, one gets the result that none of the objects in the domain of L exists according to the possibility represented by $\langle D_2, I_2 \rangle$ (since $\ulcorner \exists x (x = \text{c}) \urcorner$ is false at $\langle D_2, I_2 \rangle$ for any constant c in L), and that I exist according to the possibility represented by $\langle D_1, I_1 \rangle$ (since '$\exists x (x = \text{AR})$' is true at $\langle D_1, I_1 \rangle$).

So much for considering a-worlds in isolation. When they are considered in the context of a *space* of a-worlds, linking plays a role. So there is slightly more to be said about the possibilities that they represent. Let A be a space of a-worlds and let $\langle D, I \rangle$ be in A. Then anything that can

---

[8] See Plantinga 1976. For a critique of Plantinga, see Fine 1985.

be said about the possibility represented by $\langle D, I \rangle$ in the context of A is a consequence of the following principle:

PRINCIPLE OF REPRESENTATION (Official Version)

1. According to the possibility represented by <D, I> in the context of A, p

   if and only if there is a sentence s of $L^{\Diamond}$, such that s says that p and s is true at <D, I> in the Kripke-Model based on A.

2. Let $\langle D^*, I^* \rangle$ be an arbitrary a-world in A. Let $\ulcorner \exists x_1 \ldots x_k \, \phi(x_1 \ldots x_k) \urcorner$ and $\ulcorner \exists x_1 \ldots x_k \, \gamma(x_1 \ldots x_k) \urcorner$ be sentences of $L^{\Diamond}$ which say, respectively, that $x_1 \ldots x_k$ are F and that $x_1 \ldots x_k$ are G. Assume that $\ulcorner \exists x_1 \ldots x_k \, \phi(x_1 \ldots x_k) \urcorner$ is true at $\langle D, I \rangle$ in A and that $\ulcorner \exists x_1 \ldots x_k \, \gamma(x_1 \ldots x_k) \urcorner$ is true at $\langle D^*, I^* \rangle$ in A. Then:

   > as one is inclined to put it: some of the individuals that are F according to the possibility represented by $\langle D, I \rangle$ in the context of A are the very same individuals as some of the individuals that are G according to the possibility represented by $\langle D^*, I^* \rangle$ in the context of A

   if and only if

   > one of the sequences of pairs that witnesses $\ulcorner \exists x_1 \ldots x_k \, \phi(x_1 \ldots x_k) \urcorner$ at $\langle D, I \rangle$ in A is identical to one of the sequences of pairs that witnesses $\ulcorner \exists x_1 \ldots x_k \, \gamma(x_1 \ldots x_k) \urcorner$ at $\langle D^*, I^* \rangle$ in the Kripke-model based on A.

When A includes both $\langle D_1, I_1 \rangle$ and $\langle D_2, I_2 \rangle$, the first clause yields the result that, according to the possibility represented by $\langle D_2, I_2 \rangle$ in the context of A, there is a cellist who might have been my sister. And the two clauses together yield the slightly stronger result that—as one is inclined to put it—the individual who is a cellist according to the possibility represented by $\langle D_2, I_2 \rangle$ in the context of A is the very same object as the individual who is my sister according to the possibility represented by $\langle D_1, I_1 \rangle$ in the context of A.

A consequence of the Principle of Representation is that the possibilities represented by a-worlds are not maximally specific. Suppose, for example, that the property of tallnes is not expressible in L. Then the possibility represented by $\langle D_1, I_1 \rangle$ is compatible with a more specific possibility whereby my sister is tall and it is compatible with a more specific possibility whereby my sister is not tall. On the other hand, the possibilities represented by a-worlds *are* maximally specific as far as the language is concerned: one can only add specificity to the possibility represented by an a-world by employing distinctions that cannot be expressed in $L^{\lozenge}$.

The Principle of Representation can be used to determine which properties of an a-world are essential to its representing the possibility that it represents, and which ones are merely artifactual. It entails, for example, that $\langle D_2, I_2 \rangle$ and $\langle D_3, I_3 \rangle$ represent the same possibility when considered in isolation, so any differences between them are merely artifactual. In particular, the use of $\langle$Socrates, 'nonactual'$\rangle$ in $\langle D_2, I_2 \rangle$ is merely artifactual. On the other hand, $\langle D_2, I_2 \rangle$ and $\langle D_3, I_3 \rangle$ represent *different* possibilities when considered in the context of $\{\langle D_1, I_1 \rangle, \langle D_2, I_2 \rangle, \langle D_3, I_3 \rangle\}$. For whereas according to $\langle D_2, I_2 \rangle$ there is a cellist who might have been my sister, according to $\langle D_3, I_3 \rangle$ there is a cellist who couldn't have been my sister. So the use of $\langle$Socrates, 'nonactual'$\rangle$ in $\langle D_2, I_2 \rangle$ is essential in the context of $\{\langle D_1, I_1 \rangle, \langle D_2, I_2 \rangle, \langle D_3, I_3 \rangle\}$. This is not to say, however, that a possibility whereby there is a cellist who might have been my sister can only be represented by an a-world if the a-world contains $\langle$Socrates, 'nonactual'$\rangle$. For the possibilities represented by $\langle D_1, I_1 \rangle$, $\langle D_2, I_2 \rangle$, and $\langle D_3, I_3 \rangle$ in the context of $\{\langle D_1, I_1 \rangle, \langle D_2, I_2 \rangle, \langle D_3, I_3 \rangle\}$ are precisely the possibilities represented by $\langle D_4, I_4 \rangle$, $\langle D_3, I_3 \rangle$, and $\langle D_2, I_2 \rangle$, respectively, in the context of $\{\langle D_4, I_4 \rangle, \langle D_3, I_3 \rangle, \langle D_2, I_2 \rangle\}$.

When I speak of the possibility that an a-world represents what I will usually have in mind is the possibility that is represented in the context of the space of all *admissible* a-worlds.

6.6 The Dot-Notation

I would like to introduce a further piece of notation: the dot. The dot is a bit like a function that takes representations to the objects represented. Suppose I am seeing a play according to which I have a sister; applying the dot-function is like shifting my attention from the actor who is representing my sister to the character represented (i.e. my sister).

Consider the following two formulas:

$$[F(x)]_w \qquad\qquad\qquad [F(\dot{x})]_w$$

For w a fixed representation, the undotted formula is satisfied by all and only objects z such that w represents a possibility whereby z is an F; the dotted formula, on the other hand, is satisfied by all and only objects z such that z is used by w to represent something as being an F. Thus, if p is a performance of a play according to which I have a sister, the actor playing my sister satisfies '$[\text{Sister}(\text{AR}, \dot{x})]_p$' but not '$[\text{Sister}(\text{AR}, x)]_p$' (since the performance uses the actor to represent someone as being my sister, but the performance does not represent a scenario whereby I have that actor as my sister). And I satisfy '$[\exists y\,\text{Sister}(x, y)]_p$' but not '$[\exists y\,\text{Sister}(\dot{x}, y)]_p$' (since the performance represents a scenario whereby I have a sister, but—unlike the actors and props—I am not used by the performance to represent anything).

Now consider how the dot-notation might be cashed out from the perspective of a Lewisian. Let l_1 be a Lewisian world representing a possibility whereby I have a sister. Accordingly, l_1 contains an individual a_1, who is my counterpart, and an individual s_1, who is a_1's sister. Now consider the following two formulas:

$$[\text{Sister}(\text{AR}, x)]_{l_1} \qquad\qquad [\text{Sister}(\text{AR}, \dot{x})]_{l_1}$$

From the perspective of the Lewisian, no inhabitant of the actual world satisfies the undotted formula. For no inhabitant of the actual world could have been my sister; so—on the assumption that Lewisian worlds track metaphysical possibility—no inhabitant of the actual world is such that l_1 represents a possibility whereby *she* is my sister. The dotted formula, on the other hand, is satisfied by s_1, since she is used by l_1 to represent something as being my sister.

Here is a second pair of examples:

$$[\exists y\,\text{Sister}(x, y)]_{l_1} \qquad\qquad [\exists y\,\text{Sister}(\dot{x}, y)]_{l_1}$$

The undotted formula is satisfied by me, since l_1 represents a possibility whereby I have a sister. But it is *not* satisfied by a_1. For although it is true that a_1 has a sister in l_1, l_1 represents a possibility whereby *I* have a sister, not a possibility whereby my counterpart has a sister. The dotted formula, on the other hand, is satisfied by a_1, since a_1 is used by l_1 to represent something as having a sister (i.e. me). But the dotted formula is *not* satisfied by me, since it is only the inhabitants of l_1 that do any representing for l_1, and I am an inhabitant of the actual world.

Let me now illustrate how the dot-notation works from the perspective of the modal actualist, with a-worlds in place of Lewisian worlds. (A detailed semantics is given in Appendix A.) Here is the first pair of examples (where w_1 is the a-world $\langle D_1, I_1 \rangle$ from Section 6.3):

$$[\text{Sister}(\text{AR}, x)]_{w_1} \qquad\qquad [\text{Sister}(\text{AR}, \dot{x})]_{w_1}$$

Since $I_1(\text{'Sister'}) = \{\langle\langle \text{Agustín}, \text{'actual'}\rangle, \langle \text{Socrates}, \text{'nonactual'}\rangle\rangle\}$, w_1 represents a possibility whereby I have a sister who doesn't actually exist. Accordingly, from the perspective of a modal actualist, there is no z such that w_1 represents the possibility that z is my sister. So, from the perspective of the modal actualist, *nothing* satisfies the undotted formula. The dotted formula, on the other hand, is satisfied by $\langle \text{Socrates}, \text{'nonactual'}\rangle$, since $\langle \text{Socrates}, \text{'nonactual'}\rangle$ is used by w_1 to represent something as being my sister.

Now consider the second pair of examples:

$$[\exists y\, \text{Sister}(x, y)]_{w_1} \qquad\qquad [\exists y\, \text{Sister}(\dot{x}, y)]_{w_1}$$

Since the pair $\langle\langle \text{Agustín}, \text{'actual'}\rangle, \langle \text{Socrates}, \text{'nonactual'}\rangle\rangle$ is in $I_1(\text{'Sister'})$, w_1 represents a possibility whereby I have a sister. The undotted formula is therefore satisfied by me. But it is *not* satisfied by $\langle \text{Agustín}, \text{'actual'}\rangle$ because w_1 does not represent a possibility whereby any ordered-pairs have sisters. The dotted formula, on the other hand, is satisfied by $\langle \text{Agustín}, \text{'actual'}\rangle$, since $\langle \text{Agustín}, \text{'actual'}\rangle$ is used by w_1 to represent something as having a sister (i.e. me). But it is *not* satisfied by me, since it is only ordered-pairs that do any representing in w_1, and I am not an ordered-pair.

6.7 Inference in a Language with the Dot-Notation

The semantics for a-worlds that is supplied in Appendix A guarantees the truth of every instance of the following schemas:

1. VALIDITY
   $[\psi]_w$ (where ψ is valid in a negative free logic)
2. CONJUNCTION
   $[\psi \wedge \theta]_w \leftrightarrow ([\psi]_w \wedge [\theta]_w)$
3. NEGATION
   $[\neg\psi]_w \leftrightarrow \neg[\psi]_w$

4. QUANTIFICATION

$[\exists y(\phi(y))]_w \leftrightarrow \exists y([\dot{y} = \dot{y}]_w \wedge [\phi(\dot{y})]_w)$ (where y is a non-world-variable)[9]

$[\exists w'(\phi)]_w \leftrightarrow \exists w'([\phi]_w)$ (where w' is a world-variable)

5. TRIVIAL ACCESSIBILITY[10]

$[[\phi]_w]_{w'} \leftrightarrow [\phi]_w$

6. IDENTITY

$[v = v]_w \leftrightarrow [\exists y(y = v)]_w$

$x = y \rightarrow ([\phi(\dot{x})]_w \rightarrow [\phi(\dot{y})]_w)$

$[\dot{x} = \dot{y}]_w \rightarrow ([\dot{x} = \dot{x}]_w \wedge x = y)$

(where v may occur dotted or undotted; the first of these formulas makes clear that identity is being used in the stronger of the two senses mentioned in Section 2.4, and therefore that self-identity may be used as an existence predicate.)

7. ATOMIC PREDICATION

$[F_j^n(v_1, \ldots, v_n)]_w \rightarrow ([v_1 = v_1]_w \wedge \ldots \wedge [v_n = v_n]_w)$

(where the v_i may occur dotted or undotted)

8. NAMES

$[\psi(c)]_w \leftrightarrow \exists x(x = c \wedge [\psi(x)]_w)$ (for c a non-empty name)

Schemas 2–5 are enough to guarantee that any sentence in the actualist's language is equivalent to a sentence in which only atomic formulas occur within the scope of '$[\ldots]_w$'. For instance, the actualist rendering of '$\Diamond(\exists x(\text{Phil}(x) \wedge \Diamond(\neg\text{Phil}(x))))$':

$$\exists w[\exists x(\text{Phil}(x) \wedge \exists w'([\neg\text{Phil}(x)]_{w'}))]_w$$

is equivalent to

$$\exists w \exists x([\text{Phil}(\dot{x})]_w \wedge \exists w'(\neg[\text{Phil}(\dot{x})]_{w'})).$$

As a result, the dot-notation allows a language containing the modal operator '$[\ldots]_w$' to have the inferential behavior of a (non-modal) first-order language.

---

[9] Keep in mind that self-identity may be used as an existence predicate.

[10] If the accessibility relation is non-trivial, what one gets is the following instead:

$$[[\phi]_w]_{w'} \leftrightarrow ([\phi]_w \wedge \text{Acccessible}(w', w)).$$

6.8 The Expressive Power of the Dot-Notation

In this section we shall see that a suitably qualified version of the following claim is true: anything the Lewisian can say, the modal actualist can say too—by using the dot-notation.

Here is an example. The Lewisian can use her mighty expressive resources to capture a version of the following thought:

LINKING

>There are possible worlds w_1 and w_2 with the following properties: according to w_1, there is an individual who is a philosopher; according to w_2, that very individual is a cellist.

It is done as follows:

$$\exists w_1 \exists w_2 \exists x_1 \exists x_2 (I(x_1, w_1) \wedge I(x_2, w_2) \wedge \text{Phil}(x_1) \wedge \text{Cellist}(x_2) \wedge$$

$$C(x_1, x_2))$$

(*Read:* There are Lewisian worlds w_1 and w_2 and individuals x_1 and x_2 such that: (*a*) x_1 is an inhabitant of w_1 and x_2 is an inhabitant of w_2, (*b*) x_1 is a philosopher and x_2 is a cellist, and (*c*) x_1 and x_2 are counterparts.)

How might this be emulated by a modal actualist equipped with the dot-notation? Consider what happens when one treats the variables in the Lewisian rendering of LINKING as ranging over (admissible) *a*-worlds rather than Lewisian worlds, and carries out the following replacements:

$$I(x_n, w_n) \longrightarrow [\dot{x}_n = \dot{x}_n]_{w_n}$$

$$\text{Phil}(x_n) \longrightarrow [\text{Phil}(\dot{x}_n)]_{w_n}$$

$$\text{Cellist}(x_n) \longrightarrow [\text{Cellist}(\dot{x}_n)]_{w_n}$$

$$C(x_n, x_m) \longrightarrow x_n = x_m$$

The result is this:

$$\exists w_1 \exists w_2 \exists x_1 \exists x_2 ([\dot{x}_1 = \dot{x}_1]_{w_1} \wedge [\dot{x}_2 = \dot{x}_2]_{w_2} \wedge [\text{Phil}(\dot{x}_1)]_{w_1} \wedge$$

$$[\text{Cellist}(\dot{x}_2)]_{w_2} \wedge x_1 = x_2)$$

(*Read:* There are admissible *a*-worlds w_1 and w_2 and objects x_1 and x_2 such that: (*a*) x_1 is used by w_1 to represent something and x_2 is used by w_2 to represent something, (*b*) x_1 is used by w_1 to represent a philosopher and x_2 is used by w_2 to represent a cellist, and (*c*) $x_1 = x_2$.)

or equivalently:

$$\exists w_1 \exists w_2 \exists x([\text{Phil}(\dot{x})]_{w_1} \wedge [\text{Cellist}(\dot{x})]_{w_2})$$

(*Read:* There are admissible *a*-worlds w_1 and w_2 and an object x such that: x is used by w_1 to represent a philosopher and x is used by w_2 to represent a cellist.)

What gives the actualist's method its punch is the fact that it generalizes: one can show that there is a systematic transformation of arbitrary Lewisian sentences into dotted actualist sentences which preserves truth-values and inferential conections.[11] (See Appendix B for details.)

The actualist's transformation-method does not preserve meaning—where Lewisian sentences quantify over Lewisian possibilia, their actualist transformation quantify over *a*-worlds and ordered-pairs. But meaning-preservation is not what the actualist wants, since she doesn't want to countenance Lewisian possibilia. What she wants is a way of enjoying the theoretical benefits of quantification over Lewisian possibilia within the sober confines of an actualist framework. Here are two examples of ways in which she is able to do so:

---

[11] When I say that the transformation preserves truth-value what I mean is that there is a notion of *a*-world admissibility which guarantees that the actualist transformation of an arbitrary Lewisian sentence is true just in case the original Lewisian sentence would count as true from the perspective of the Lewisian. When I say that the transformation preserves inferential role, what I mean is that a Lewisian sentence ϕ follows from a set of Lewisian sentences Γ just in case ϕ's transformation follows from the the transformations of sentences in Γ.

The result assumes that atomic predicates in the Lewisian's language other than 'I', 'C' and '=' (and any set-theoretic vocabulary) be *projectable*. For a monadic predicate P to be projectable is for it to be the case that a Lewisian world represents a possibility whereby something is P by containing an inhabitant who is P. (And similarly for many-place predicates.) Thus, 'Philosopher' is projectable because a Lewisian world represents a possibility whereby something is a philosopher by containing an inhabitant who is a philosopher; but 'inhabits a Lewisian world which is part of a pluriverse containing many Lewisian worlds' is not projectable because a Lewisian world does *not* represent a possibility whereby something inhabits a Lewisian world which is part of a pluriverse containing many Lewisian worlds by containing an inhabitant who inhabits a Lewisian world which is part of a pluriverse containing many Lewisian worlds.

Firstorderizing Modal Sentences By quantifying over Lewisian possibilia, the Lewisian is able to render any sentence in the language of first-order modal logic in (non-modal) first-order terms. The sentence,

$$\Diamond(\exists x(\text{Phil}(x) \wedge \Diamond(\text{Cellist}(x))))$$

> (*Read:* there might have been a philosopher who might have been a cellist),

for example, gets rendered as the (non-modal) first-order sentence:

$$\exists w_1 \exists w_2 \exists x_1 \exists x_2 (\text{I}(x_1, w_1) \wedge \text{I}(x_2, w_2) \wedge \text{Phil}(x_1) \wedge \text{Cellist}(x_2) \wedge \text{C}(x_1, x_2))$$

And Lewis (1968) shows that it can be done in general.[12]

The (non-modal) firstorderizability of modal sentences brings two immediate advantages. The first is that it allows one to think of the inferential connections amongst modal sentences in terms of the inferential connections amongst the corresponding non-modal sentences; the second is that it allows one to read off a semantics for modal sentences from the semantics of the corresponding non-modal sentences.

The actualist transformation-method allows actualists equipped with the dot-notation to enjoy both of these advantages.

Characterizing Intensions On a standard way of doing intensional semantics for natural languages, characterizing the semantic value of an expression calls for quantification over possibilia.[13] Oversimplifying a bit, the semantic value of, e.g. 'philosopher' might be taken to be the set of pairs $\langle w, z \rangle$ where w is a possible world and z is an (actual or merely possible) individual who is a philosopher at w.

As emphasized in Lewis 1970, the Lewisian is able to do the job by quantifying over Lewisian possibilia:

$$[\![\text{'philosopher'}]\!] = \{\langle w, z \rangle : \text{I}(z, w) \wedge \text{Phil}(z)\}$$

---

[12] As Lewis observes, a feature of the 1968 translation is that '$\forall x \Box(\exists y(x = y))$' turns out to be true. For this reason, I prefer a modification of the translation whereby $(\Box \phi)^\beta$ is $\forall \beta_1(W(\beta_1) \rightarrow (\phi)^{\beta_1})$, $(\Diamond \phi)^\beta$ is $\exists \beta_1(W(\beta_1) \wedge (\phi)^{\beta_1})$ and $(P(x_1, \ldots, x_n))^\beta$ is $\exists \gamma_1 \ldots \exists \gamma_n(\text{I}(\gamma_1, \beta) \wedge \text{C}(\gamma_1, x_1) \wedge \ldots \text{I}(\gamma_n, \beta) \wedge \text{C}(\gamma_n, x_n) \wedge P(\gamma_1 \ldots, \gamma_n)$ (for P atomic). The modified translation delivers the same truth-values as a version of Kripke-semantics in which atomic formulas (including identity-statements) can only be satisfied at a world by objects that exist at that world.

[13] For a representative textbook, see Heim and Kratzer 1998.

But the actualist transformation-method allows actualists armed with the dot-notation to follow suit, by quantifying over a-worlds and ordered pairs:

$$[\![\text{'philosopher'}]\!] = \{\langle w, z \rangle : [\dot{z} = \dot{z}]_w \wedge [\text{Phil}(\dot{z})]_w\}$$

or, equivalently,

$$[\![\text{'philosopher'}]\!] = \{\langle w, z \rangle : [\text{Phil}(\dot{z})]_w\}.$$

Since the actualist transformation-method preserves inferential connections, the actualist semantics is guaranteed to deliver the same theorems as its Lewisian counterpart. And since the transformation-method preserves truth-value the actualist's axioms will be true just in case their Lewisian counterparts would count as true from the perspective of the Lewisian.

In particular, one can expect the actualist semantics to deliver every instance of the (world-relative) T-schema. For instance:

$$\text{True}(\text{'}\exists x\,\text{Phil}(x)\text{'}, w) \leftrightarrow ([\exists x\,\text{Phil}(x)]_w)$$

or, equivalently,

$$\text{True}(\text{'}\exists x\,\text{Phil}(x)\text{'}, w) \leftrightarrow \exists x([\text{Phil}(\dot{x})]_w)$$

(*Read:* The object-language sentence '$\exists x\,\text{Phil}(x)$' is true at admissible a-world w just in case there is an individual which is used by w to represent a philosopher.)

6.9 Limitations of the Proposal

A-worlds are subject to an important limitation.[14] Whereas differences between a-worlds are no more fine-grained than is required to make distinctions expressible in one's language, there might be differences amongst Lewisian worlds too fine-grained to be expressed in one's language.[15]

---

[14] For discussion of related issues, see Lewis 1986a: §3.1. It is worth noting that Lewis's critique is not meant to apply to the sort of project that is the focus of the present essay. Here is Lewis:

When I complain, as I shall, that there are various ways for different possibilities to get conflated in their linguistic descriptions, that may be harmless when we want to use ersatz *possibilia* to characterize the content of thought for a subject who has no way to distinguish the conflated possibilities in his perception and conduct. (p. 144, footnote)

[15] More precisely, there might be different Lewisian worlds such that every inhabitant of the one world is a counterpart of an inhabitant of the other, and every predicate in the

Because of this limitation, some of the metaphysical work that the Lewisian gets out of Lewisian possibilia cannot be replicated by an actualist equipped with the dot-notion. Here is an example. Lewis (1986a) treats properties as sets of worldbound individuals. Up to a certain point, the actualist is able to follow suit. When the Lewisian claims that the property of being a philosopher is to be identified with the set of philosophers inhabiting actual or non-actual Lewisian worlds, for instance, the actualist could claim that the set $\{\langle z, w\rangle : [\mathrm{Phil}(\dot{z})]_w\}$ is to be used as a *surrogate* for the property of being a philosopher. But the strategy breaks down when it comes to properties making finer distinctions than can be expressed in one's language.[16]

In general, whether or not the actualist's limitation turns out to get in the way will depend on whether the job at hand calls for using possibilia to make finer distinctions than can be expressed in one's language. When the job at hand is a piece of semantic theorizing, the extra resources are unnecessary: since a semantic theory is ultimately an effort to explain how language is used, it need not be concerned with distinctions too fine-grained to figure in our explanations. But when the job at hand is metaphysical reduction, matters are otherwise.

language which is projectable in the sense of footnote 11 is satisfied by inhabitants of one world just in case it is satisfied by the counterparts of those individuals at the other. The distinct possibilities represented by such Lewisian worlds would both be compatible with the less-specific possibility represented by an a-world in which the behavior of the predicates mirrors the behavior of the predicates at the Lewisian worlds.

[16] Any set of worldbound individuals containing an inhabitant of one of the Lewisian worlds described in footnote 15 but not its counterpart at the other corresponds to a Lewisian property with no actualist surrogate.

7

Paraphrase

Philosophers of mathematics have often been concerned with the question of whether mathematical statements can be paraphrased as sentences containing no mathematical vocabulary (Field 1980; Hodes 1984; Yablo 2001). To what extent would the availability of such paraphrases be important to a mathematical trivialist of the sort described in Chapter 3?

Here is one way in which the paraphrases could be useful. Suppose one's interlocutor doesn't understand arithmetic, and one wants to get her to see what truth-conditions a mathematical trivialist would wish to associate with arithmetical sentences. One way to do so would be to teach her a method for paraphrasing each arithmetical sentence as a sentence containing no mathematical vocabulary with the desired truth-conditions. As far as Mathematical Trivialism is concerned, however, it is not clear that this is a particularly urgent project, since it's not clear why it would be interesting to assume that one's interlocutor doesn't understand arithmetic. And if she does understand arithmetic, paraphrase is unnecessary. A semantics of the sort described in Section 3.3.1 can be used to convey the desired assignment of truth-conditions.

The availability of non-mathematical paraphrases for mathematical statements would enable the trivialist to claim that a mathematical fact can always be described using non-mathematical vocabulary. This would be a nice result. But it is not a result that the trivialist is committed to. For trivialism is a view about the truth-conditions of mathematical sentences, not a view about whether such truth-conditions can be expressed using a particular kind of vocabulary. More generally, it seems to me that philosophers of mathematics should be weary of putting too much emphasis on paraphrase. For the existence of suitable paraphrases turns crucially on the expressive resources of one's non-mathematical vocabulary. The result is that any claim to the effect that a suitable paraphrase-function exists or fails to exist must be tied to a non-trivial claim about the legitimacy or illegitimacy of a given set of expressive resources. And it seems dangerous to rest any substantial conclusions in the philosophy of mathematics on one's views about the legitimacy of a potentially controversial piece of vocabulary. (For further discussion, see Section 1.4.)

The purpose of this chapter is to get clear on the sorts of expressive resources that would be needed to supply interesting paraphrase functions for the language of arithmetic.

7.1 Paraphrase-Functions

A *trivialist paraphrase-function* is a mapping that takes each arithmetical sentence ϕ to a sentence whose truth-conditions are the truth-conditions that the trivialist would wish to associate with ϕ (that is, the truth conditions that the semantics of Section 3.3.1 associates with ϕ when arithmetic is assumed to be true). We will insist, moreover, that the mapping be *uncontroversial*: that it be possible to show that the mapping delivers the desired truth-conditions independently of whether one assumes that trivialism is true. (The function that maps every arithmetical sentence onto itself won't count as uncontroversial, for example, since it can only be shown to deliver the desired truth-conditions on the assumption that trivialism is true.)

We will investigate the question of whether it is possible to specify a trivialist paraphrase-function for the language of arithmetic. Attention will be restricted to paraphrase-functions that can be characterized algorithmically. Without this restriction, it is obviously true that there is a trivialist paraphrase-function for the language of pure arithmetic: map every true sentence to a tautology and every false sentence to a contradiction.

The possibility of specifying a suitable paraphrase-function will depend on the expressive resources of the language in which paraphrases are given.

7.2 Higher-Order Languages

Suppose, first, that one takes the paraphrase-language to be an nth-order language, for some finite n. Then, assuming the Church-Turing Thesis, *it is impossible to specify a trivialist paraphrase-method for the language of arithmetic.* (For a proof of this result, see Rayo 2008.)

There are a few paraphrase-methods that have the right flavor, but don't quite give us what we're after. Consider, for example, the method of *universal Ramseyfication*. If ϕ is a sentence in the language of pure arithmetic, its universal Ramseyfication is the universal closure of $\ulcorner(\mathscr{D} \to \phi)^*\urcorner$, where $\mathscr{D}$ is the conjunction of the (second-order) Dedekind-Peano Axioms and $(\ldots)^*$ is the result of uniformly substituting variables for mathematical vocabulary in $(\ldots)$.

The method of universal Ramseyfication only delivers the right results on the assumption that the world is infinite. To see this, consider an arithmetical falsehood, such as '$0 = 1$'. If the world is finite, the Dedekind-Peano Axioms, $\mathscr{D}$, will turn out to be false. So '$0 = 1$'s universal Ramseyfication (i.e. the universal closure of $\ulcorner(\mathscr{D} \to 0 = 1)^*\urcorner$) will turn out to be true, which is contrary to what we want. Of course, a *trivialist* will think that finite worlds are incoherent, and therefore that commitment to infinitely many objects is no commitment at all. So a trivialist will think that the method of universal Ramseyfication does, after all, deliver the right assignment of truth-conditions. But universal Ramseyfication still won't count as an *uncontroversial* trivialist paraphrase-function because such a conclusion depends on the truth of trivialism.

Other higher-order paraphrase-methods that have the right flavor but depend on infinity-assumptions to deliver the right results include Hodes 1984; Fine 2002: II.5; and Rayo 2002.

7.3 Languages of Very High Order

If one's paraphrase-language includes variables of *transfinite* order, then a trivialist paraphrase-method for the language of arithmetic is available.

For α an arbitrary ordinal, let $\mathscr{L}_{\in}^{\alpha}$ be a version of the language of set-theory in which each occurrence of a quantifier is restricted by some V_{β} ($\beta < \alpha$). Any sentence in the language of first-order arithmetic can be 'translated' as a sentence of $\mathscr{L}_{\in}^{\omega+1}$. What one does is replace arithmetical quantifiers by set-theoretic quantifiers restricted to finite ordinals, and replace each occurrence of arithmetical vocabulary by its counterpart in ordinal arithmetic. (This procedure presupposes that all the relevant set-theoretic notions can be adequately characterized in $\mathscr{L}_{\in}^{\omega+1}$, but it is straightforward to check that this is indeed the case.)

Linnebo and Rayo (forthcoming) show that, for arbitrary α, every sentence of $\mathscr{L}_{\in}^{\alpha}$ can be paraphrased as a sentence in a language of order $\alpha + 2$ (or order α, if α is a limit ordinal). From this it follows that one can use the 'translation' of first-order arithmetical sentences into $\mathscr{L}_{\in}^{\omega+1}$ to characterize a trivialist paraphrase-method from the language of first-order arithmetic into a language of order $\omega + 3$.

7.4 Infinitary Languages

Another way of characterizing a trivialist paraphrase-function is by allowing for infinite conjunctions and disjunctions.

Because we will be dealing with infinite sentences, our paraphrase-function won't be algorithmic in the standard sense (i.e. it won't be computable in finite time). But it will still count as algorithmic in a derived sense: one could write a finite computer program that approximates the paraphrase asymptotically, and outputs it after infinitely many steps.

Our paraphrase-function will consist of a four-step transformation. We shall assume that the input formula is a sentence of the language of pure first-order arithmetic, excluding mixed identities. (To make life simpler, we shall also assume that the input formula is in prenex normal form, and that only atomic formulas are in the scope of a negation sign.)

The basic strategy is due to Yablo (2002):

STEP 1

Replace each subformula $\ulcorner \exists n \phi(n) \urcorner$ by the infinite disjunction $\ulcorner \phi(0) \vee \phi(1) \vee \phi(2) \vee \ldots \urcorner$, and each subformula $\ulcorner \forall n \phi(n) \urcorner$ by the infinite conjunction $\ulcorner \phi(0) \wedge \phi(1) \wedge \phi(2) \wedge \ldots \urcorner$.

For instance, the result of applying STEP 1 to '$\forall n \exists m(n + 1 = m)$' is an infinite conjunction of infinite disjunctions:

$(0 + 1 = 0 \vee 0 + 1 = 1 \vee 0 + 1 = 2 \vee \ldots) \wedge (1 + 1 = 0 \vee 1 + 1 = 1 \vee 1 + 1 = 2 \vee \ldots) \wedge (2 + 1 = 0 \vee 2 + 1 = 1 \vee 2 + 1 = 2 \vee \ldots) \wedge \ldots$

In general, the result of applying STEP 1 is a (possibly infinite) sentence in which every atomic formula is an identity statement $\ulcorner t_1 = t_2 \urcorner$, where t_1 and t_2 contain no free variables.

We must now deal with atomic formulas. Yablo suggests that we do so by substituting a suitable non-arithmetical paraphrase for each occurrence of $\ulcorner t_1 = t_2 \urcorner$. An unnegated occurrence of $\ulcorner \bar{k} + \bar{l} = \bar{m} \urcorner$, for example, gets replaced by:

$$[\exists!_k x Fx \land \exists!_l x Gx \land \forall x \neg(Fx \land Gx)] \rightarrow \exists!_m x(Fx \lor Gx)$$

(*Read:* if there are exactly k Fs, there are exactly l Gs and nothing is an F-and-G, then there are exactly m F-or-Gs.)

This procedure succeeds in eliminating all mathematical vocabulary from the original arithmetical sentence. But what one gets is a formula that is only guaranteed to have the right truth-value on the assumption that the world is infinite. Consider, for example, the arithmetical falsehood '$\exists n(n + 1 = n)$'. The result of applying STEP 1 is an infinite disjunction:

$$(0 + 1 = 0) \lor (1 + 1 = 1) \lor (2 + 1 = 2) \lor \ldots$$

But now suppose that there are exactly k objects, and consider the $(k + 1)$th disjunct in the series: $\ulcorner \bar{k} + 1 = \bar{k} \urcorner$. According to Yablo's procedure, this disjunct should be replaced by

$$[\exists!_k x Fx \land \exists!_1 x Gx \land \forall x \neg(Fx \land Gx)] \rightarrow \exists!_k x(Fx \lor Gx)$$

which is guaranteed to be true in a world with k objects (since its antecedent is guaranteed to be false). From this it follows that the result of applying Yablo's procedure is true, even though '$\exists n(n + 1 = n)$' is false.

Fortunately, there is a way around the problem. As Santos (typescript) points out, one can make the following changes to the output of STEP 1:

STEP 2
Replace each occurrence of $\ulcorner \bar{k} + \bar{l} \urcorner$ by '$\underbrace{SS \ldots S}_{k+l}(0)$', and each occurrence of $\ulcorner \bar{k} \times \bar{l} \urcorner$ by '$\underbrace{SS \ldots S}_{k \times l}(0)$'. (Make sure you apply the procedure to subordinate formulas first.)

STEP 3
Replace occurrences of '$\underbrace{SS \ldots S}_{k}(0) = \underbrace{SS \ldots S}_{l}(0)$' by $\top$ whenever $k = l$; replace them by $\bot$ whenever $k \neq l$.

(Here $\top$ is a logical truth from a finitary language containing no mathematical vocabulary, and $\perp$ is a logical falsity from a finitary language containing no mathematical vocabulary.)

The result is a (possibly infinite) sentence that contains no arithmetical vocabulary and can be shown to have the right truth-value regardless of the identity statements one presupposes in the metatheory. In fact, every truth of pure arithmetic gets mapped onto a truth of infinitary logic and every falsity of pure arithmetic gets mapped onto a falsity of infinitary logic.

By adding a final step to the process, one can get the transformation to output a *finite* sentence:

STEP 4

Substitute $\top$ for infinite conjunctions all of whose conjuncts are true and infinite disjunctions some of whose conjuncts are true; substitute $\perp$ for infinite disjunctions all of whose conjuncts are false and infinite disjunctions some of whose conjuncts are false. (Make sure you apply the procedure to subordinate formulas first.)

When the original input sentence is true, the result of applying steps 1–4 will be a logical truth from a finitary language with no mathematical vocabulary; otherwise, the result will be a logical falsehood from a finitary language with no mathematical vocabulary.

A nice feature of this procedure is that it delivers a completeness theorem for an infinitary version of the Dedekind-Peano Axioms, in which the Induction Axiom is replaced by rules stating that a universal quantifier is equivalent to the conjunction of its numerical instances and an existential quantifier is equivalent to the disjunction of its numerical instances. All one needs to do to prove the result is carry out the transformation, and note that each of its four steps can be justified on the basis of our axioms. (To justify the fourth step one needs to assume that one is working with a suitable infinitary logic.)

7.5 Intensional Operators

The presence of intensional operators makes it much easier to define a trivialist paraphrase-function (Hellman 1989; Yablo 2001; Dorr 2007). A particularly straightforward strategy would be to map each sentence of pure arithmetic to the result of adding a box in front of its universal

Ramseyfication. This will deliver the right results on the assumption that there *might have been* infinitely many objects. Perhaps it is uncontroversial that there might have been infinitely many objects. If so, the method of necessitated universal Ramseyfication counts as an uncontroversial trivialist paraphrase-function for the special case of pure arithmetic.

If one wishes to accommodate applied arithmetic, something more elaborate is needed. Here are two familiar proposals:

COUNTERFACTUALISM
> Paraphrase an arbitrary arithmetical sentence ϕ as:
>> if the world contained an infinity of extra objects playing the role of numbers, it would be the case that ϕ.

FICTIONALISM
> Paraphrase an arbitrary arithmetical sentence ϕ as:
>> According to a fiction whereby the world is as it actually is except for the addition of an infinity of extra objects playing the role of numbers, ϕ.

Properly construed, both of these strategies can be made to deliver the desired assignment of correctness-conditions. But they are both potentially misleading. For it is easy to overestimate their ability to shed light on the truth-conditions that a trivialist would associate with arithmetical sentences. In fact, neither of them is any more illuminating than the following:

THE NO-FRILLS STRATEGY
> Paraphrase an arbitrary arithmetical sentence ϕ as:
>> ϕ, except for all that stuff about numbers.

Appearances to the contrary come from the fact that we have a satisfying story to tell about what it takes for ϕ to be true at a world (or fiction): one gives a standard compositional semantics for the language in question, and relativizes it to worlds (or fictions). But that is not the difficult part. The difficult part is *not* to explain what it takes for a world (or fiction) to verify ϕ, but to explain what it would take for a world (or fiction) *to be like a world (or fiction) that verifies ϕ in all non-mathematical respects.* And on this issue the more familiar paraphrase-strategies do no better than the No-Frills Strategy.

One way to see that there is a non-trivial issue here is to note that all three strategies presuppose a *subtraction* claim: the claim that it makes sense to subtract the mathematical part of the requirement imposed on the the world by the truth-conditions of a mathematical sentence. But, as emphasized in Section 5.2.2, subtraction claims are highly non-trivial. Wittgenstein illustrates the point in the *Philosophical Investigations* by asking: 'what is left over if I subtract the fact that my arm goes up from the fact that I raise my arm?' (§621) Here is a more contemporary example. A friend of narrow content might think that one can get to the narrow content of a mental state by subtracting away 'environmental factors'. (Perhaps one can get to a narrow concept 'watery' by subtracting environmental factors from the ordinary concept of water.) But foes of narrow content will protest that the needed subtractions are not generally well defined. (See Yablo (forthcoming) for further discussion.)

It is easy to show that mathematical-subtraction is, indeed, well-defined when it comes to toy examples. One might suggest, for example, that the non-mathematical part of the requirement that the world be such that the number of the planets is Eight is the requirement that the world contain exactly eight planets. But the real challenge is to defend the claim that mathematical-subtraction is well-defined *in general*. I know of only two ways of doing so. The first is to supply a *non-intentional* paraphrase-method for the language of arithmetic. The second is to supply a specification of truth-conditions of the sort described in Section 3.3.1. But if either of these methods is available, we get more than just an assurance that the factoring claim is satisfied. We get an illuminating explanation of the truth-conditions that a trivialist would wish to associate with arithmetical sentences. So it is not clear that there is much to be gained by deploying an intensional paraphrase strategy of the kind that has been described here.

7.6 Conclusion

Characterizing a trivialist paraphrase-method for the language of arithmetic is not as straightforward as one might have thought. One option is to avail oneself of potentially controversial logical resources, such as variables of very high type or infinitary operations. Another option is to make use of intensional operators.

Intensional paraphrase-functions need to be treated with care, however. On the one hand, they are potentially misleading, since they might be thought to shed more light on the truth-conditions of arithmetical sentences than they actually succeed in shedding. On the other hand, they presuppose a non-trivial subtraction claim. And although it is a claim that can be shown to be true, the very methods that might be used to buttress its truth cast doubt on the interest of finding an intensional paraphrase-method in the first place.

8

Introducing Mathematical Vocabulary

A familiar way of introducing mathematical vocabulary is by linguistic stipulation. One sets forth an axiom system, and stipulates that the new vocabulary is to be understood in such a way that the axioms turn out to be true (or necessarily true).

This chapter is a compositionalist account of linguistic stipulation. I will explain how the compositionalist should think of stipulation, and suggest a sufficient condition for successful stipulation, from a compositionalist point of view.

8.1 Linguistic Stipulation for Compositionalists

Metaphysicalists and compositionalists agree that the goal of a linguistic stipulation is to specify an assignment of *truth-conditions* to sentences involving the newly introduced vocabulary. They also agree that an assignment of truth-conditions presupposes an assignment of *reference* to the relevant terms. But, as noted in Section 1.3, they disagree about what it takes for a singular term to succeed in referring. Whereas the metaphysicalist would insist that a singular term can only succeed in referring if it is paired with one of the objects carved out by the world's metaphysical structure, the compositionalist will claim that all it takes is a suitable specification of truth-conditions for sentences involving the term. In particular, the compositionalist thinks that a sufficient condition for a singular term t to refer is that the following four conditions obtain:

1. SYNTAX

   t behaves *syntactically* like a singular term: it generates *grammatical* strings when placed in the right sorts of syntactic contexts.

2. TRUTH-CONDITIONS

Truth-conditions have been assigned to every sentence involving t that one wishes to make available for use.

3. LOGICAL FORM

This assignment of truth-conditions is such as to respect any inferential connections that are guaranteed by the *logical forms* of the relevant sentences. In particular:

> If the sentences in Φ and Ψ have all been assigned truth-conditions, and if it is a logical consequence of the sentences in Φ that at least one of the sentences in Ψ must be true, then joint satisfaction of the truth-conditions assigned to any sentences in Φ is at least as strong a requirement on the world as the requirement that the truth-conditions of at least one sentence in Ψ be satisfied.

4. TRUE EXISTENTIAL

The world is such as to satisfy the truth-conditions that have been associated with the sentence '$\exists x(x = t)$' (or an inferential analogue thereof).

As noted in Section 3.2.3, a metaphysicalist would claim that if the singular terms t_1 and t_2 both have referents, then it must be possible to meaningfully ask whether $\ulcorner t_1 = t_2 \urcorner$ is true. For she believes that each of t_1 and t_2 is paired with one of the objects carved out by the metaphysical structure of the world. So the question whether $\ulcorner t_1 = t_2 \urcorner$ is true can be cashed out as the question whether t_1 and t_2 are paired with the same such object. For a compositionalist, in contrast, there is no tension between thinking that t_1 and t_2 both have referents and denying that one has asked a meaningful question when one asks whether $\ulcorner t_1 = t_2 \urcorner$ is true. For t_1 and t_2 can satisfy the compositionalist's conditions for reference even if no truth-conditions have been associated with $\ulcorner t_1 = t_2 \urcorner$. All it takes is a suitable assignment of truth-conditions *for whichever sentences involving t_1 and t_2 one wishes to make available for use.*

A more colorful way of putting the point is by saying that t_1 and t_2 might correspond to different ways of carving up the world into objects and properties. But, as emphasized in Section 1.5, a carving of the world is simply a compositional system of representation for carving the world. So to say that t_1 and t_2 correspond to different ways of carving up the world is to say that t_1 and t_2 are to be counted as building blocks of different compositional systems.

The moral of all this is that, whereas metaphysicalists treat any two terms as corresponding to the same system of representation—and should therefore treat arbitrary identity statements as well-formed—compositionalists might think that the terms correspond to different systems of representation—and may therefore wish to treat the relevant identity statement as ill-formed. Accordingly, compositionalists would divide linguistic stipulations into two kinds. Stipulations of the first kind are *extensions* of an existing compositional system. So the newly introduced terms should yield meaningful sentences when combined with extant vocabulary of the right semantic category. Say I introduce the new term 'Muncle' with the stipulation that 'Muncle is Marcus's favorite uncle' is to count as true at the time of the stipulation. One would expect both 'Muncle = Julius Caesar' and 'Muncle isn't much of a conversationalist' to count as meaningful.

Stipulations of the second kind result in the *introduction* of a new system of compositional representation: a new way of carving up the world. So there should be no general expectation that the new vocabulary will yield meaningful sentences when combined with extant vocabulary of the right semantic category. Suppose, for example, that the language of arithmetic is introduced as a new way of carving up the world. Then there should be no expectation that '7 = Julius Caesar' will be counted as meaningful. At the same time, some combinations of old and new vocabulary may be assigned truth-conditions, and therefore counted as meaningful: '$\#_x \text{Planet}(x) = 8$', for example, or '$2^3 = 8 \wedge$ Caesar is a Roman'.

Just because different fragments of one's discourse correspond to different carvings of the world, it doesn't mean that one is barred from using a single language to formalize one's theorizing. A multi-sorted language can use terms and predicates of different sorts to talk about objects corresponding to different carvings. And one can indicate which 'mixed' formulas have been assigned truth-conditions by treating the rest as ill-formed.

8.2 Success Conditions

The aim of the preceding section was to explain how compositionalists think of linguistic stipulations. In the present section I will suggest a sufficient condition for successful stipulation, from a compositionalist point of view.

8.2.1 Pure Stipulations

Let us begin with the simplest case. Say that a *pure* mathematical stipulation is a stipulation in which:

1. one makes clear that one's stipulation is meant to *introduce* a new system of compositional representation, rather than extend an existing system;
2. one uses the new vocabulary to build an axiom system in which all the variables and non-logical constants are of the new sort, and stipulates that the new vocabulary is to be understood in such a way that the axiom system is counted as necessarily true;
3. one makes clear that any atomic formula that mixes vocabulary of old and new sorts is to be counted as ill-formed.

From the perspective of a compositionalist, all it takes for a pure mathematical stipulation to be successful is for the relevant axiom system to be *internally coherent* (i.e. for it not to have a logical absurdity as a logical consequence).

The reason internal coherence is sufficient for success is that it guarantees the availability of an assignment of truth-conditions with two properties: (*a*) it counts the axioms as necessarily true; and (*b*) it allows for genuine singular terms, by satisfying Condition 3 of Sections 1.3 and 8.1. The assignment in question is as follows. Let $\mathcal{L}^{new}$ be the fragment of the language in which all the variables and non-logical constants are of the new sort. Then: (1) a sentence of $\mathcal{L}^{new}$ is taken to have trivial truth-conditions if it is a logical consequence of the axioms; (2) a sentence of $\mathcal{L}^{new}$ is taken to have trivially unsatisfiable truth-conditions if its negation is a logical consequence of the axioms; and (3) other sentences of $\mathcal{L}^{new}$ are taken to lack well-defined truth-conditions.

Since the axiom system is internally coherent, this procedure is guaranteed not to deliver more than one assignment of truth conditions to a given sentence of $\mathcal{L}^{new}$.[1] And since atomic formulas that mix vocabulary

---

[1] Here I assume that the background logic is not paraconsistent. Note, however, that if one's background logic is paraconsistent, one need not see contradictory assignments of truth-conditions as inherently problematic.

of old and new sorts are counted as ill-formed, the sentences of $\mathcal{L}^{new}$ float free, inferentially speaking, from sentences that contain no new vocabulary. This means, in particular, that the new axiom system is *conservative*[2] over sentences with no new vocabulary. So the proposed assignment of truth-conditions is guaranteed to have no effect on sentences that contain no new vocabulary.

8.2.2 Internal Coherence

We have seen that, from the perspective of the compositionalist, all it takes for a pure mathematical stipulation to succeed is internal coherence (assuming the stipulation gives rise the the right sort of linguistic practice).

It would be a mistake to conclude from this, however, that it is generally a straightforward matter to determine whether a pure mathematical stipulation will succeed. For it is not, in general, a straightforward matter to determine whether an axiom system is internally coherent. Suppose, for example, that one sets forth a pure mathematical stipulation based on Quine's NF. The consistency of NF remains an open question.[3] So it is by no means clear that knowledge that the stipulation would succeed is within our reach.

As I emphasized in Chapter 4, acquiring a warrant for the internal coherence of an axiom system is a tricky affair. One can sometimes prove the consistency of one formal system in another. But it is a consequence of Gödel's Second Theorem that (when the systems in question are consistent and sufficiently strong) the system in which the proof is carried out cannot be a subsystem of the system the proof is about. There is therefore reason to expect that one's warrant for the internal coherence of a formal system will turn on more than just consistency proofs. It might turn on whether one has a good feel for the sorts of things that can be proved in the system, or on whether one has a good feel for the sorts of things that can be proved

---

[2] For axiom system $\mathcal{A}$ to be conservative over sentences containing no new vocabulary is for the following condition to be satisfied: let O be a set of sentences containing no new vocabulary, and let ϕ be a sentence containing no new vocabulary; then ϕ is only a (semantic) consequence of O and $\mathcal{A}$ if it is a (semantic) consequence of O. (In the case of systems whose logic fails to be complete—second-order systems, for example—the choice of semantic, rather than syntactic, consequence is significant. For relevant discussion, see Field 1980; Shapiro 1983; and Field 1985.)

[3] There is, on the other hand, a consistency proof for New Foundations with Urelements (Jensen 1969).

in formal systems within which one has been able to produce a consistency proof. It might also turn on whether one has a good feel for what a model for the axiom system in question would look like.

As a result, one should expect one's warrant for the internal coherence of an axiom system to be *defeasible* (whether or not it is also *a priori*). And since one's warrant for the truth of an axiom system that has been set forth as a pure mathematical stipulation will be no better than one's warrant for the system's internal coherence, one should also expect one's warrant for the truth of the system to be defeasible.

The picture of mathematical knowledge that we are left with is a messy one. One's warrant for the truth of the axioms of pure mathematics will be typically defeasible. It will sometimes turn on informal considerations, such as whether one has a good feel for the sorts of things that can be proved on the basis of the axioms, or for what a model for the axioms would look like. And it will sometimes depend on one's warrant for the truth of further mathematical theories.

This is as it should be. One wouldn't want one's account of mathematical knowledge to yield the result that mathematical knowledge is easier to come by than the practice of mathematicians would suggest.

8.2.3 Applied Mathematics

The claim that internal coherence is sufficient for success depends on the assumption that the mathematical stipulation in question is *pure*. To see this, imagine a case in which we introduce arithmetical vocabulary by way of a (second-order) axiom system which entails (1) that every number is finite, (2) that any material objects can be numbered, and (3) that the number of the Fs is n just in case there are precisely n Fs. Such an axiom system is internally coherent. But one certainly wouldn't want to count it as necessarily true, since it entails that there are only finitely many stars, and one shouldn't be able to settle the question of whether there are finitely many stars on purely mathematical grounds.

The problem with this axiom system is that it fails to be *conservative* (see footnote 2). In the case of *pure* mathematical stipulations conservativeness is guaranteed by the fact that mixed atomic formulas are always counted as ill-formed. But when it comes to applied arithmetic we have no choice but to allow for mixed atomic formulas, and therefore countenance substantial inferential interactions between sentences built from new vocabulary and sentences built from old vocabulary.

Fortunately, the role that was played by internal coherence in the case of pure mathematics can be played by conservativeness in the case of applied mathematics. Say that a *generalized* mathematical stipulation is a stipulation in which:

1. one makes clear that one's stipulation is meant to *introduce* a new system of compositional representation, rather than extend an existing system;
2. one uses the new vocabulary to build an axiom system which may or may not include vocabulary of the old sort, and stipulates that the new vocabulary is to be understood in such a way that the axiom system is counted as necessarily true;
3. one makes clear which mixed atomic formulas are to be counted as ill-formed.

From the perspective of a compositionalist, all it takes for a generalized mathematical stipulation to succeed is for the relevant axiom system to be *conservative*.

The reason conservativeness is sufficient for success is that, as before, it guarantees the availability of an assignment of truth-conditions with two properties: (*a*) it counts the axioms as necessarily true; and (*b*) it allows for genuine singular terms, by satisfying Condition 3 of Sections 1.3 and 8.1. The assignment in question is as follows. Let $\mathcal{A}$ be the relevant axiom system, ϕ be a sentence containing new vocabulary, w be a world and O be the set of sentences containing no new vocabulary that are true at w. Then: (1) ϕ is counted as true at w just in case ϕ is a logical consequence of $\mathcal{A} \cup O$; (2) ϕ is counted as false at w just in case $\ulcorner \neg \phi \urcorner$ is a logical consequence of $\mathcal{A} \cup O$; and (3) ϕ is otherwise counted as lacking a well-defined truth-value relative to w. (The fact that the axiom system is conservative guarantees that this procedure will have no effect on sentences containing only vocabulary of the old sort.)

It is worth noting that the proposed assignment of truth-conditions does not take into account features of the world that are not expressible in the language of O. Suppose, for example, that O is couched in a first-order language with no mathematical vocabulary, and that our stipulation introduces set-theoretic vocabulary by way of the standard axioms. Now consider a world w in which there are infinitely many particles. Since O is couched in a first-order language with no mathematical vocabulary, it doesn't entail an answer to the question of whether there are exactly

$\aleph_0$-many particles in w. So a set-theoretic sentence that would standardly be interpreted as stating that the cardinality of the stars is $\aleph_0$ will be counted as lacking well-defined truth-value relative to w (and so will its negation). In order for the additional information about w to be reflected in the proposed assignment of truth-conditions, one would need to couch one's old vocabulary in a more expressive language: a language with infinitary resources, for example, or a higher-order language.

The stipulations that we have considered in this chapter are *language-based* in a very strong sense. They assume that the truth-conditions of sentences containing newly introduced vocabulary are to be fixed entirely on the basis of the truth-conditions of other sentences—be it axioms stipulated to be necessarily true, or sentences whose truth-conditions have been fixed independently of the stipulation. I do not mean to suggest, however, that there couldn't be other ways of rendering mathematical terms meaningful.

8.3 Conclusion

I have argued for two main claims. The first is that, from the perspective of the compositionalist, it would be a mistake to assume from the outset that a linguistic stipulation *extends* systems of compositional representation that were already in place. The effect of the stipulation may be to introduce a new system of compositional representation, and therefore a new way of carving up the world into objects and properties.

The second claim is that, from the perspective of the compositionalist, it doesn't take much for a linguistic stipulation to be successful. In the case of pure mathematics, all it takes is for the relevant axiom system to be *internally coherent*; in the case of applied mathematics, all it takes is for the theory to be *conservative* over sentences in the original language.

PART III

Appendices

Appendix A

A Semantics for a Language with the Dot-Notation

I give a formal semantics for a language $\mathcal{L}^w$ which allows for empty names and contains both the intensional operator $[\ldots]_w$ (read 'according to $w,\ldots$') and the dot-notation. $\mathcal{L}^w$ consists of the following symbols:

1. for $n > 0$, the n-place (non-modal) predicate letters: $\ulcorner F_1^n \urcorner$, $\ulcorner F_2^n \urcorner,\ldots$ (each with an intended interpretation);
2. for $n > 0$, the one-place modal predicate letters: $\ulcorner B_1 \urcorner, \ulcorner B_2 \urcorner,\ldots$ (each with an intended interpretation);
3. the identity symbol '=';
4. for $n > 0$, the individual non-empty constant-letter $\ulcorner c_n \urcorner$ (each with an intended referent);
5. for $n > 0$, the individual empty constant-letter $\ulcorner e_n \urcorner$;
6. the individual constant 'α'
7. the dot '';
8. the monadic sentential operator '$[\ldots]$';
9. the monadic sentential operator '$\neg$';
10. the dyadic sentential operators '$\wedge$',
11. the quantifier-symbol '$\exists$';
12. the modal variables: 'w', 'v' 'u' with or without numerical subscripts;
13. the non-modal variables: 'x', 'y', 'z' with or without numerical subscripts;
14. the auxiliaries '(' and ')'.

Undotted terms and formulas are defined as follows:

1. any modal variable is an undotted modal term;
2. 'α' is an undotted modal term;
3. any non-modal variable or individual constant-letter is an undotted non-modal term;

4. if $\tau_1, \ldots, \tau_n$ are undotted non-modal terms, then $\ulcorner F_i^n(\tau_1, \ldots, \tau_n) \urcorner$ is an undotted formula;

5. if τ_1 and τ_2 are either both undotted non-modal terms or both undotted modal terms, then $\ulcorner \tau_1 = \tau_2 \urcorner$ is an undotted formula;

6. if w is an undotted modal term, then $\ulcorner B_i(w) \urcorner$ is an undotted formula;

7. if ϕ is an undotted formula and w is an undotted modal term, then $\ulcorner [\phi]_w \urcorner$ is an undotted formula;

8. if v is an undotted (modal or non-modal) variable and ϕ is an undotted formula, then $\ulcorner \exists v(\phi) \urcorner$ is an undotted formula;

9. if ϕ and 'ψ' are undotted formulas, then $\ulcorner \neg\phi \urcorner$, $\ulcorner (\phi \wedge \psi) \urcorner$, $\ulcorner (\phi \vee \psi) \urcorner$ and $\ulcorner (\phi \supset \psi) \urcorner$ are undotted formulas;

10. nothing else is an undotted term or formula.

A *non-modal term* is either an undotted non-modal term or the result of dotting a non-modal variable; a *modal term* is an undotted modal term; a *formula* is the result of dotting any free or externally bounded occurrences of non-modal variables in an undotted formula.[1]

Next, we characterize the notion of an *a*-world and of a variable assignment. An *a*-world is a pair $\langle D, I \rangle$ with the following features:

1. D is a set of individuals in the range of the non-modal variables, each of which is either of the form $\langle x, \text{'actual'} \rangle$ or of the form $\langle x, \text{'nonactual'} \rangle$.

2. I is a function assigning a subset of D to each 1-place predicate-letter, and a subset of D^n to each n-place predicate letter (for $n < 1$). In addition, if e is an empty name, I may or may not assign a referent to e (and if a referent is assigned, it may or may not be in D).

The *actualized* *a*-world $\langle D_\alpha, I_\alpha \rangle$ will be singled out for special attention. D_α is the set of pairs $\langle z, \text{'actual'} \rangle$ for z an individual in the range of the non-modal variables; and $I_\alpha(\text{'}F_j^n\text{'})$ is the set of sequences $\langle \langle z_1, \text{'actual'} \rangle, \ldots \langle z_n, \text{'actual'} \rangle \rangle$ such that $z_1 \ldots z_n$ are in the range of the non-modal variables and satisfy F.

A variable assignment is a function σ with the following features:

1. σ assigns an *a*-world to each modal variable.
2. σ assigns an individual to each non-modal variable.

---

[1] An occurrence of a non-modal variable in an undotted formula is *free* if it is not bound by a quantifier; an occurrence of a non-modal variable in an undotted formula is *externally bounded* if it is bound by a quantifier which is not within the scope of '[. . .]'.

This puts us in a position to characterize notions of quasi-denotation and quasi-satisfaction. (With a suitable notion of admissibility on board, one can characterize truth and satisfaction for $\mathcal{L}^w$. Satisfaction is the special case of quasi-satisfaction in which attention is restricted to admissible a-worlds, and truth is the special case of quasi-truth in which attention is restricted to admissible a-worlds.) For v a non-modal variable, σ a variable assignment, ϕ a formula and w an a-world, we characterize the quasi-denotation function $\delta_{\sigma,w}(v)$ and the quasi-satisfaction predicate $Sat(\phi, \sigma)$. In addition, we characterize an auxiliary (a-world-relative) quasi-satisfaction predicate $Sat(\phi, \sigma, w)$. We proceed axiomatically, by way of the following clauses:

- If v is a (modal or non-modal) variable, $\delta_{\sigma,w}(v)$ is $\sigma(v)$;
- If v is a non-modal variable, w is an a-world and $\sigma(v)$ is an ordered pair of the form $\langle z, \text{'actual'}\rangle$, then $\delta_{\sigma,w}(\ulcorner \dot{v} \urcorner)$ is the first member of $\sigma(v)$; otherwise $\delta_{\sigma,w}(\ulcorner \dot{v} \urcorner)$ is undefined;
- if c is a non-empty constant-letter and w is an a-world, $\delta_{\sigma,w}(c)$ is the intended referent of c.
- if e is an empty constant-letter and w is an a-world, $\delta_{\sigma,w}(e)$ is the w-referent of e if there is one, and is otherwise undefined;
- $\delta_{\sigma,w}(\text{'}\alpha\text{'})$ is $\langle D_\alpha, I_\alpha \rangle$;
- if τ_1 and τ_2 are terms (both of them modal or both of them non-modal) and neither of them is an empty constant-letter, then $Sat(\ulcorner \tau_1 =, \tau_2) \urcorner, \sigma)$ if and only if $\delta_{\sigma,w}(\tau_1) = \delta_{\sigma,w}(\tau_2)$ for arbitrary w;
- if τ_1 and τ_2 are non-modal terms at least one of which is an empty constant-letter, then not-$Sat(\ulcorner \tau_1 =, \tau_2) \urcorner, \sigma)$;
- if $\tau_1, \dots \tau_n$ are non-modal terms none of which is an empty constant-letter, then $Sat(\ulcorner F_i^n(\tau_1, \dots, \tau_n) \urcorner, \sigma)$ if and only if $F_i^n(\delta_{\sigma,w}(\tau_1), \dots, \delta_{\sigma,w}(\tau_n))$, where w is arbitrary and $\ulcorner F_i^n \urcorner$ is intended to express F_i^n-ness;
- if $\tau_1, \dots \tau_n$ are non-modal terms at least one of which is an empty constant-letter, then not-$Sat(\ulcorner F_i^n(\tau_1, \dots, \tau_n) \urcorner, \sigma)$;
- if v is a modal variable, $Sat(\ulcorner B_i(v) \urcorner, \sigma)$ if and only if $B_i(\delta_{\sigma,w}(v))$ for arbitrary w, where B_i is intended to express B_i-ness;
- if v is a non-modal variable, $Sat(\ulcorner \exists v(\phi) \urcorner, \sigma)$ if and only if there is an individual z in the range of the non-modal variables such that $Sat(\ulcorner \phi \urcorner, \sigma^{v/z})$, where $\sigma^{v/z}$ is just like σ except that it assigns z to v;
- if v is a modal variable, $Sat(\ulcorner \exists v(\phi) \urcorner, \sigma)$ if and only if there is an a-world z such that $Sat(\ulcorner \phi \urcorner, \sigma^{v/z})$, where $\sigma^{v/z}$ is just like σ except that it assigns z to v;
- $Sat(\ulcorner \neg\phi \urcorner, \sigma)$ if and only if it is not the case that $Sat(\phi, \sigma)$;

- $Sat(\ulcorner \phi \wedge \psi \urcorner, \sigma)$ if and only if $Sat(\phi, \sigma)$ and $Sat(\psi, \sigma)$;
- $Sat(\ulcorner [\phi]_w \urcorner, \sigma)$ if and only if $Sat(\phi, \sigma', \sigma(w))$, where $\sigma'(x) = \sigma(x)$ for x a modal variable and $\sigma'(x) = \langle \sigma(x), \text{'actual'} \rangle$ for x a non-modal variable;

- if τ_1 and τ_2 are non-modal terms neither of which is an empty constant-letter without a w-reference, then $Sat(\ulcorner \tau_1 =, \tau_2) \urcorner, \sigma, w)$ if and only if $\delta_{\sigma,w}(\tau_1)$ is in the domain of w and is identical to $\delta_{\sigma,w}(\tau_2)$;
- if τ_1 and τ_2 are non-modal terms at least one of which is a constant-letter without a w-reference, then not-$Sat(\ulcorner \tau_1 =, \tau_2) \urcorner, \sigma, w)$;
- if τ_1 and τ_2 are modal terms, then $Sat(\ulcorner \tau_1 =, \tau_2) \urcorner, \sigma, w)$ if and only if $\delta_{\sigma,w}(\tau_1) = \delta_{\sigma,w}(\tau_2)$ for arbitrary w;
- if $\tau_1, \ldots \tau_n$ are non-modal terms none of which is a constant-letter without a w-reference, then $Sat(\ulcorner F_i^n(\tau_1, \ldots, \tau_n) \urcorner, \sigma, w)$ if and only if $\langle \delta_{\sigma,w}(\tau_1), \ldots, \delta_{\sigma,w}(\tau_n) \rangle$ is in the w-extension of $\ulcorner F_i^n \urcorner$;
- if $\tau_1, \ldots \tau_n$ are non-modal terms at least one of which is a constant-letter without a w-reference, then not-$Sat(\ulcorner F_i^n(\tau_1, \ldots, \tau_n) \urcorner, \sigma, w)$;
- if v is a modal term, $Sat(\ulcorner B_i(v) \urcorner, \sigma, w)$ if and only if $B_i(\delta_{\sigma,w}(v))$, where $\ulcorner B_i \urcorner$ is intended to express B_i-ness;
- if v is a non-modal variable, $Sat(\ulcorner \exists v(\phi) \urcorner, \sigma, w)$ if and only if there is an individual z in the domain of w such that $Sat(\ulcorner \phi \urcorner, \sigma^{v/z}, w)$, where $\sigma^{v/z}$ is just like σ except that it assigns z to v;
- if v is a modal variable, $Sat(\ulcorner \exists v(\phi) \urcorner, \sigma, w)$ if and only if there is an a-world z such that (a) any empty constant-letter which is assigned a referent by w is assigned the same referent by z, and (b) $Sat(\ulcorner \phi \urcorner, \sigma^{v/z}, w)$, where $\sigma^{v/z}$ is just like σ except that it assigns z to v;
- $Sat(\ulcorner \neg \phi \urcorner, \sigma, w)$ if and only if it is not the case that $Sat(\phi, \sigma, w)$;
- $Sat(\ulcorner \phi \wedge \psi \urcorner, \sigma, w)$ if and only if $Sat(\phi, \sigma, w)$ and $Sat(\psi, \sigma, w)$;
- $Sat(\ulcorner [\phi]_u \urcorner, \sigma, w)$ if and only if $Sat(\phi, \sigma, \sigma(u))$.

Finally, we say that a formula ϕ is *quasi-true* if and only if $Sat(\phi, \sigma)$ for any variable assignment σ.

Appendix B

If Lewis Can Say It, You Can Too

In Section 6.8, I described a transformation from Lewisian sentences to dotted actualist sentences. The purpose of this appendix is to explain how the transformation works in general. I shall assume that the Lewisian language is a two-sorted first-order language, with *world-variables* 'w_1', 'w_2', etc. ranging over Lewisian worlds, and *individual-variables* 'x_1', 'x_2', etc. ranging over world-bound individuals in the Lewisian pluriverse. The language contains no function-letters; there is a world-constant 'α' referring to the actual Lewisian world and individual-constants 'c_1', 'c_2', etc. referring to world-bound individuals. The only atomic predicates are 'I' (which takes an individual-variable and a world-variable), 'C' (which takes two individual-variables), '=' (which takes (*i*) two world-variables, (*ii*) two individual-variables, (*iii*) a world-constant and a world-variable, or (*iv*) an individual-constant and an individual-variable) and, for each j, $\ulcorner P_j^n \urcorner$ (which takes n individual-variables). (If one likes, one can also take the language to contain set-theoretic vocabulary.) Finally, I shall assume that universal quantifiers are defined in terms of existential quantifiers in the usual way, and that logical connectives other than '$\wedge$' and '$\neg$' are defined in terms of '$\wedge$' and '$\neg$' in the usual way.

The plan is to proceed in two steps. The first is to get the Lewisian sentence into a certain kind of normal form; the second is to convert the normal-form sentence into a dotted actualist sentence. Here is a recipe for getting an arbitrary Lewisian sentence into normal form:

1. Start by relabeling variables in such a way that no world-variable has the same index as an individual-variable;
2. next, replace each occurrence of $\ulcorner I(x_j, w_k) \urcorner$ by $\ulcorner w_j = w_k \urcorner$;
3. then replace each occurrence of the atomic formula $\ulcorner P_j^n(x_{k_1}, \ldots, x_{k_n}) \urcorner$ by

$$(P_j^n(x_{k_1}, \ldots, x_{k_n}) \wedge w_{k_1} = w_{k_2} \wedge \ldots \wedge w_{k_1} = w_{k_n}),$$

each occurrence of $\ulcorner c_j = x_k \urcorner$ by $\ulcorner (c_j = x_k \wedge \alpha = w_k) \urcorner$, and each occurrence of $\ulcorner x_j = x_k \urcorner$ by $\ulcorner (x_j = x_k \wedge w_j = w_k) \urcorner$.[2]

4. finally, replace each occurrence of $\ulcorner \exists x_j (\ldots) \urcorner$ by $\ulcorner \exists x_j \exists w_j (I(x_j, w_j) \wedge \ldots) \urcorner$.

On the assumption that $\ulcorner P_j^n \urcorner$ is projectable (and, hence, that $\ulcorner P_j^n (x_{k_1}, \ldots, x_{k_n}) \urcorner$ can only be true if $x_{k_1}, \ldots, x_{k_n}$ are world-mates), it is easy to verify that this procedure respects truth-value. (For a characterization of projectability, see footnote 11 of Chapter 6.)

Here is an example. The Lewisian sentence

$$\exists w_{17} \exists x_2 \exists x_5 (I(x_2, w_{17}) \wedge \text{Sister}(x_2, x_5))$$

(*Read:* There is a Lewisian world w_{17} an individual x_2 and an individual x_5 such that x_2 is an inhabitant of w_{17} and x_2 has x_5 as a sister.)

gets rewritten as:

$$\exists w_{17} \exists x_2 \exists w_2 (I(x_2, w_2) \wedge \exists x_5 \exists w_5 (I(x_5, w_5) \wedge$$

$$w_2 = w_{17} \wedge \text{Sister}(x_2, x_5) \wedge w_2 = w_5))$$

(*Read:* There is a Lewisian world w_{17}, an individual x_2 inhabiting Lewisian world w_2, and an individual x_5 inhabiting Lewisian world w_5 such that w_2 is identical to w_{17}, x_2 has x_5 as a sister and w_2 is identical to w_5.)

Once one has a Lewisian sentence in normal form, it can be transformed into a dotted actualist sentence by carrying out the following replacements:

$$I(x_j, w_j) \longrightarrow [\exists y(y = \dot{x}_j)]_{w_j}$$

$$P_j^n(x_{k_1}, \ldots, x_{k_n}) \longrightarrow [P_j^n(\dot{x}_{k_1}, \ldots, \dot{x}_{k_n})]_{w_{k_1}}$$

$$C(x_j, x_k) \longrightarrow x_j = x_k$$

$$c_j = x_k \longrightarrow [c_j = \dot{x}_k]_{w_k}$$

Here is an example. The Lewisian rendering of '$\Diamond (\exists x_1 \exists x_2 \text{Sister}(x_1, x_2))$' is

$$\exists w_3 \exists x_1 \exists x_2 (I(x_1, w_3) \wedge I(x_2, w_3) \wedge \text{Sister}(x_1, x_2))$$

---

[2] These three replacements are needed to secure the base clause in the induction below.

whose normal form

$$\exists w_3 \exists x_1 \exists w_1 (\mathrm{I}(x_1, w_1) \wedge \exists x_2 \exists w_2 (\mathrm{I}(x_2, w_2) \wedge$$
$$w_1 = w_3 \wedge w_1 = w_3 \wedge \mathrm{Sister}(x_1, x_2) \wedge w_1 = w_2))$$

gets transformed by the actualist into

$$\exists w_3 \exists x_1 \exists w_1 ([\exists y(y = \dot{x}_1)]_{w_1} \wedge \exists x_2 \exists w_2 ([\exists y(y = \dot{x}_2)]_{w_2} \wedge$$
$$w_1 = w_3 \wedge w_1 = w_3 \wedge [\mathrm{Sister}(\dot{x}_1, \dot{x}_2)]_{w_1} \wedge w_1 = w_2))$$

which boils down to:

$$\exists w_3 \exists x_1 \exists x_2 ([\mathrm{Sister}(\dot{x}_1, \dot{x}_2)]_{w_3})$$

(*Read:* There are objects x_1 and x_2 and an admissible *a*-world w_3 such that x_1 and x_2 are used by w_3 to represent someone's having a sister.)

and is guaranteed by the Appendix A semantics to be equivalent to

$$\exists w_3 ([\exists x_1 \exists x_2 \, \mathrm{Sister}(x_1, x_2)]_{w_3})$$

(*Read:* There is an admissible *a*-world w_3 according to which there are individuals x_1 and x_2 such that x_1 has x_2 as a sister.)

which is the actualist's rendering of '$\Diamond(\exists x_1 \exists x_2 \, \mathrm{Sister}(x_1, x_2))$'.

Here is a slightly more complex example. The Lewisian's rendering of

> There are possible worlds w_4 and w_5 with the following properties: according to w_4, there is an individual who is my sister and a philosopher; according to w_5, that very individual is a cellist rather than a philosopher.

is

$$\exists w_4 \exists w_5 \exists x_1 \exists x_2 \exists x_3 ($$
$$\mathrm{I}(x_1, w_4) \wedge \mathrm{I}(x_2, w_4) \wedge \mathrm{I}(x_3, w_5) \wedge$$
$$\exists x_6 (\mathrm{AR} = x_6 \wedge \mathrm{C}(x_6, x_1)) \wedge \mathrm{C}(x_2, x_3) \wedge$$
$$\mathrm{Sister}(x_1, x_2) \wedge \mathrm{Phil}(x_2) \wedge \mathrm{Cellist}(x_3) \wedge \neg \mathrm{Phil}(x_3))$$

whose normal form

$$\exists w_4 \exists w_5 \exists x_1 \exists w_1 (I(x_1, w_1) \wedge \exists x_2 \exists w_2 (I(x_2, w_2) \wedge \exists x_3 \exists w_3 (I(x_3, w_3) \wedge$$

$$w_1 = w_4 \wedge w_2 = w_4 \wedge w_3 = w_5 \wedge$$

$$\exists x_6 \exists w_6 (I(x_6, w_6) \wedge \text{AR} = x_6 \wedge \alpha = w_6 \wedge C(x_6, x_1)) \wedge C(x_2, x_3) \wedge$$

$$\text{Sister}(x_1, x_2) \wedge \text{Phil}(x_2) \wedge \text{Cellist}(x_3) \wedge \neg\text{Phil}(x_3))))$$

gets transformed by the actualist into

$$\exists w_4 \exists w_5 \exists x_1 \exists w_1 ([\exists y (y = \dot{x}_1)]_{w_1} \wedge \exists x_2 \exists w_2 ([\exists y (y = \dot{x}_2)]_{w_2} \wedge$$

$$\exists x_3 \exists w_3 ([\exists y (y = \dot{x}_3)]_{w_3} \wedge w_1 = w_4 \wedge w_2 = w_4 \wedge w_3 = w_5 \wedge$$

$$\exists x_6 \exists w_6 ([\exists y (y = \dot{x}_6)]_{w_6} \wedge [\text{AR} = \dot{x}_6]_{w_6} \wedge \alpha = w_6 \wedge x_6 = x_1) \wedge x_2 = x_3 \wedge$$

$$[\text{Sister}(\dot{x}_1, \dot{x}_2)]_{w_1} \wedge w_1 = w_2 \wedge [\text{Phil}(\dot{x}_2)]_{w_2} \wedge [\text{Cellist}(\dot{x}_3)]_{w_3}$$

$$\wedge \neg[\text{Phil}(\dot{x}_3)]_{w_3})))$$

which boils down to

$$\exists w_4 \exists w_5 \exists x_2 ([\text{Sister}(\text{AR}, \dot{x}_2)]_{w_4} \wedge [\text{Phil}(\dot{x}_2)]_{w_4} \wedge [\text{Cellist}(\dot{x}_2)]_{w_5}$$

$$\wedge [\neg\text{Phil}(\dot{x}_2)]_{w_5})$$

(*Read:* there are admissible *a*-worlds w_4 and w_5 and an individual x_2 such that: (*i*) x_2 is used by w_4 to represent my sister and a philosopher, and (*ii*) x_2 is used by w_5 to represent a cellist rather than a philosopher.)

Finally, we show that there is a notion of *a*-world admissibility which guarantees that the actualist transformation of an arbitrary Lewisian sentence has the truth-value that the Lewisian sentence would receive on its intended interpretation. (The proof relies on the assumption that the Lewisian language is rich enough—and the space of Lewisian worlds varied enough with respect to predicates occurring in the language—that the set of true sentences has a model in which any two worlds are such that some atomic predicate is satisfied by a sequence of objects inhabiting one of the worlds, but not by the result of replacing each object in the sequence by its counterpart in the other world.) Start by enriching the Lewisian language with a standard name for each inhabitant of the actual world, and let *S* be the set of true sentences in the extended language. One can use the Completeness Theorem to generate a model *M* of *S* in which the domain consists of '='-equivalence classes of terms and in which the assumption above is satisfied. If a_1 is an object in the individual-variable domain of M, let a_1^* be the set of individuals a_2 such that '$C(x_1, x_2)$' is satisfied by a_1 and a_2. (I assume that 'C' is an equivalence relation, and therefore that $*$ partitions the individual-variable domain of M into equivalence classes.) If a_1 is an object in the individual-variable domain of M, let $a^\dagger$ be $\langle z, \text{'actual'}\rangle$ if the standard name of z is in the transitive closure of a^*, and $\langle a^*, \text{'nonactual'}\rangle$ otherwise.

For each c in the world-variable domain of M, we construct an a-world w_c, as follows: the domain of w_c is the set of $a^\dagger$ such that '$I(x_1, w_1)$' is satisfied by a and c in M; the w_c extension of $\ulcorner P_j^n \urcorner$ is the set of sequences $\left\langle a_1^\dagger, \ldots, a_n^\dagger \right\rangle$ such that '$I(x_1, w_1) \wedge \ldots \wedge I(x_n, w_1) \wedge P_j^n(x_1 \ldots, x_n)$' is satisfied by $a_1, \ldots, a_n, c$ in M. In addition we let individual constants receive their intended interpretations, and let 'α' be w_c, where c is the M-referent of 'α'. Say that an a-world is admissible just in case it is a w_c for some c in the world-variable domain of M. If σ is a variable-assignment function in M, let $\sigma^\dagger$ be such that $\sigma^\dagger(\ulcorner x_j \urcorner)$ is $\sigma(\ulcorner x_j \urcorner)^\dagger$, $\sigma^\dagger(\ulcorner w_j \urcorner)$ is w_c if $\ulcorner x_j \urcorner$ occurs in ϕ (where c is such that '$I(x_1, w_1)$' is satisfied by $\sigma(\ulcorner x_j \urcorner)$ and c in M), and $\sigma^\dagger(\ulcorner w_j \urcorner)$ is $w_{\sigma(\ulcorner w_j \urcorner)}$ if $\ulcorner x_j \urcorner$ does not occur in ϕ. An induction on the complexity of formulas shows that a Lewisian formula ϕ is satisfied by an assignment function σ in M just in case the actualist transformation of its normal form is satisfied by $\sigma^\dagger$ when the world-variables range over admissible a-worlds and the individual-variables range over the union of the domains of admissible a-worlds.

Appendix C

The Canonical Space
of Worlds

This appendix contains proofs of the technical results described in Chapter 5, and presupposes the machinery described in Chapter 6.

Preliminaries   Let L be a first-order language, $L^\Diamond$ be the result of adding '$\Diamond$' to L, and A be an assignment of truth-values to sentences in L and basic 'just is'-statements built up from vocabulary in L. I shall assume that L has a set-sized vocabulary and a set-sized domain.

We will construct the canonical space of worlds in stages. At each stage, we do two things: (1) we introduce a set of objects and assign each of them an 'essence', and (2) we introduce a set of a-worlds for $L^\Diamond$.

I will begin by explaining what an essence is, and then describe the construction in further detail.

Essences   We start with the notion of a constitutive predicate. Where $\vec{v}$ is a sequence of variables $v_1, \ldots, v_k$, which we will think of as *parameters*, we will refer to $\phi(z_1, \ldots, z_m, \vec{v})$ as an m-place predicate, and say that $\phi(z_1, \ldots, z_m, \vec{v})$ is *constitutive* by the lights of A (or A-constitutive) just in case the basic statement

$$\frac{\phi(z_1, \ldots, z_m, \vec{v})}{x_1 = z_1 \wedge \ldots \wedge x_m = z_m \gg_{x_1, \ldots, x_m} \phi(x_1, \ldots, x_m, \vec{v})}$$

is true according to A.

Informally speaking, an 'essence' is a set of m-place constitutive predicates in which any parameters have been filled by objects from a given domain.

Formally speaking, essences are defined as follows. Let D be a domain of objects, and let o be an arbitrary object not in D, which we shall refer to as the 'outside object'. (The 'outside object' will be used to keep track of the behavior of constitutive predicates whose parameters have been filled with objects which lie outside the domain of the world with respect to which the predicate is being evaluated.) If $\phi(z_1, \ldots, z_m, \vec{v})$ is an (m-place) predicate of L, we say that an (m-place) D-completion of $\phi(z_1, \ldots, z_m, \vec{v})$ is a pair $\langle \phi(z_1, \ldots, z_m, \vec{v}), f \rangle$ where f is a function that assigns an element of $D \cup \{o\}$ to each variable in $\vec{v}$. A set E of (m-place) D-completions of A-constitutive predicates is an (m-place) D-*essence* just in case a sequence of objects $a_1, \ldots, a_m$ could consistently instantiate every D-completion in E, in the following sense:

> There is an a-world w with domain D such that: (1) w verifies (the modal analogue of) every unconditional 'just is'-statement that is counted as true by A, and (2) some sequence of objects $a_1, \ldots, a_m \in D$ is such that for any $\langle \phi(z_1, \ldots, z_m, \vec{v}), f \rangle$ in E, $\phi(z, \vec{v})$ is true in w relative to a variable assignment that assigns a_j to z_j and $f(w_i)$ to each w_i in $\vec{v}$.

(Since the 'outside object' o is not in the domain D of w, constitutive predicates whose parameters have been filled with o will behave in w like predicates containing empty names.)

The Construction   The intuitive picture is very simple. Our construction proceeds in stages. At stage 0 we introduce the 'actualized' a-world. At each later stage we introduce as varied a set of a-worlds as we can, while respecting the essences assigned to sequences of objects introduced earlier in the process.

Here is how the construction works in greater detail. At stage 0, we introduce the 'actualized' a-world for $L^{\Diamond}$, that is, the a-world whose domain D_0 consists of pairs $\langle x, \text{'actual'} \rangle$ for x in the domain of L, and in which every predicate receives its intended interpretation (corrected for the fact that the domain consists of ordered pairs $\langle x, \text{'actual'} \rangle$ instead of their first components). For each $z_1, \ldots, z_m \in D_0$, we let the (m-place) D_0-essence of $z_1, \ldots, z_m$ be the set of D_0-completions of (m-place) A-constitutive predicates that are true of $z_1, \ldots, z_m$ in the actualized a-world. (I shall assume that the 'outside object' o is not an ordered pair, and therefore not in D_0.)

For k a natural number, stage $k + 1$ is constructed as follows. We let μ be the maximum of: (a) ω, (b) the cardinality of D_0, and (c) the cardinality of L. Next, we let D_{k+1} be the union of D_k and of the set of objects $\langle \alpha_{k+1}, \text{'non-actual'} \rangle$ for $\alpha \in \mu$. (Since the 'outside object' is not an ordered pair, it is not in D_{k+1}.) Each sequence $d_1, \ldots, d_m \in D_{k+1}$ is then assigned an (m-place) D_{k+1}-essence in such a way that:

1. D_k-essences are preserved (that is, if $d_1, \ldots, d_m \in D_k$, then the m-place D_{k+1}-essence of $d_1, \ldots, d_m$ is just the m-place D_k essence of $d_1, \ldots, d_m$).

2. Essences are distributed as diversely as possible.

    Let me be more specific. For each $n \geq 1$, let an n-distribution of essences be a function f such that, for each $i \leq n$, f assigns an i-place essence to each i-membered sequence built from numbers less than n. Then we shall require our assignment of essences to be such that each n-distribution of essences applies to μ sequences $d_1, \ldots, d_n \in D_{k+1}$ (where an n-distribution 'applies' to a sequence of objects $d_1, \ldots, d_n$ just in case each i-membered sequence built from $d_1, \ldots, d_n$ is assigned the essence that the n-distribution assigns to the corresponding sequence of numbers).

    This procedure guarantees that our assignment of essences is unique, up to isomorphism.

Finally, we introduce an a-world w just in case it meets the following conditions:

C0 w respects the intended interpretations of singular terms (all of which must refer to objects in the domain of the actualized a-world, D_0.)

C1   The domain of w is a subset of D_{k+1}.

C2   If $\ulcorner \phi(x_1, \ldots, x_n) \equiv_{x_1, \ldots, x_n} \psi(x_1, \ldots, x_n) \urcorner$ is counted as true by A, $\ulcorner \forall x_1 \ldots \forall x_n(\phi(x_1, \ldots, x_n) \leftrightarrow \psi(x_1, \ldots, x_n)) \urcorner$ is true at w.

C3   Let $\phi(z_1, \ldots, z_m, \vec{v})$ be an (m-place) A-constitutive predicate, let $x_1, \ldots, x_m$ be objects in the domain of w, and let $\langle \phi(z_1, \ldots, z_m, \vec{v}), f \rangle$ be a D_{k+1}-completion of $\phi(z_1, \ldots, z_m, \vec{v})$. Let $s \leq k + 1$ be the first stage at which $x_1, \ldots, x_m$ were all introduced, and let f^* be just like f except that whenever $f(v_i)$ is an object outside D_s, $f^*(v_i)$ is the 'outside object' o.

     Then $x_1, \ldots, x_m$ satisfies $\phi(z_1, \ldots, z_m, \vec{v})$ in w relative to the parameters assigned to $\vec{v}$ by f just in case $\langle \phi(z_1, \ldots, z_m, \vec{v}), f^* \rangle$ is in the (m-place) D_{k+1}-essence assigned to $x_1, \ldots, x_m$.

We let the canonical space of worlds, M_A, consist of all and only a-worlds w such that w is introduced at some finite stage of this process, and designate the actualized a-world as M_A's center.

It is clear from the construction that M_A has been specified uniquely (up to isomorphism). We can also prove:

Theorem C.1 M_A *satisfies the following two conditions:*

1. If $\phi(\vec{x}) \equiv_{\vec{x}} \psi(\vec{x})$ is true according to A, then $M_A \models \Box(\forall \vec{x}(\phi(\vec{x}) \leftrightarrow \psi(\vec{x})))$.

2. If

$$\frac{\phi(z_1, \ldots, z_m, \vec{v})}{x_1 = z_1 \wedge \ldots x_m = z_m \gg_{x_1, \ldots, x_m} \phi(x_1, \ldots, x_m, \vec{v})}$$

is true according to A, then

$$M_A \models \Box(\forall z_1, \ldots, z_m, \vec{v}(\phi(z_1, \ldots, z_m, \vec{v}) \rightarrow$$

$$\Box(\exists y_1, \ldots, y_m(y_1 = z_1 \wedge \ldots \wedge y_m = z_m) \rightarrow \phi(z_1, \ldots, z_m, \vec{v}))))$$

Proof: It is straightforward to check that the first condition is verified. To see that the second condition is verified, assume that $\phi(z_1, \ldots, z_m, \vec{v})$ is A-constitutive. Let w be an a-world in M_A and suppose that $a_1, \ldots, a_m, b_1, \ldots, b_k$ is a sequence of objects in the domain of w such that $\phi(z_1, \ldots, z_m, \vec{v})$ is true at w relative to $a_1, \ldots, a_m, b_1, \ldots, b_k$. We show that, if $w' \in M_A$ has $a_1, \ldots, a_m$ in its domain, then $\phi(z_1, \ldots, z_m, \vec{v})$ is true at w' relative to $a_1, \ldots, a_m, b_1, \ldots, b_k$. Let the sequence $b_1^*, \ldots, b_k^*$ be just like the sequence $b_1, \ldots, b_k$ except that b_i^* is the 'outside object' o whenever the $a_1, \ldots, a_m$ were all introduced before b_i in our construction. Since $\phi(z_1, \ldots, z_m, \vec{v})$ is A-constitutive, it follows from condition C3 above that $\phi(z_1, \ldots, z_m, \vec{v})$ is true at w relative to $a_1, \ldots, a_m, b_1, \ldots, b_k$ just in case $\langle \phi(z_1, \ldots, z_m, \vec{v}), f^* \rangle$ is in the essence of $a_1, \ldots, a_m$, where $f^*(v_i) = b_i^*$. So $\langle \phi(z_1, \ldots, z_m, \vec{v}), f^* \rangle$ is in the essence of $a_1, \ldots, a_m$. But it also follows from C3 that $\phi(z_1, \ldots, z_m, \vec{v})$ is true at w' relative to $a_1, \ldots, a_m, b_1, \ldots, b_k$ just in case $\langle \phi(z_1, \ldots, z_m, \vec{v}), f^* \rangle$ is in the essence of the $a_1, \ldots, a_m$. So $\phi(z_1, \ldots, z_m, \vec{v})$ is true at w' relative to $a_1, \ldots, a_m, b_1, \ldots, b_k$.

Possibility   Let a *possibility statement* be a sentence of $L^\Diamond$ of the following form:

$$\exists \vec{x}_1(\phi_1(\vec{x}_1) \wedge \Diamond(\exists \vec{x}_2(\phi_2(\vec{x}_1, \vec{x}_2) \wedge \Diamond(\exists \vec{x}_3(\phi_3(\vec{x}_1, \vec{x}_2, \vec{x}_3) \wedge \ldots))))$$

where none of the ϕ_i contain boxes or diamonds.

Intuitively speaking, a possibility statement will be said to be 'good' just in case it meets the following three constraints: (1) '$\phi_1(\vec{x}_1)$' is satisfied by the actualized a-world of M_A, (2) each of the '$\phi_i(\vec{x}_1, \ldots, \vec{x}_i)$' is consistent with the unconditional basic statements that are true by the lights of A, and (3) there are no clashes amongst the ϕ_i regarding the constitutive properties demanded of the referents of a given sequence of variables.

We wish to prove the following result:

Theorem C.2 *Every good possibility statement is true in M_A.*

Before turning to the proof, we need to give a proper definition of 'good'. Say that a possibility statement ϕ is *good* just in case there is:

(a) an essence-assignment η such that, for any variables $x_1, \ldots, x_m$ occurring in ϕ, there is a k such that η assigns $x_1, \ldots, x_m$ some D_k-essence; and

(b) a decision δ as to which variables to treat as coreferential;

such that η and δ satisfy the following condition:

Start by expanding the language with a new individual constant for each of the objects filling parameters in the essences that η assigns to sequences of variables in ϕ (including an empty individual constant 'o' corresponding to the 'outside object' o).

Next modify the possibility statement so as to get the following:

$$\exists \vec{x}_1 (E_1(\vec{x}_1) \wedge I_1(\vec{x}_1) \wedge \phi_1(\vec{x}_1) \wedge \Diamond(\exists \vec{x}_2 (E_2(\vec{x}_1, \vec{x}_2)$$
$$\wedge I_2(\vec{x}_1, \vec{x}_2) \wedge \phi_2(\vec{x}_1, \vec{x}_2) \wedge \ldots)))$$

(Here $E_i(\vec{x}_1, \ldots, \vec{x}_1)$ is the (possibly infinite) conjunction of formulas θ whose D_k-completions are in the D_k-essence that η assigns to subsets of $\vec{x}_1, \ldots, \vec{x}_i$, where each free variable in θ to which the D_k-completion assigns an object has been replaced with the new constant that refers to that object (and where each variable 'z_i' has been replaced by an appropriate variable x_j). And $I_i(\ldots)$ is the conjunction consisting of a conjunct '$\exists y \exists z (x_i = y \wedge x_j = z) \rightarrow x_i = x_j$' whenever x_i and x_j are treated as coreferential by χ and a conjunct '$\exists y \exists z (x_i = y \wedge x_j = z) \rightarrow x_i \neq x_j$' whenever x_i and x_j are treated by χ as referring to different objects.

Then each of the following conditions is satisfied:

1. $\exists \vec{x}_1 (E_1(\vec{x}_1) \wedge I_1(\vec{x}_1) \wedge \phi_1(\vec{x}_1))$ is true in the actualized a-world (when all constants are assigned their intended interpretations, whether or not they refer to objects in the domain of the actualized a-world).

2. For each $i > 1$, there is an a-world w and a way of further expanding the language with a family of interpreted constants c_α (which may or may not refer to objects in the domain of w such that: (1) w satisfies C2, and (2) $\exists \vec{x}_i (E_i(\vec{c}_1, \ldots, \vec{c}_{i-1}, \vec{x}_i) \wedge I_i(\vec{c}_1, \ldots, \vec{c}_{i-1}, \vec{x}_i) \wedge \phi_i(\vec{c}_1, \ldots, \vec{c}_{i-1}, \vec{x}_i))$ is true at w (when all constants are assigned their

intended interpretations, whether or not they refer to objects in the domain of the actualized a-world).

We now turn to the proof of the theorem.

Let ψ be a good possibility statement containing n diamonds. We know that there are assignments η and χ of essences and coreferentiality, respectively, such that a version of ψ modified as above satisfies conditions 1 and 2. Since modified-ψ entails ψ, it will suffice to show that modified-ψ is true in M_A.

We proceed by *reductio*. For $k \leq n+1$, let the k-truncation of modified-ψ be the result of eliminating from modified-ψ the subformula beginning with the kth diamond and the conjunction sign that precedes it (or doing nothing, if $k = n+1$). Suppose that modified-ψ is false in M_A. It follows from condition 1 of the definition of goodness, and the fact that the M_A's center is the actualized a-world, that the 1-truncation of modified-ψ is true in M_A. So there must be some $k \leq n$ such that the kth-truncation of modified-ψ is true in M_A and the $k+1$th truncation is false in M_A.

Since the kth-truncation of modified-ψ is true, there must be a sequence of a-worlds $w_1, \ldots w_k$ in M_A and a sequence of objects $\vec{a}_1, \ldots, \vec{a}_k$ such that: (1) w_1 is the actualized a-world, (2) each of the $\vec{a}_i$ is in the domain of w_i, and (3) w_i verifies the subformula of the kth-truncation of modified-ψ that follows the string of existential quantifiers that binds $\vec{x}_i$ when each variable in $\vec{x}_j$ is assigned the corresponding $\vec{a}_j$ as a value ($j \leq i$). By condition 2 of the definition of goodness, there is an a-world w verifying every 'just is'-statement counted as true by A and such that the subformula $\exists \vec{x}_{k+1}(E_{k+1}(\vec{x}_1 \ldots, \vec{x}_{k+1}) \wedge I_{k+1}(\vec{x}_1, \ldots \vec{x}_{k+1}) \wedge \phi_{k+1}(\vec{x}_1, \ldots \vec{x}_{k+1}))$ of ψ is true when the $\vec{x}_j$ ($j < k+1$) are replaced by suitable new constants. Where m is the maximum of the stages at which $w_1, \ldots w_k$ were introduced to M_A and stages k such that η assigns to some sequence of variables in ψ a D_k-essence, one can verify that there is a world w^* which is isomorphic to w and is introduced to M_A at stage $m+1$.

To see this, we assume with no loss of generality that w has a countable domain, and replace each object z in the domain of w by z^*, where $(\ldots)^*$ is defined as follows:

1. If c_j^i is the new constant introduced to take the place of the ith member of $\vec{x}_j$, and if the referent z of c_j^i is in the domain of w, then z^* is ith member of $\vec{a}_j$.

(This assignment is guaranteed to be one-one because we know that the result of substituting new constants for variables in $I_{k+1}(\vec{x}_1, \ldots \vec{x}_{k+1})$ is true at w.)

2. To each remaining object z in the domain of w, $(\ldots)^*$ assigns a distinct $m + 1$-stage object whose essence matches the distribution of constitutive predicates that are satisfied by z in w.

The construction of M_A guarantees that some a-world introduced to M_A at stage $m + 1$ is isomorphic to w under $(\ldots)^*$.

This can be used to show that the $k + 1$th truncation of modified-ψ is true in M_A, and therefore to complete our *reductio*. It suffices to check that the subformula $\exists \vec{x}_{k+1}(E_{k+1}(\vec{x}_1, \ldots, \vec{x}_{k+1}) \wedge I_{k+1}(\vec{x}_1, \ldots \vec{x}_{k+1}) \wedge \phi_{k+1}(\vec{x}_1, \ldots \vec{x}_{k+1}))$ of modified-ψ is true in w^* when the values of the $\vec{x}_1, \ldots, \vec{x}_k$ are taken to be $\vec{a}_1, \ldots, \vec{a}_k$. Start by fixing referents $\vec{b}_{k+1}$ for $\vec{x}_{k+1}$ in the domain of w that witness the truth of $\exists \vec{x}_{k+1}(E_{k+1}(\vec{x}_1, \ldots, \vec{x}_{k+1}) \wedge I_{k+1}(\vec{c}_1, \ldots \vec{c}_k, \vec{x}_{k+1}) \wedge \phi_{k+1}(\vec{c}_1, \ldots \vec{c}_k, \vec{x}_{k+1}))$ in w. Let σ be a variable-assignment that assigns the referent of a new constant replacing a given variable to that variable and assigns $\vec{b}_{k+1}$ to $\vec{x}_{k+1}$; let σ^* be a variable-assignment that assigns $\vec{a}_1, \ldots, \vec{a}_k$ to $\vec{x}_1, \ldots, \vec{x}_k$, assigns z^* to a variable v whenever $\sigma(v) = z$ and z is in the domain of w, and assigns an object outside the domain of w^* to v whenever $\sigma(v)$ is an object outside the domain of w.

To prove the result, it suffices to show that $\phi_{k+1}(\vec{x}_1, \ldots \vec{x}_{k+1})$ is true in w relative to σ just in case it is true in w^* relative to σ^*. We proceed by induction on the complexity of ϕ_{k+1}:

- $\phi_{k+1}(\vec{x}_1, \ldots \vec{x}_{k+1})$ is $P(\vec{x}_1, \ldots \vec{x}_{k+1})$ for P atomic.
  I am assuming that atomic formulas (including formulas of the form '$y = z$') are false at an a-world whenever they involve empty terms. So the empty-term case follows from the observation that the result of applying σ to $\vec{x}_1, \ldots, \vec{x}_{k+1}$ is outside the domain of w just in case the result of applying σ^* to $\vec{x}_1, \ldots, \vec{x}_{k+1}$ is outside the domain of w^*. When there are no empty terms, the result follows from the observation that w and w^* are isomorphic under $(\ldots)^*$.
- $\phi_{k+1}(\vec{x}_1, \ldots \vec{x}_{k+1})$ is $\exists z(\theta(\vec{x}_1, \ldots \vec{x}_{k+1}, z))$. Suppose $\exists z(\theta(\vec{x}_1, \ldots \vec{x}_{k+1}, z))$ is true in w relative to σ, then there is some y in the domain of w such that $\theta(\vec{x}_1, \ldots \vec{x}_{k+1}, z)$ is true in w relative to $\sigma[y/z]$. By inductive hypothesis, $\theta(\vec{x}_1, \ldots \vec{x}_{k+1}, z)$ is true in w^* relative to $\sigma[y^*/z]$. So $\exists z(\theta(\vec{x}_1, \ldots \vec{x}_{k+1}, z))$ is true in w^* relative to σ^*. The converse is analogous.
- The remaining cases are trivial.

Reduction Assume that every object a in the domain of the actualized a-world of M_A has a unique name c_a. If w is an a-world in M_A, let S_w be the (possibly infinite) sentence that is constructed as follows:

1. Assign a variable x_a to each member a of the domain of w.
2. Form the (possibly infinite) conjunction whose conjuncts are: (*i*) the formulas $P(x_{a_1}, \ldots, x_{a_n})$ such that $\langle a_1, \ldots, a_n \rangle$ satisfies the atomic predicate P in w, (*ii*) the formulas $x_{a_i} \neq x_{a_j}$ for $a_i \neq a_j$, (*iii*) the formulas $c_{a_i} \neq x_{a_j}$ for $a_i \neq a_j$, (*iv*) the formulas $c_{a_i} = x_{a_i}$, and (*v*) the (possibly infinite) formula $\forall z(z = x_{a_1} \vee z = x_{a_2} \vee \ldots)$.
3. Bind the free variables with a (possibly infinite) initial string of existential quantifiers.

If ϕ is a sentence of $L^{\Diamond}$, let ϕ^L be the (possibly infinite) disjunction of (possibly infinite) sentences S_w such that ϕ is true at w.

Theorem C.3 *For every $w \in M_A$, $w \models \phi$ if and only if $w \models \phi^L$.*

The left-to-right direction is trivial, in light of the definition of ϕ^L. To verify the right-to-left direction, we begin by proving a lemma:

Let v and v' be a-worlds in M_A and assume that there is an isomorphism g from v onto v'. (An 'isomorphism' is a function from the domain of v onto the domain of v' that respects the interpretation of every piece of vocabulary in L.) Let s be a variable assignment with the special feature that (1) whenever s assigns to some variable a value x outside the domain of v, x is also outside the domain of v', and (2) there is some k such that every object in the range of s was introduced by the kth stage of the construction of M_A. Then a formula ϕ of $L^{\Diamond}$ is true at v relative to s just in case it is true at v' relative to the variable assignment s^g (which is just like s except that if the value that s assigns to a variable is an object x in the domain of v, then the value that s^g assigns to that variable is $g(x)$).

We prove the lemma by induction on the number of occurrences of $\Diamond$ in ϕ. Assume, first, that ϕ has no occurrences of $\Diamond$. We proceed by induction on the complexity of ϕ. Every case is straightforward except when ϕ is atomic. So all we need to show is that, for ϕ atomic, ϕ is true at v relative to s just in case ϕ is true at v' relative to s^g. We verify the left-to-right direction. (The converse is analogous.) Assume that ϕ is true at v relative to s. If every free variable in ϕ is assigned by s a value in the domain of v, it follows from the fact that g is an isomorphism from v onto v' that ϕ is true at v' relative to s^g. If, on the other hand, there are free variables in ϕ to which s assigns values outside the domain of v, the truth-value of ϕ

at v relative to s doesn't depend on the particular choice of those values (as long as they are chosen to be outside the domain of v). Likewise, the truth-value of ϕ at v' relative to s^g doesn't depend on the particular choice of values for those variables (as long as they are chosen to be outside the domain of v'). But we are working on the assumption that any object in the range of s that is outside the domain of v is also outside the domain of v'. So if s assigns to a free variable in ϕ an object outside the domain of v, s (and therefore s^g) assigns to that variable an object outside the domain of v'. Since ϕ is true at v relative to s it must therefore be the case that ϕ is true at v' relative to s^g.

Let us now assume that the lemma holds for the case in which ϕ has k or less occurrences of $\Diamond$, and show that it holds when ϕ has $k + 1$ or less occurrences of $\Diamond$.

We proceed by induction on the complexity of ϕ. Every case is straightforward except when ϕ is of the form $\Diamond\psi$. So all we need to show is that $\Diamond\psi$ is true at v relative to s just in case $\Diamond\psi$ is true at v' relative to s^g.

We verify the left-to-right direction. (The converse is analogous.) Assume that $\Diamond\psi$ is true at v relative to s. Then there is an a-world u in M_A such that ψ is true at u relative to s. The construction of M_A—together with the fact that every object in the range of s was introduced by stage k of the construction—guarantees that there is a world u' in M_A which is isomorphic to u and which is such that the relevant isomorphism, h, has three properties: (1) $h(x) = g(x)$ for any x in the domain of v, (2) $h(x) = x$ for any x such that s assigns x to some variable occurring free in ψ and x is outside the domain of v, and (3) if s assigns to some variable an object x outside the domain of u, x is also outside the domain of u'. Since ψ is true at u relative to s, it follows from our (outer) inductive hypothesis (and from property (3) of h) that ψ is true at u' relative to s^h. But—thanks to properties (1) and (2) of h—s^g agrees with s^h on the values of any variables occurring free in ψ. So the fact that ψ is true at u' relative to s^h entails that $\Diamond\psi$ is true at v' relative to s^g.

This concludes the proof of our lemma. To prove the theorem, suppose that ϕ^L is true at w. Then some disjunct S_t of ϕ^L is true at w, which entails that t and w are isomorphic. But the definition of ϕ^L guarantees that ϕ is true at t. So our lemma guarantees that ϕ is true at w.

References

Alston, William (1957). Ontological commitments. *Philosophical Studies*, **9**, 8–17.

Beall, J. C. (2009). *Spandrels of Truth*. Oxford University Press, Oxford.

Beaney, Michael (ed.) (1997). *The Frege Reader*. Blackwell, Oxford.

Benacerraf, Paul (1973). Mathematical truth. *Journal of Philosophy*, **70**, 661–79. Reprinted in (Benacerraf and Putnam 1983).

Benacerraf, Paul and Putnam, Hilary (ed.) (1983). *Philosophy of Mathematics* (2nd edn). Cambridge University Press, Cambridge.

Bennett, Karen (2009). Composition, colocation and metaontology. In (Chalmers, Manley, and Wasserman 2009).

Block, Ned (2002). The harder problem of consciousness. *The Journal of Philosophy*, **99**, 391–425.

Block, Ned and Stalnaker, Robert (1999). Conceptual analysis, dualism, and the explanatory gap. *Philosophical Review*, **108**, 1–46.

Boolos, George (1971). The iterative conception of set. *The Journal of Philosophy*, **68**, 215–31. Reprinted in (Boolos 1998).

Boolos, George (1998). *Logic, Logic and Logic*. Harvard, Cambridge, MA.

Bottani, Andrea, Carrara, Massimiliano, and Giaretta, Pierdaniele (eds.) (2002). *Individuals, Essence, and Identity: Themes of Analytic Metaphysics*. Kluwer Academic Publishers, Dordrecht and Boston.

Braddon-Mitchel, David and Nola, Robert (eds.) (2009). *Conceptual Analysis and Philosophical Naturalism*. MIT Press, Cambridge, MA.

Burgess, John (2005). Being explained away. *Harvard Review of Philosophy*, **13**, 41–56.

Byrne, Alex (2006). Review of *There's Something about Mary*. *Notre Dame Philosophical Reviews*, **January 20**. Available at <http://ndpr.nd.edu/review.cfm?id=5561>.

Cameron, Ross (2010). The grounds of necessity. *Philosophical Compass*, **4**, 348–58.

Carnap, Rudolf (2003). *The Logical Structure of the World*. Open Court Publishing Company, Chicago and La Salle, IL. Translated from the German by Rolf A. George.

Cartwright, Nancy (1999). *The Dappled World*. Cambridge University Press, Cambridge.

Castellani, E. (ed.) (1998). *Interpreting Bodies: Classical and Quantum Objects in Modern Physics*. Princeton University Press, Princeton.

Chalmers, David (1996). *The Conscious Mind: In Search of a Fundamental Theory*. Oxford University Press, New York.

Chalmers, David and Jackson, Frank (2001). Conceptual analysis and reductive explanation. *The Philosophical Review*, **110**, 315–60.

Chalmers, David, Manley, David, and Wasserman, Ryan (eds.) (2009). *Metametaphysics*. Oxford University Press, New York.

Claridge, M., Dawah, H., and Wilson, M. (eds.) (1997). *Species—The Units of Biodiversity*. Chapman and Hall, London.

Cook, Roy (ed.) (2007). *The Arché Papers on the Mathematics of Abstraction*. The Western Ontario Series in Philosophy of Science. Springer, Dordrecht.

Dorr, Cian (2007). There are no abstract objects. In (Hawthorne, Sider, and Zimmerman 2007).

Dummett, Michael (1981). *Frege: Philosophy of Language* (2nd edn). Harvard University Press, Cambridge, MA.

Eklund, Matti (2008). The picture of reality as an amorphous lump. In (Sider, Hawthorne, and Zimmerman 2008).

Eklund, Matti (2009). On some recent criticisms of the 'linguistic' approach to ontology. *Dialectica*, **63**, 313–23.

Ewald, William (1996). *From Kant to Hilbert: A Source Book in the Foundations of Mathematics*, Volume 2. Oxford University Press, Oxford.

Field, Hartry (1980). *Science Without Numbers*. Basil Blackwell and Princeton University Press, Oxford and Princeton.

Field, Hartry (1985). On conservativeness and incompleteness. *Journal of Philosophy*, **82**, 239–78. Reprinted in (Field 1989).

Field, Hartry (1986). Stalnaker on intentionality: On Robert Stalnaker's *Inquiry*. *Pacific Philosophical Quarterly*, **67**, 98–112. Reprinted in (Field 2001).

Field, Hartry (1989). *Realism, Mathematics and Modality*. Basil Blackwell, Oxford.

Field, Hartry (2001). *Truth and the Absence of Fact*. Oxford University Press, Oxford.

Field, Hartry (2005). Recent debates about the *a priori*. In (Gendler and Hawthorne 2005).

Field, Hartry (2008). *Saving Truth from Paradox*. Oxford University Press, Oxford.

Fine, Kit (1985). Plantinga on the reduction of possibilist discourse. In (Tomberlin and van Inwagen 1985). Reprinted in (Fine 2005).

Fine, Kit (1994). Essence and modality. *Philosophical Perspectives*, **8**, 1–16.

Fine, Kit (1995a). The logic of essence. *Journal of Philosophical Logic*, **24**, 241–73.

Fine, Kit (1995b). Senses of essence. In (Sinnott-Armstrong 1995).

Fine, Kit (2000). Semantics for the logic of essence. *Journal of Philosophical Logic*, **29**, 543–84.

Fine, Kit (2001). The question of realism. *Philosophers' Imprint*, **1**, 1–30.

Fine, Kit (2002). *The Limits of Abstraction*. Oxford University Press, Oxford.

Fine, Kit (2003). The problem of possibilia. In (Loux and Zimmerman 2003). Reprinted in (Fine 2005).

Fine, Kit (2005). *Modality and Tense*. Oxford University Press, Oxford.

Fine, Kit (2006). Relatively unrestricted quantification. In (Rayo and Uzquiano 2006).

Frege, Gottlob (1884). *Die Grundlagen der Arithmetik*. English translation by J. L. Austin, *The Foundations of Arithmetic*, Northwestern University Press, Evanston, IL, 1980.

Frege, Gottlob (1892). On concept and object. *Vierteljahrsschrift für wissenschaftliche Philosophie*, **16**, 192–205. English translation by Peter Geach in (Beaney 1997).

Gendler, Tamar Szabo and Hawthorne, John (eds.) (2005). *Oxford Studies in Epistemology*, Volume 1. Oxford University Press, Oxford.

Gödel, Kurt (1933). The present situation in the foundations of mathematics. In (Gödel 1995).

Gödel, Kurt (1944). Russell's Mathematical Logic. In (Benacerraf and Putnam 1983).

Gödel, Kurt (1995). *Collected Works*, Volume III. Oxford University Press, Oxford.

Goldfarb, Warren (1997). Metaphysics and nonsense: On Cora Diamond's *The Realistic Spirit*. *Journal of Philosophical Research*, **22**, 57–73.

Graham, Andrew J. (2011). The significance of metaphysics. Ph.D. thesis, MIT, Cambridge, MA.

Hacker, P. M. S. (1986). *Insight and Illusion: Themes in the Philosophy of Wittgenstein*. Oxford University Press, Oxford.

Hale, Bob and Wright, Crispin (2001a). *The Reason's Proper Study: Essays towards a Neo-Fregean Philosophy of Mathematics*. Clarendon Press, Oxford.

Hale, Bob and Wright, Crispin (2001b). To bury Caesar.... In (Hale and Wright 2001a), 335–96.

Hare, Caspar (2009). *On Myself, and Other, Less Important Subjects*. Princeton University Press, Princeton.

Haslanger, Sally (2012). *Resisting Reality: Social Construction and Social Critique*. Oxford University Press, New York and Oxford.

Hawthorne, J., Sider, T., and Zimmerman, D. (eds.) (2007). *Contemporary Debates in Metaphysics*. Blackwell, Oxford.

Heck, Richard (1997a). The Julius Caesar objection. Reprinted in (Heck 1997b).

Heck, Richard (ed.) (1997b). *Language, Thought and Logic: Essays in Honour of Michael Dummett*. Clarendon Press, Oxford.

Heil, John (2003). *From an Ontological Point of View*. Clarendon Press, Oxford.

Heim, Irene and Kratzer, Angelika (1998). *Semantics in Generative Grammar*. Blackwell Textbooks in Linguistics. Blackwell, Oxford.

Hellman, Geoffrey (1989). *Mathematics Without Numbers*. Clarendon Press, Oxford.

Hirsch, Eli (2002). Quantifier variance and realism. *Philosophical Issues*, **12**, 51–73.

Hodes, Harold T. (1984). Logicism and the ontological commitments of arithmetic. *Journal of Philosophy*, **81**, 123–49.

Hofweber, Thomas (2009). Ambitious, yet modest, metaphysics. In (Chalmers, Manley, and Wasserman 2009).

Jackson, Frank (1982). Epiphenomenal qualia. *Philosophical Quarterly*, **32**, 127–36.

Jackson, Frank (1986). What Mary didn't know. *The Journal of Philosophy*, **83**, 291–95.

Jackson, Frank (1998). *From Metaphysics to Ethics: A Defence of Conceptual Analysis*. Oxford University Press, Oxford.

Jensen, R.B. (1969). On the consistency of a slight(?) modification of Quine's NF. *Synthese*, **19**, 250–63.

Kanger, S. and Öhman, S. (eds.) (1980). *Philosophy and Grammar*. Reidel Publishing Company, Dordrecht.

Kitcher, Philip (1984). Species. *Philosophy of Science*, **51**, 308–35.

Kment, Boris (2006). Counterfactuals and the analysis of necessity. *Philosophical Perspectives*, **20**, 237–302.

Kripke, Saul A. (1980). *Naming and necessity*. Harvard University Press, Cambridge, MA.

Lewis, David (1968). Counterpart theory and quantified modal logic. *The Journal of Philosophy*, **65**, 113–26. Reprinted in (Lewis 1983b).

Lewis, David (1970). General semantics. *Synthese*, **22**, 18–67. Reprinted in (Lewis 1983b).

Lewis, David (1980). Index, context, and content. In (Kanger and Öhman 1980). Reprinted in (Lewis 1998).

Lewis, David (1982). Logic for equivocators. *Noûs*, **16**, 431–41.

Lewis, David (1983a). New work for a theory of universals. *Australasian Journal of Philosophy*, **61**, 343–77. Reprinted in (Lewis 1999).

Lewis, David (1983b). *Philosophical Papers, Volume I*. Oxford.

Lewis, David (1984). Putnam's paradox. *The Australasian Journal of Philosophy*, **62**, 221–36. Reprinted in (Lewis 1999).

Lewis, David (1986a). *On the Plurality of Worlds*. Blackwell, Oxford and New York.

Lewis, David (1986b). *Philosophical Papers, Volume II*. Oxford.

Lewis, David (1988). What experience teaches. *Proceedings of the Russellian Society*, **13**, 29–57. Reprinted in (Lewis 1999).

Lewis, David (1998). *Papers in Philosophical Logic*. Cambridge University Press, Cambridge.

Lewis, David (1999). *Papers in Metaphysics and Epistemology*. Cambridge University Press, Cambridge.

Lewis, David (2009). Ramseyan humility. In (Braddon-Mitchell and Nola 2009).

Linnebo, Øystein (2009). Bad company tamed. *Synthese*, **170**, 371–91.

Linnebo, Øystein (2010). Pluralities and sets. *Journal of Philosophy*, **107**, 144–64.

Linnebo, Øystein (typescript). The potential hierarchy of sets.

Linnebo, Øystein and Rayo, Agustín (forthcoming). Hierarchies ontological and ideological. *Mind*.

Loux, M. (ed.) (1979). *The Possible and the Actual*. Cornell University Press, Ithaca, NY.

Loux, M. and Zimmerman, D. (2003). *The Oxford Handbook of Metaphysics*. Oxford University Press, Oxford.

MacBride, Fraser (2003). Speaking with shadows: A study of neo-Fregeanism. *British Journal for the Philosophy of Science*, **54**, 103–63.

MacBride, F. (ed.) (2006). *Identity and Modality*. Oxford University Press, Oxford.

McMichael, Alan (1983). A problem for actualism about possible worlds. *The Philosophical Review*, **92**, 49–66.

Maudlin, Tim (1998). Part and whole in quantum mechanics. In (Castellani 1998).

Melia, Joseph (2001). Reducing possibilities to language. *Analysis*, **61**, 19–29.

Morton, Adam and Stich, Stephen (eds.) (1996). *Benacerraf and his Critics*. Basil Blackwell, Oxford.

Nuffer, Gerhard (2009). Stalnaker on mathematical information. *The Southern Journal of Philosophy*, **47**, 187–204.

Parikh, Rohit (2009). Sentences, belief and logical omniscience, or what does deduction tell us? *The Review of Symbolic Logic*, **1**, 459–76.

Parsons, Charles (1974). Sets and classes. *Noûs*, **8**, 1–12. Reprinted in (Parsons 1983).

Parsons, Charles (1983). *Mathematics in Philosophy*. Cornell University Press, Ithaca, NY.

Peacocke, Christopher (1999). *Being Known*. Clarendon Press, Oxford.

Pears, D. (1987). *The False Prison: A Study of the Development of Wittgenstein's Philosophy*, Volume 1. Oxford University Press, Oxford.

Perry, John (2001). *Knowledge, Possibility, and Consciousness*. MIT Press, Cambridge, MA.

Plantinga, A. (1976). Actualism and possible worlds. *Theoria*, **42**, 139–60. Reprinted in (Loux 1979).

Potter, Michael (2004). *Set Theory and Its Philosophy: A Critical Introduction*. Oxford University Press, Oxford.

Price, Huw (2009). Metaphysics after Carnap: The ghost who walks? In (Chalmers, Manley, and Wasserman 2009), 320–46.

Priest, Graham (2006). *In Contradiction: A study of the Transconsistent* (2nd edn). Oxford University Press, Oxford.

Putnam, Hilary (1980). Models and reality. *The Journal of Symbolic Logic*, **45**, 464–82.

Putnam, Hilary (1987). *The Many Faces of Realism*. Open Court, La Salle, IL.

Rayo, Agustín (2002). Frege's unofficial arithmetic. *The Journal of Symbolic Logic*, **67**, 1623–38.

Rayo, Agustín (2003). Success by default? *Philosophia Mathematica*, 305–22.

Rayo, Agustín (2005). Logicism reconsidered. In (Shapiro 2005).

Rayo, Agustín (2008). On specifying truth-conditions. *The Philosophical Review*, **117**, 385–443.

Rayo, Agustín and Uzquiano, Gabriel (eds.) (2006). *Absolute Generality*. Oxford University Press, Oxford.

Rosen, Gideon (1993). The refutation of nominalism (?). *Philosophical Topics*, **21**, 149–86.

Rosen, Gideon (2006). The limits of contingency. In (MacBride 2006).

Roy, T. (1995). On defence of linguistic ersatzism. *Philosophical Studies*, **80**, 217–42.

Salmon, Nathan (1989). The logic of what might have been. *The Philosophical Review*, **98**, 3–34.

Salmon, Nathan U. (1995). *Reference and Essence* (2nd edn). Prometheus Books, Amherst, NY.

Santos, Pedro F. (typescript). Logicism without ontology.

Schaffer, Jonathan (2009). On what grounds what. In (Chalmers, Manley, and Wasserman 2009).

Shapiro, Stewart (1983). Conservativeness and incompleteness. *Journal of Philosophy*, **80**, 521–31.

Shapiro, Stewart (1987). Principles of reflection and second-order logic. *Journal of Philosophical Logic*, **16**, 309–33.

Shapiro, Stewart (ed.) (2005). *The Oxford Handbook for Logic and the Philosophy of Mathematics*. Clarendon Press, Oxford.

Sider, Theodore (2002). The ersatz pluriverse. *Journal of Philosophy*, **99**, 279–315.

Sider, Theodore (2012). *Writing the Book of the World*. Oxford University Press, Oxford and New York.

Sider, Theodore, Hawthorne, John, and Zimmerman, Dean (eds.) (2008). *Contemporary Debates in Metaphysics*. Blackwell, Cambridge, MA.

Sinnott-Armstrong, W. (ed.) (1995). *Modality, Morality and Belief*. Cambridge University Press, Cambridge.

Skow, Brad (2011). Experience and the passage of time. *Philosophical Perspectives*, **25**, 359–87.

Sober, E. (1984). Discussion: Sets, species, and evolution: Comments on Philip Kitcher's 'species'. *Philosophy of Science*, **51**, 334–41.

Stalnaker, Robert C. (1979). Assertion. *Syntax and Semantics*, **9**, 315–22. Reprinted in (Stalnaker 1999).

Stalnaker, Robert C. (1984). *Inquiry*. MIT Press, Cambridge, MA.

Stalnaker, Robert C. (1996). On what possible worlds could not be. In (Morton and Stich 1996). Reprinted in (Stalnaker 2003).

Stalnaker, Robert C. (1999). *Context and Content*. Oxford University Press, Oxford.

Stalnaker, Robert C. (2001). On considering a possible world as actual. *Supplement to the Proceedings of The Aristotelian Society*, **75**, 141–56. Reprinted in (Stalnaker 2003).

Stalnaker, Robert C. (2003). *Ways a World Might Be: Metaphysical and Anti-Metaphysical Essays*. Clarendon Press, Oxford.

Tomberlin, J.E. and van Inwagen, P. (eds.) (1985). *Alvin Plantinga*. Reidel Profiles Series 5. Reidel, Dordrecht.

Van Heijenoort, Jean (ed.) (1967). *From Frege to Gödel*. Harvard University Press, Cambridge, MA.

van Inwagen, Peter (1990). *Material Beings*. Cornell University Press, Ithaca, NY.

Williamson, Timothy (2010). Necessitism, contingentism, and plural quantification. *Mind*, **119**, 657–748.

Wittgenstein, Ludwig (1921). *Tractatus Logico-Philosophicus*. Published as 'Logisch-Philosophische Abhandlung', in *Annalen der Naturphilosophische* Vol. XIV, **3/4**, 184–262.

Wright, Crispin (1983). *Frege's Conception of Numbers as Objects*. Aberdeen University Press, Aberdeen.

Wright, Crispin (1997). The philosophical significance of Frege's theorem. In (Heck 1997*b*), 201–44.

Yablo, Stephen (2001). Go figure: A path through fictionalism. *Midwest Studies in Philosophy*, **XXV**, 72–102.

Yablo, Stephen (2002). Abstract objects: A case study. *Noûs*, **36, supp. 1**, 255–86. Originally appeared in (Bottani, Carrara, and Giaretta 2002).

Yablo, Stephen (forthcoming). *Aboutness*. Princeton University Press, Princeton and Oxford.

Zermelo, Ernst (1908). Untersuchungen über die grundlagen der mengenlehre i. *Mathematische Annalen*, **65**, 261–81. English translation by Stefan Bauer-Mengelberg, 'Investigations in the Foundations of Set Theory I', in (Van Heijenoort 1967).

Zermelo, Ernst (1930). Über grenzzahlen und mengenbereiche: Neue untersuchungen über die grundlagen der mengenlehre. *Fundamenta Mathematicae*, **16**, 29–47. Translated in (Ewald 1996).

Index